GHOST SHIPS OF THE GREAT LAKES

Also by Dwight Boyer

TRUE TALES OF THE GREAT LAKES

GREAT STORIES OF THE GREAT LAKES

GHOST SHIPS
OF THE
GREAT LAKES

by Dwight Boyer

Illustrated with photographs and maps

DODD, MEAD & COMPANY ⚓ *NEW YORK*

*To my wife, Virginia, whose patience and help made
it all possible, this book is affectionately dedicated*

First published as a Dodd, Mead Quality Paperback in 1984

Copyright © 1968 by Dwight Boyer
All rights reserved
No part of this book may be reproduced in any form
without permission in writing from the publisher
Published by Dodd, Mead & Company, Inc.
79 Madison Avenue, New York, N.Y. 10016
Distributed in Canada by
McClelland and Stewart Limited, Toronto
Manufactured in the United States of America

The Library of Congress cataloged the first
printing of this title as follows:

Boyer, Dwight.
  Ghost ships of the Great Lakes. Illustrated with photos
and maps. New York, Dodd, Mead ₁1968₎
    xxvi, 294 p. illus., maps, ports. 21 cm. $6.50
    Bibliography: p. 277-279.
    1. Shipwrecks—Great Lakes. I. Title.
G525.B78   917.7   68-23094

ISBN 0-396-08346-3 (pbk.)

Acknowledgments

Once again it is time to tender sincere thanks to those whose special knowledge and help have played a major role in making this book a reality.

One would be hard pressed, indeed, without the dedicated and patient help of Janet Coe Sanborn of the Cleveland Public Library, and the editor of *Inland Seas*, the superb quarterly of the Great Lakes Historical Society. The task would be long and difficult, too, without the willing help of those whose passion is the accurate compilation of Great Lakes lore and records . . . people like Richard J. Wright; Walter and Teddy Remick; the Reverend Edward J. Dowling, S.J.; Robert J. MacDonald; the Reverend Alexander C. Meakin; Rowley W. Murphy; Frank A. Myers; Lee C. Hinslea; William D. Carle III; Cletus Schneider; Captains John Kelsner and James Hallahan of the Great Lakes Towing Company; and Leslie D. Weston of the American Bureau of Shipping.

Foremost among those who gave help and encouragement are Ernest H. Rankin, Executive Director of the Marquette County Historical Society; Beryl H. Scott; Clinton Young; Scott Worden, Jr.; Lloyd Chambers; Elsie Mohr King; John A. Chisholm of the Muskegon *Chronicle*; William F. Rapprich; George M. Steinbrenner III, President of the American Ship Building Company; Captain H. C. Inches, curator of the Great Lakes Historical Society's Marine Museum in Vermilion, Ohio; and Ross Mortimer and Frank Fauver of the Great Lakes Towing Company.

Invaluable assistance came, too, from Mrs. Joseph B. Rodebaugh of Ashtabula, Ohio, whose unrelenting researching made possible the full recounting of the tragic loss of the *Marquette & Bessemer No. 2*. Another who made heroic contributions of time and talent is Vince Matteucci, the well-known artist of the Cleveland *Plain Dealer's Sunday Magazine*. And long hours were spent at the typewriter by Bertha Kelly, transposing horrendously butchered "rough" chapters into something readable.

Librarians, frequently imposed upon by authors, were kind and generous in their responses to what must have seemed like vague and unusual requests. Among them were J. C. Arnot of the Port Arthur Public Library; Michael Pearson of the Canadian History and Manuscript Section of the Toronto Public Library; Ray A. Smith of the Parry Sound Public Library; and Alice E. Wright of the Morley Library, Painesville, Ohio.

Appreciated, too, is the assistance of Rear Admiral Charles Tighe, Commander of the Ninth Coast Guard District, and a capable staff that includes, among others, Captain Willis Bruso; Commander Warren D. Andrews; Ensign Ronald H. Coonin and Albert L. McGinty.

Editors are busy people; among those who gave of their time in locating obscure clippings or directing the author to various sources are Denis Harvey, Executive Editor of the Hamilton, Ontario, *Spectator*; Bernard Lyons, Managing Editor of the Port Huron *Times-Herald*; Phil Richards, Editor of the Alpena *News*; Arthur L. Davies, publisher, and Robert D. Owen, executive editor, respectively, of the Kingston, Ontario, *Whig-Standard*; Mrs. L. J. Skuderin, Editor of the *Great Lakes Red Book*, published by the Penton Publishing Company of Cleveland; and Gordon R. McKean, Editor of the *Imperial Oil Fleet News*.

In the seemingly endless task of accumulating bits and nuggets of information and compiling a collection of photographs that fit into specific Great Lakes scenes, a debt of gratitude is owed to the Parry Sound Historical Society; the Kingston Historical Society; Captain Clyde C. Clattenburg of Upper Lakes Shipping Limited; Lyle A. Myers, Sr.; Milton J. Brown; Fred Trelfa; Ronald Rosie, Jr.; Dudley Brumbach, senior photographer of the Cleveland *Plain Dealer*; photographer John A. Tyler of Conneaut, Ohio; Alex Walton, the popular Kincardine and Wingham, Ontario, newsman; the late A. E. "Ernie" Williams; Captain Ervin L. Malloch and the Kenosha County Historical Society.

From Ross J. Plaisted came valuable recollections of the early days of wireless on the Great Lakes, while Bill Wade and Captain George Skuggen of Wilson Marine Transit Company, and Jack D. Cain, executive vice president of the Lorain Electronics Corporation were very helpful in documenting the pioneer installations of ship-to-shore, radiotelephones in the Wilson fleet.

To all these fine people, and the few I may have forgotten but to whom I am, nevertheless, greatly indebted, my sincere appreciation.

—DWIGHT BOYER

Mentor, Ohio

Foreword

The Great Lakes, long recognized as the world's greatest fresh-water transportation system and the prime catalyst around which evolved the steel-oriented, heavy-industry centers of midwestern America, also provide some of man's most inexplicable and eerie mysteries. Vast and lonely, there is something hauntingly compulsive about their dangers and hazards. In pursuit of commerce inspired by the lakes' strategic geographic location joining the nation's major deposits of natural resources, great ships have left their ports, never to be seen again. "Ghost ships" they are called—phantom vessels that sailed away into the unknown. They were sturdily built, well-found, and manned by capable crews. Yet, through the years, many were lost without a trace, each one adding another name to the long list of vanished ships on the Great Lakes . . . strange disappearances that will plague fresh-water mariners as long as ships and men go to sea. Only the lakes have the answers, and they rarely yield a clue.

The *L. R. Doty*, a fine big steamer only five years old, loaded corn at Chicago on October 24, 1898, and left that port towing the schooner barge *Olive Jeanette*. They were headed for Midland, Ontario, on Georgian Bay, but encountered nasty weather late the following day. When the towline parted, the *Doty* steamed off into the dusk, presumably to swing in a wide circle to pick up her tow again, or at least stay in the vicinity until the weather moderated. The battered *Olive Jeanette* was sighted two days later, but the *L. R. Doty* was never found. The *Olive Jeanette* may have been a bad-luck ship, for seven years later, when she was being towed down to Lake Superior by the steamer *Iosco*, the steamer went down with all hands. So did the *Olive Jeanette*.

The new steel steamer *W. H. Gilcher*, with three thousand long tons of coal in her holds, steamed through the Straits of Mackinac one evening in October of 1892, bound for Milwaukee. Captain Leeds H. Weeks chose the east shore, or Manitou Passage course, down Lake Michigan. Sometime during the night the steamer and her crew simply vanished.

The propeller *Nashua*, Georgian Bay to Toledo with lumber, steamed out of the Main Channel between Cove and Fitzwilliam Islands and into Lake Huron—with all, apparently, well aboard. She was sighted by two vessels a short time later, but never again. A year later, on the same lake, the same mysterious fate befell the staunch schooner *Newell A. Eddy*. Coal was the cargo of the large schooner *Celtic*, upbound to the Soo from Buffalo in November of 1902. Somewhere in Lake Huron the *Celtic* sailed into eternity, going down without a trace.

The big steamer *D. M. Clemson* locked through the Soo at 9:30 A.M. on Sunday, December 1, 1908, bound for Duluth with six thousand tons of coal under her hatches and with Captain Sam Chamberlain in command of a crew of twenty-two. She is unreported to this day! Fourteen years later the *Lambton*, a Canadian government vessel, disappeared with all hands in the vicinity of Caribou Island. As ships "gone missing" in Lake Superior, the *Clemson* and *Lambton* have plenty of company. The *Manistee, Merchant, W. W. Arnold*,

Magellan, John Owen,[1] *Atlanta, Gilbert Mollison, Superior,* and *Pearl B. Campbell* (the latter a tug), all vanished in this largest and deepest of the Great Lakes.

Mariners were puzzled when the big schooner *Thomas Hume,* sailing from Chicago to Muskegon on the evening of May 21, 1891, never made her scheduled port of call, or any other port. Why a fine big vessel, in first-class condition and in the charge of a skilled navigator and an able crew, should be so totally obliterated seems quite remarkable.

The schooner *Radiant,* carrying general cargo and a crew of ten, sailed from Toledo and was never again sighted. From Toledo, too, the *Maumee Valley,* bound for Port Stanley with coal, spread her canvas to the winds in Maumee Bay and wandered off into the unknown. A fine trim vessel, she was sailed by Captain Eugene Winchester for years. Sometime before she was lost an itinerant marine artist painted a picture of her, a superb likeness that is still valued highly by the Winchester family. Through the years many other vessels, of wood and steel, sail and steam, have joined the *Radiant* and *Maumee Valley* as Lake Erie "ghost ships." Two of

---

1 After reading the story of the tragic disappearance of the steamer *John Owen* in *Great Stories of the Great Lakes,* George H. Johnston of Parry Sound, Ontario, chief officer of the Canadian Coast Guard vessel *C. P. Edwards,* revealed this heart-warming sequel:

My father, George W. Johnston, was lightkeeper at the Caribou Island station in Lake Superior from 1912 until 1921. After the foundering of the *John Owen,* he found several pieces of wreckage, including her forward spar, on which was a large brass ship's bell with the name "John Owen" engraved on it.

My father kept the bell for some years and, upon moving to Parry Sound, brought the bell with him.

A small Anglican mission church in the nearby village of Sprucedale was canvasing for money to buy and install a bell in the new belfry they had built on their church. They approached my father, vestry clerk at Trinity Church in Parry Sound. He offered, instead, to donate the bell of the *John Owen,* suggesting that it would be a fitting memorial to her gallant crew as it called others to worship and prayer.

A local blacksmith fitted it with balance wheels and the Canadian National Railway transported it to Sprucedale, the above services without charge. All in all, it was a fitting tribute to a brave ship and crew.

them, the *Jersey City* and the *Dacotah*, chose to "go missing" on the same November night in 1860, the lost crews numbering forty-three.

Not a clue or scrap of wreckage remained to tell where the brig, *Iceberg*, went down in Lake Ontario. She just "sailed away," never to be seen again. The same lake, which had mysteriously claimed the schooners *Willis*, *Neptune*, and *Kentuckian* and the propeller *Bay State*, swallowed up the big tug *Frank C. Barnes*, and her crew in 1915. A prolonged search was made but the *Barnes* was gone forever.

Years ago there were many yarns of ghost ships being sighted again, sometimes years after they disappeared. Superstitious sailors swore their visions were true . . . phantom ships off in the distance on a night when shafts of light from a bright moon dapple the sea and enliven the imagination. The *Bannockburn*, the famous "Flying Dutchman" of Lake Superior, was supposedly sighted a year after she disappeared, beating toward the Soo off Caribou Island. A steward, tossing potato peelings from the fantail of a steamer on Lake Huron, told of seeing a mysterious ship without lights skimming by in the darkness off Thunder Bay . . . a ship that bore a remarkable likeness to the steamer, *Water Witch*, missing for many months with twenty-eight souls aboard. Deckhands on a lumber barge told of seeing the ghost of the coal-laden schooner *Wells Burt* romp past them on a foggy night while off Death's Door, near Washington Island. Strange and weird are these visions of old sailors, but when one considers the unexplainable things that have happened at sea over the centuries, who can doubt but that the Great Lakes have their gray ghosts . . . riding the endless waves of the past, bound for mysterious ports they will never make, on voyages from which they will never return.

An accomplished poet and Great Lakes buff, Lyle A. Myers, Sr., of Silver Creek, New York, has always been fascinated by the lore of vanished ships. His "feeling" for them is expressed in the following:

PHANTOM SHIPS THAT PASS IN THE NIGHT

Shimmering ripples on the lakes below
The full moon's eerie silver glow
In the stillness of the summer night
Reveal weird shadows in translucent light.

Strange forms take shape, tall masts and spars
Like fairy wands, touch the twinkling stars,
Then through the magic of mind and sight
We see the Phantom Ships that pass in the night.

Unfolding the mysteries of long, long ago
Lost vessels and crews lying deep down below
Return as ghosts and sail on once more
Toward that beacon light on the distant shore.

The Master of all ships is now in command
The course is charted to that promised land;
Not a sound breaks the silence in the pale moonlight
On those Phantom Ships that pass in the night.

The roster of ghost ships on the Great Lakes is impressive. Yet, many more would have been included in that category, were it not that luck or superb physical condition, perhaps both, permitted a single sailor, perhaps two or three, to live and thus account for the loss.

Only Harry W. Stewart, a young and strong swimmer, lived to tell how the big new steamer *Western Reserve* had suffered a major structural failure on Lake Superior, breaking in two and foundering in minutes.

Joe Frazer, a wheelsman, was the only survivor as the passenger steamer *Sunbeam* succumbed to a Lake Superior summer storm. He told how she was caught in the trough of the waves and lay on her beam ends, held there by the wind and seas until she filled and sank.

Of the twenty-one men aboard the package freighter *Idaho* when she surrendered to a Lake Erie gale in 1897, only Second Mate Louis LaForce and deckhand William Gill survived. They were clinging to the tip of the *Idaho*'s foremast, nearly frozen to death when Captain Frank Root brought his steamer, the *Mariposa*, right up to the mast, where his men pried LaForce and Gill from their perch. The rescued men told how Captain Alexander Gillies foolishly bypassed the shelter of Long Point, although a severe gale was blowing, to continue his course to Detroit. When rising waters put out the steamer's fires and left her helpless, Lake Erie soon pounded her to pieces.

Nearly dead from exposure after floating for many hours on the ship's life raft, Captain Walter Grashaw was the only survivor of the sinking of the whaleback steamer *James B. Colgate*, lost in the great October storm of 1916. He related how the seas had mauled his ship's hatches and bashed in her forward deck turret, allowing tons of water to flood her cargo of hard coal.

On Lake Michigan, in November of 1958, only First Mate Elmer Fleming and deck watchman Frank Mays, tossing on a life raft for hours as their clothing became encrusted with ice, lived to tell how their ship, the 615-foot *Carl D. Bradley*, broke in half and went down quickly, drowning their thirty-three shipmates.

Sometimes the testimony of survivors has led to important changes, enabling shipbuilders and operators to send out safer vessels.

Charlie Pitz was the only man to live and, consequently, report on how the new and supposedly watertight hatch covers on the twenty-five-day-old steamer *Cyprus* proved not to be watertight at all. On only the second voyage of her career, the *Cyprus* was lost in a modest Lake Superior storm of 1907. He told how the water gained access through the hatch covers and eventually caused the ship to capsize. The hatch design was changed on later ships, but it was too late to help the twenty-one men who perished.

The loss of the 580-foot steamer, *Daniel J. Morrell*, on Lake Huron in 1966 inspired several safety-at-sea advances on the Great Lakes. In this case only Dennis N. Hale, who huddled in a life raft under the ice-covered bodies of three shipmates, lived to tell of the last moments of his ship. He explained how she suddenly broke in half during a furious gale, thus severing the electrical lines from the after end and preventing an SOS (or Mayday) call from being sent from the ship-to-shore radio-telephone in the pilothouse. This has led to the installation of auxiliary battery-powered radio units. Hale's thirty-six hour ordeal in the life raft also graphically illustrated the inadequacy of existing equipment and has inspired, in many cases, the abandonment of the old-type life rafts in favor of inflatable rafts provided with a protective canopy under which survivors can stay dry and relatively warm, despite freezing winds and seas.

The *Morrell* disaster, with the loss of twenty-eight crewmen, has also brought about a new concept of maritime safety on the lakes. Made possible by the efficiency of present-day communications, "LAVERS" (Lake Vessel Reporting System) will allow the Coast Guard to keep track of ships crossing open waters on the Great Lakes.

All ships over one hundred tons, regardless of nationality, that use the lakes, are encouraged to participate in the voluntary system. A ship does this by filing its intended destination, estimated time of arrival, and intended route with the Coast Guard when it leaves its port of departure. The information is updated periodically throughout the ship's voyage.

"LAVERS is designed to reduce the amount of time in which a ship may be in distress and no one know about," says Rear Admiral Charles Tighe, Commander of the Ninth Coast Guard District. "This is what happened when the *Morrell* (she was overdue thirty hours) sank in Lake Huron with the loss of twenty-eight lives. Because of the sudden storms associated with the lakes and the low air and water temperatures that considerably reduce the chances of survival in the water, every minute counts when a ship is endangered."

If a participating vessel is four hours overdue in reporting to the next checkpoint in the system, or its destination, the LAVERS Center at the Ninth District headquarters in Cleveland will begin an immediate communications search for her. If the vessel is still unreported an hour later, Coast Guard ships and aircraft begin an immediate search. The Coast Guard stations serving as checkpoints are connected by a teletype network to the Ninth District search-and-rescue base in Cleveland.

But while new and stronger ships, better navigational aids, and improved communications are evident, the old yarns and stories of long-lost ships being sighted are not forgotten. Call them old-wives' tales, sailors' myths, halucinations, metaphysical manifestations, or what you will, the fact remains that knowledgeable and reputable people have experienced strange and seemingly unexplainable sights and sounds and, while they cannot account for the visual and audible phenomena revealed to them, they can most certainly vouch for their existence. A case in point is the remarkable experience of Rowley W. Murphy, the distinguished Canadian artist and Great Lakes historian. It involved eleven men, including Murphy, all of them reputable citizens of Canada. What they saw and heard on a summer night in 1910 remained indelibly imprinted upon their minds, yet there is no obvious or reasonable explanation. But let Mr. Murphy tell about it in his own words:

Another appearance from the past was seen by the crews of three yachts one beautiful night with a full moon (like cool daylight) in August, 1910. My father, a cousin, and I were on a holiday cruise around the west end of Lake Ontario, and as we were late getting underway from Toronto Island, and were running before a light easterly, decided to spend the night in the quiet, sheltered, and beautiful basin at the mouth of the creek, spelled "Etobicoke" . . . but always pronounced "Tobyco" by old-timers.

Our cruising yawl, with a larger sister of the same rig and a still larger Mackinaw (one of several "fish boats" converted to cruising yachts with great success), were the only occupants of the harbour this perfect night. The crews of the three yachts numbered eleven in all, and as is generally the case, after dinner was over and dishes done, gathered on deck in the moonlight to engage in the best conversation known to man.

All hands turned in earlier than usual, there being no distractions ashore, and by midnight were deep in happy dreams, helped by the quiet ripple alongside. At what was about 1:30 A.M., the writer was wakened by four blasts on a steamer's whistle. After waiting for a repetition . . . to be sure it was not part of a dream . . . he put his head out of the companionway.

There, flooded by moonlight, was a steamer heading about WSW . . . at about half speed, and approximately half a mile off shore. She had a good chime whistle but not much steam . . . like *Noronic* on that awful night of September 17, 1949, who also repeated her four blasts many times.

But who was she? On this amazingly beautiful night, with memory strained to the utmost, it was difficult to do more than think of who she was not! She was considerably smaller than the three famous Upper Lakers, *China*, *India*, and *Japan* (about this date under Canadian registry, known as *City of Montreal*, *City of Ottawa*, and *City of Hamilton*). She was not as small as *Lake Michigan*, but like her, did appear to be of all wooden construction. However, there were many in the past, of quite related design and size. The vessel seen had white topsides and deckhouses, and appeared to be grey below her main deck, like the Welland Canal-sized freighters (at this date, the big wooden steamers of the Ogdensburg Line of the Rutland Transportation Company), *Persia* and *Ocean*, were like her in size and arrangement, but were all white and came to known ends, and, of course, *Arabian* was of iron, and was black.

In this appearance off "Toby Coke" (a variant of spelling), the starboard light, deck lights and some seen through cabin windows, had the quality of oil lamps; and her tall mast, with fitted topmast, carried a gaff and brailed up mainsail. Her smokestack was all black, and she had no hog beams . . . but appeared to have four white boats. Her chime whistle was a good one, but was reduced in volume as previously mentioned, and was sounded continuously for perhaps ten minutes. Very soon all hands now watching on the beach decided that something should be done. So a dinghy was quickly hauled over from the basin, and, with a crew of four made up from some of those aboard the three yachts, started to row out with all speed to the vessel in distress, to give her what assistance might be possible.

As the boys in the dinghy reached the area where something definite should have been seen, there was nothing there beyond clear and powerful moonlight, a few gulls wakened from sleep . . . but something else, impossible to ignore. This was a succession of long curving ripples in a more or less circular pattern, which just might have been the last appearance of those caused by the foundering of a steamer many years before on a night of similar beauty. In any case, the four in the dinghy returned in about an hour, reporting also small scraps of wreckage which were probably just old driftwood, seldom seen with any fresh breezes blowing.

But something more there was. This was the reappearance to the visual and audible memory, which those on the beach and those afloat had seen and heard, of something that had occurred in the more or less distant past, and which had returned to the consciousness of living men after a long absence.

Whatever the cause, the experienced crews of the three yachts mentioned were of one mind as to what they had seen and heard. At least eleven lake sailors would be unlikely to agree on the character of this reappearance without good reason! And the reason was certainly not firewater working on the mass imagination, as no one of the three yachts had any aboard. So, what was the answer?

What, indeed, did the eleven yachtsmen see that night? Was some supernatural manifestation projected before them in the moonlight on Lake Ontario? Did some unearthly power cause an old steamer to rise from her grave to live once more her final minutes afloat? Or did eleven sober and dependable citizens, against the incalculable odds of coincidence, all suffer the same halucination at the same time? Not likely. Whatever the name of the phantom ship looming so eerily in the moonlight, something was there, beyond a doubt. And it was thoroughly consistent with the stories told by many old sailors, before and since, of specter ships of the past riding the seas once more. The incident cited by Rowley W. Murphy and verified by ten companions of unquestioned integrity gives them credibility and substance.

The phantom fleet of vessels "gone missing" on the Great Lakes numbers in the hundreds, sail and steam . . . brigs, schooners, tow barges, package freighters, passenger ships, and long bulk freighters . . . all lost far from home, where the tossing seas are the only monument they will ever have. In a sense it is most fitting, although only those who make their living from the fresh-water seas can appreciate this appropriateness.

Because it is a following inherent with many dangers, there too often exists in the maritime industry a philosophical acceptance of lost ships and missing men as a regrettable but inevitable fact of seafaring life . . . a fact that, while brutal, constitutes the calculated risks that have been part and parcel of the sailor's and shipowner's lot since men began to go to sea. It is an atmosphere that does not inspire sudden or significant changes, particularly in the area of safety-at-sea aids and devices. Adoption of new equipment standards or deviations from traditional procedures are matters that seemingly require a protracted series of industry conferences, international agreements, and, above all, a great passage of time.

The whole world thrilled to the accounts of Jack Binns, wireless operator on the White Star liner, *Republic*, tapping out the first "CDQ" (now SOS) in history after his ship collided with the steamship, *Florida*, in a dense fog off Nantucket Lightship in 1909. Here was irrefutable evidence, as testified by the many lives thus saved, that wireless should be standard equipment on all ships at sea. Still, no official action was taken until after the *Titanic* rammed an iceberg in 1912, with a death toll of over 1500. This tragic loss of life, it was proved, could have been minimized had nearby ships been equipped with wireless, had a universal code been in use, and if operators had been compelled to man their sets around the clock or at specific intervals. Belatedly then, the "Radio Act of 1913," the result of the International Wireless Convention held in London in 1912, and ratified by the United States Senate early in 1913, made it mandatory for vessels carrying more than fifty people to be equipped with wireless and qualified operators before leaving any United States port. These requirements were incumbent upon ships of all nations. The Act also called for the standardization or adoption of a single International Code at sea. Previously, three different codes had been in general use.

Like their salt-water brethren, the Great Lakes passenger ships adapted to the new regulations. And even though it was not required of them, many of the ore and package freighters plying fresh water, somehow made space for a wireless room and operator. A few had been wireless-equipped for years and could already attest to its value.

Soon, the fringe or added benefits began to overshadow and supersede the original safety-at-sea application. Pleased vessel managers found it highly convenient to know exactly where their ships were and, if necessary, to advise the skipper of changes in discharge ports. Details in cargo makeup, loading schedules, personnel matters, fueling, provisioning, and all the manifold problems that are traditionally the vessel manager's lot in life were vastly simplified. Best of all, hours in advance, thanks to the up-to-the-minute weather information gleaned from the airwaves by "Sparks," a vessel's arrival time at a dock could be plotted almost to the minute.

Obviously, though, there was some opposition to wireless, and strangely enough most of it came from those who stood to benefit most from it in times of peril. Grizzled old skippers who had navigated the lakes for years with only a compass, clock, taffrail log, and their own highly personalized "weather sense" often looked suspiciously upon wireless operators as "spies" from the front office. Most of the old captains preferred to keep their contacts with superiors at an irreducible minimum. Only when space-consuming wireless sets had been superseded, in the early 1930s, by compact ship-to-shore radio-telephones, did the safety-at-sea devices more frequently become standard equipment in pilothouses.

The first such instrument, pioneered by the Lorain County Radio Corporation,[2] was installed on the progressive Wilson Marine Transis Company's steamer *William C. Atwater* in 1934. It was a highly efficient unit destined quickly to dramatize its value aboard ship.

The very next season, as the coal-laden *Atwater* was upbound and six hours out of Whitefish Bay, in Lake Superior, Captain Edward Morton fell down a companionway, suffering serious facial, hip, and rib injuries. With the ship's new radio-telephone, the *Atwater*'s first mate arranged to divert the ship from Duluth to nearby Marquette, Michigan. There, a doctor, an ambulance, and relief skipper Bill Coles waited

2 The Lorain County Radio Corporation, now the Lorain Electronics Corporation, handles a wide range of navigating equipment in addition to the radio-telephone gear they developed.

at the dock. Wilson Marine Transit officials almost immediately ordered radio-telephone equipment for all their vessels, and other enlightened operators soon followed suit. Still, the radio-telephone did not become a mandatory requirement of the United States Coast Guard until 1954.

If the early proponents of wireless communication for all Great Lakes ships had sought specific incidents to illustrate its life-saving potentials, they could have found no better rostrum for espousing the cause than that which Lake Michigan provided in September and October of 1929. Nor could any stage be more advantageously managed for a dramatic comparison between the communication-equipped vessels and those whose owners still considered the wireless sets an unnecessary and costly luxury. Four big ships went down in a space of fifty days, two with wireless and two without. The grim inventory of people and wreckage plucked from the lake and its shoreline rendered its own poignant judgment.

Contents

Illustrations

Following page 166

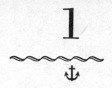

The Luck of Mr. Murphy

Second Mate Charles Murphy, of the steamer *Kaliyuga*, did not consider himself a lucky man. Quite to the contrary, he often felt that chronic ill fortune was his cross to bear. He was very conscious of his curious affinity for the abuses of fate on the afternoon of October 26, 1905, as he entered the Cleveland office of his employer, Jasper H. Sheadle, the astute manager of several fleets of steamboats. Mr. Murphy had missed his boat at Erie, Pennsylvania, and fully expected to be discharged. But, truly, he felt that he was not to blame.

Mr. Sheadle, when Murphy entered his office, turned pale, half rose from his chair and gasped, "Good God, man, where have you been?" "In Erie, sir," the mate stammered. "I missed the boat, but it really wasn't my fault. Captain Tonkin very kindly gave me permission to . . . but what's wrong, sir?"

Mr. Sheadle, still ashen-faced, sat down again and handed him a telegram. It was from Port Huron and was signed jointly by Captain C. E. Sayre of the steamer, *Centurion*, and Captain Thomas E. Murray of the steamer, *Pontiac*:

HAVE MADE THOROUGH SEARCH OF EAST AND NORTH SHORE LAKE HURON. NO SIGN OF THE "KALIYUGA" OR WRECKAGE FROM HER.

It was mate Murphy's turn to collapse in a chair, dazed and almost speechless.

"You mean . . . she's gone, sir?"

"She's missing, at any rate." Sheadle sighed. "A week overdue now and not a sign of her. I'm very much afraid that she's lost."

"I've been hearing about the storm, sir, and about the other vessels that were lost, but never a hint about the *Kaliyuga*."

"That was because we had assumed that Captain Tonkin had taken her over on the east shore and was in shelter behind some island, waiting for weather. It was the very devil of a storm, you know."

This was considerably an understatement. The gale, the first of two prolonged and disastrous fall storms of 1905, had sunk or wrecked some twenty-seven vessels. More than one had gone unreported for several days, but Mr. Sheadle had remained optimistic, assuming that the *Kaliyuga* would show up in due time. When the ship was two days overdue, he had asked the Great Lakes Towing Company to send out a tug from the Soo to search along Manitoulin Island and other islands that the larger vessels could not approach. The tug had found nothing. Mr. Sheadle was now very pessimistic.

Only an hour before Mr. Murphy's arrival, anxious to hold out some hope to the families of the ship's crew, but quite contrary to his own personal convictions, he had issued a statement to the marine reporters of the Cleveland papers:

> The mere fact that no sign of wreckage has appeared anywhere, leaves us with some hope that the vessel may still be safe. If the boat had gone down, something would certainly have appeared on the surface by this time. But no report of any wreckage whatever has been received.

Mr. Sheadle had taken some measure of comfort from the rather humorous report of another ship, missing on Lake

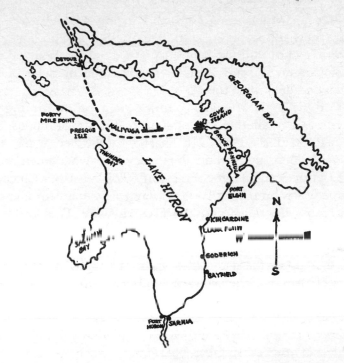

Huron for many hours before passing the reporting station at Port Huron. She was the *Alexander Nimick*. When a representative of the Lynn Brothers ship-reporting firm placed some mail and packages aboard her and solicitously inquired of her captain where he had been, that testy individual told him to mind his own damn business.

Mr. Sheadle was certain that Captain Fred Tonkin of the *Kaliyuga* would be happy to give the ship-reporter's man a civil answer, should the opportunity, happily, present itself.

Mate Murphy was still obviously shaken and distraught.

"Well, now," said Sheadle. "You, as it turned out, are a very lucky man. But now that you're here, let's see what we can do to straighten out this crew list of the *Kaliyuga*. There were about seventeen aboard, I believe?"

"Sixteen, without me," replied Murphy. "Unless, when I didn't show up, Captain Tonkin requested a replacement."

"No, I heard nothing from Captain Tonkin about taking on another mate," said Sheadle. "Only a routine wire of his anticipated departure time."

"Well, sir," said Murphy, counting them off on his fingers, "there was Captain Tonkin, of course, and Mr. Simmons, the first mate. And there was Mr. Sharpe, the first engineer, and Ernie Madden, the second engineer. The wheelsmen were Paul Deitman and Tom Carr, a couple of lads from Chicago. George Foster and Tom Wright were the watchmen; Charlie Beaugrand, the oiler; and the firemen were Tom Sullivan and Frank McKay. The three deckhands were all fellows named John—John Ross, John Rush, and John Yotter—or at least those were the names they gave. And, finally, there was Harry Laflamme, the steward, and his wife, the assistant steward. Let's see now . . . yes, sir, that makes sixteen, all told."

"Good, at least that's settled. Now, let's hear about this business of your missing the boat."

"It was this way, sir," explained the mate. "We got into Erie with a cargo of ore from Marquette late in the day. There were a couple of other ships in line ahead of us. Then the dock manager came aboard and told Captain Tonkin that there was some sort of breakdown in the unloading rigs and that only part of them were working. The way he saw it, we'd be hanging around for several days, waiting our turn. Then I asked Captain Tonkin if I could take a little time off and go home to Buffalo to see some friends of mine. The captain kindly gave me permission and I caught a Lake Shore & Michigan Southern train, right away. I got back in what I thought was plenty of time, but I missed the boat by a couple of hours. They must have gotten the rigs fixed sooner than they expected. I felt bad and hung around Erie for a few days, figuring I would be out of a job, but finally I decided to come here and explain it all to you. It really wasn't my fault, you see."

Mr. Murphy's enumeration of the crew and their respective responsibilities revealed some rather odd statistics. By any standards of the day the *Kaliyuga* was seriously undermanned, compared to other vessels of her size engaged in the same trade. He had named only two firemen and not a single coal passer.[1] Four would normally have been the minimum number of firemen needed to feed the ship's two Scotch boilers. They would have been augmented with a similar number of coal passers to relay the coal from the bunkers to the boilerroom deck. Most vessels had six firemen and six coal passers. Moreover, no third engineer was listed, and no third mate. The third mate could be dispensed with if Captain Tonkin stood one of the pilothouse watches, which he obviously did. But, in the engineroom, first engineer Charles Sharpe and second engineer Ernest Madden must have been working long, alternating watches. How Captain Tonkin solved the problem of firemen is a matter of conjecture. Probably the men Murphy classed as seamen were pressed into duty down below. Most vessels had crews of twenty-four or twenty-six, although the *Kaliyuga* got along with only seventeen . . . sixteen when Mr. Murphy got back to Erie a couple of hours late. There had been more men when the *Kaliyuga* was fitted out in the spring, but when men left, for one reason or another, they were simply not replaced. Early in the season, for example, Charles Skellie had quit to take a job on the barge, *Constitution.* His place on the crew roster had not been filled. Later, just the trip

1 The so-called "La Follette Act" of 1915, subsequent legislation, and enforcement of the United States Coast Guard-manning requirements brought an end to the days when deckhands or deck watchmen might be required to perform the duties of coal passers, and vice versa.

Other legislation included the important "Watch-and-Watch" bill, establishing the three-watch system and limiting the working hours for seamen to eight in a given twenty-four-hour period.

before her final one, Norman Hammond had left the ship with no replacement named. The ranks of the black gang had obviously been thinned, too, drastically so, judging from Murphy's recollection of only two firemen and not a single coal passer.

To a degree, the situation was understandable. The *Kaliyuga*, a wooden steamer, a 1941 gross-ton vessel, some 269 feet long and forty feet of beam, had been built at St. Clair, Michigan, in 1887. It was an unfortunate era in which to build a wooden ship, for Great Lakes shipyards were soon to be launching big steel freighters, twice the length of the *Kaliyuga* and capable of carrying three times her cargo tonnage. The economics of operating a relatively small vessel in competition with the larger carriers undoubtedly inspired a close watch on costs, a major item being the crew payroll. Captain Tonkin, who lived near Painesville, Ohio, was a young man in his first year of command. He was anxious to make his initial season a successful one for the ship's owners, and he probably trimmed costs to the bone, although his policy of operating his vessel so outrageously shorthanded was highly questionable.

It was a strange situation, but no less curious than the manner in which the ship itself had received her rather odd name. She was nearing completion in the St. Clair yards when the group of men financially interested in her began to cast about for a suitable name. The matter came up for discussion several times without an agreement being reached. The conversations were spirited but friendly . . . but also unproductive of an acceptable name. Finally, one of the men, in a fit of frustration, said, "Oh, we'll leave it to Langell; let him name her." Mr. Langell, one of the brothers who operated the shipyard, chanced at the time to be reading a magazine article relating to the iron-ore trade. In it appeared the word, kaliyuga, with the statement that it meant "age of iron." It was a fitting name, although someone else pointed out that in Sanskrit, according to an encyclopedia, the word meant "age of strife." But Mr. Langell had no interest in the Hindu language and opined that few people in the Great Lakes trade would know or care. So, *Kaliyuga* she became.

The working day was drawing to a close. Mate Murphy and Mr. Sheadle were still together when the office secretary brought the manager another telegram. This one seemed to settle the painful issue. It was a second message from Port Huron, relayed from Point Edward, Ontario:

> At about midnight on Thursday night the steamer *Lillie Smith* reported finding wreckage in Georgian Bay. It consisted of a pilothouse and sections of cabin, painted yellow outside, white inside. The nameboard on the pilothouse said *Kaliyuga*. All hands on the *Lillie Smith* were called on deck to witness and affirm the discovery.

Mr. Sheadle was a practical man, as all vessel managers are, or learn to be. There was now the unpleasant task of informing the next of kin that the *Kaliyuga* had certainly been lost and that all hope had been abandoned.

Then, too, and he knew it would be so, it was the beginning of a long and trying period of making numerous reports and depositions, handling insurance claims and filling out official form. Just the matter of trying to locate the survivors of the ship's itinerant crew members would involve a seemingly endless trail of correspondence.

Detail work was nothing new to him. In handling the affairs of many ships a man in his position must be in possession of a vast fund of knowledge . . . technical and otherwise, dealing with the operation, manning, loading, unloading, and scheduling . . . all of which demand close attention to details.

Mr. Sheadle was, first of all, vessel manager for the Cleveland Cliffs Iron Company's fleet of eight freighters. Beyond that, he had the same managerial responsibilities for several ships in which he, and others, were financially interested. They were operated under various company names, probably for tax purposes, and because each ship had a different group of owners. The steamer *Centurion* was operated by the Hopkins Steamship Company. The steamers *Angeline* and *Presque Isle* made their voyages under the house flag of the Presque Isle Transportation Company. The *Kaliyuga* was registered to the St. Clair Steamship Company. Mr. Sheadle was the guiding genius behind their efficient and profitable operation.

Now he had much to do, and after promising mate Murphy a job for the 1906 season and bidding him adieu, he began work immediately. There were telegrams to be sent . . . sixteen of them.

Marine men, some of them convinced that Captain Tonkin's policy of operating his vessel with practically a skeleton crew in the firehold and engineroom may have contributed to his undoing, have reconstructed his last voyage many times . . . up to a point. Beyond that, everything is mystery. Larger ships, and smaller ones, too, had survived the terrible gale on Lake Huron. She was eighteen years old, but many vessels that rode out the storm were older, much older.

After departing Erie earlier than expected, thus embarrassing Second Mate Murphy, the *Kaliyuga* made an uneventful voyage back to Marquette to load another cargo of iron ore. She steamed away from the loading spouts about two o'clock on the afternoon of Wednesday, September eighteenth. At five o'clock on the morning of Thursday, the nineteenth, she locked through the Soo. That fact had been duly noted by the canal's official ship-reporting service. Mr. Sheadle, as a matter of everyday routine, had found a telegram to that effect on his desk when he reported for work at eight o'clock.

The next official word of the ship's progress, via the ship-reporting services, would come from Port Huron, at the southerly tip of Lake Huron, and at the *Kaliyuga*'s modest pace, a good thirty hours' steaming time from the Soo.

The storm began about the time the *Kaliyuga* left the lower St. Marys River at Detour and began plugging south. Ship captains reported that the leaden skies seemed almost to touch the seas. The wind began to blow from the northeast, gaining in velocity with each passing hour. By noon, the seas were like heaving mountains, pounding the length of Lake Huron. Vessels in port put out extra hawsers and stayed moored to their docks. Those not far from a harbor of refuge, or a lee shore, steamed to safe anchorages under a full head of steam. For some, such as the *Kaliyuga*, it was too late to run. They were caught. There was nothing they could do but make the best of it. The best, in many cases, as the weather front broadened out to encompass all the Great Lakes, was not enough. Off Southeast Shoal, in Lake Erie, a scant thirty miles from the Rockefeller Building office of Mr. Sheadle, the schooner barge *Tasmania* foundered with all hands. Even closer, the steamers *Sarah E. Sheldon* and *Wisconsin* were aground off Lorain. The Gilchrist Transportation Company was frantically seeking word of its big steamer, *S. J. Hecker*; the managers of the Corrigan fleet were seriously concerned about their steamer, *Progress*, four days overdue at the Soo. At Elk Rapids, on the easterly shore of Grand Traverse Bay, on Lake Michigan, the schooner *Three Sisters* came piling ashore, overturning and spewing her cargo out. Off Harbor Beach, on Lake Huron, the schooner *Minnedosa*, in tow of a steamer, plunged to the bottom with her entire crew. Elsewhere, the steamers *Siberia*, *Prince*, and *Joseph Fay* were lost, the wreckage mingling along the shore with that from the schooners *Commerce*, *Yukon*, *Mautenee*, *Rhodes*, *Kathadin*, *Neilson*, *J. V. Jones*, *Vega*, *Kate Lyons*, *Glen Cuyler*, *Lydia*, *Foster*, *Alta*, *Olga*, *Oregon*, *Nirvana*, and the *Galatea*. Citizens along the west shore of Lake Huron, at Au Sable, Tawas, and Alpena, found the beaches a veritable bonanza of lumber, cordage, luggage, and the inevitable collection of mementoes that follow disaster offshore.

But what of the *Kaliyuga*? Like other vessels unable to withstand the pounding of monstrous seas for a prolonged period, she probably put her head to the seas and tried to reach the lee shore on the eastern side of Lake Huron. She was not a powerful vessel by any standards. Her progress would have been slow, very slow. From accounts of the two men who sighted her on Thursday and made the fact known when they later learned that the *Kaliyuga* was missing, Captain Tonkin was obviously trying to do just that. His course, until the weather dictated otherwise, was apparently going to be the normal one, just a few miles off the west shore. From all indications he had made his decision to head for the east shore at about four o'clock that afternoon, for when he was sighted by the captain of the steamer *Frontenac* a few minutes after that hour, he was seven miles off Presque Isle, and steering directly toward the east shore.

At dusk the *Kaliyuga* was sighted again, this time by Captain John Duddleson of the steamer *L. C. Waldo*. This time the vessel was between Middle Island and Thunder Bay Island, considerably to the south of the first sighting. Captain Tonkin was still steering east. The wind at the time, Captain Duddleson reported, was still blowing hard from the northeast. The *Kaliyuga* had made little progress crawling eastward in the face of the seas, but she had been driven some distance to the south.

Very probably Captain Tonkin came quite near reaching his goal during the night. The wreckage from his ship, found in Georgian Bay, near Cove Island, would indicate that he had been within reach of safety, only to face danger from another direction. In reporting his sighting of the *Kaliyuga*, at dusk on Thursday, Captain Duddleson had also given the wind direction as "blowing hard from the northeast." He added, however, that at about two o'clock on Friday morning the wind had shifted rapidly to the northwest and blew a gale, kicking up a terrible sea.

The dilemma faced by Captain Tonkin then would be a desperate one. After plugging for hours through a head sea to reach the lee shore, he would suddenly have found himself being assaulted by on-shore gale winds. It is doubtful if the *Kaliyuga* could have stood up under a return trip across the lake. The captain's nearest refuge, and it would be a dangerous trip at best, would involve steaming into Georgian Bay to seek the lee of Cove Island, or round Wingfield Point, at the northeasterly tip of the Bruce Peninsula, there to anchor in a comfortable depth of water. But this would require a safe passage through the Main Channel, north of Cove Island. It was not much of a choice. The channel was laced with rocks, flanked by shoals and studded with small islands. Under the circumstances, it must have been a choice between the very difficult and the impossible. Captain Tonkin would undoubtedly have chosen the Main Channel.

There were later developments that cast serious doubts as to whether Captain Tonkin ever got close enough to the east shore to be forced into such a decision. On October twenty-ninth the body of oiler Charles Beaugrand was washed ashore south of Kincardine. In a vest-pocket memorandum book he had written:

> Dear father, goodbye. I have a bank book at the Cleveland Society of Savings.
> Goodbye, mother, dear sister and brother.
> A kiss for all.

Three days later, at Port Elgin, just north of Kincardine, the body of another sailor, apparently a fireman, came drifting ashore. Both wore life preservers marked *Kaliyuga*. The strange and curious fact is that both men were found on the Lake Huron, or opposite, side of the long Bruce Peninsula, many miles away from where the ship's pilothouse was found floating in, Georgian Bay. Had they been washed overboard before Captain Tonkin was forced to try the Main Channel into Georgian Bay? Or had the *Kaliyuga* really foundered far from shore in Lake Huron? The latter would be a reasonable assumption, considering that the unfortunate crewmen, with a northwesterly gale blowing, would have ended up just where they did. But what of the *Kaliyuga's* pilothouse, found bobbing in the water a good sixty miles away and on the opposite side of the Bruce Peninsula? Surely it would have been carried in the same direction as the luckless crewmen, not in a different direction and through the Main Channel into Georgian Bay! Some hold that Captain Tonkin may have misjudged his position and mistaken the shallow Macgregor Channel, between Cove Island and Cape Hurd, for the wider and deeper Main Channel, thereby wrecking the *Kaliyuga* in the shoals of Southwest Bank, Middle Bank, or any of a hundred submerged rocks. Thereafter, they assume, the northwest gale bore the seamen southward to the sands of Kincardine and Port Elgin, while a freak current may have taken the battered pilothouse through the channel, past Russel Island and into Georgian Bay. Many were wondering, no matter what theory they held to, if Captain Tonkin, during the hours when his ship was sore beset by wind and water, had not sincerely regretted his cost-paring in the firehold. Steam, lots of it, would have been his only weapon in turning his vessel while trying to claw away from the east shore after the wind had shifted again, assuming that he had gotten that far. Steam was the only thing that would get her out of those dreadful troughs and heading into the seas again. He would not be likely to get it from two exhausted firemen or deckhands pressed into duty as coal passers.

Just where the ship went down or the exact cause of her disappearance are as much a mystery today as during that bleak fall of 1905, when some of her former crewmen patrolled the beaches looking for the bodies of their one-time shipmates. Captain Duddleson was the last man to see her. At that time she, like every other vessel on Lake Huron, was encountering seas that burst over her bows and combed her deck. She was, apparently, making the best of it and gave no signal of trouble or distress. She was heading east, in the face of the gale, an entirely proper maneuver, considering her modest size and cargo of iron ore. She carried lifeboats, flares, and the other approved lifesaving equipment. Had Captain Tonkin judged his ship to be in difficulty, or had he anticipated that the *Kaliyuga* would not last the night out, a few flares would have brought the *L. C. Waldo* and Captain Duddleson to his assistance. But there is no pride like that of a man in his first year of command. The situation would have to be desperate before he would call for help. Perhaps, in the gloomy dusk of that September evening, the situation was not yet critical, or even serious.

All through the long winter, as the lake vessels were moored at their docks and the beached wreckage of others became festooned with ice, the fate of the *Kaliyuga* was a popular subject. In all the waterfront saloons and in the warm lofts of ship chandlers, busy preparing for another season, a dozen theories were advanced—each accounting for the loss of the *Kaliyuga*. Who knows which one, if any, was the correct one.

Back in Buffalo, Second Mate Charles Murphy was a man of distinction. He recounted his story of missing the ship a hundred times, always to entranced audiences. Toasts were offered to his continued good health. Old friends gathered near, and even strangers sought him out. It was rather flattering, being a celebrity, of sorts.

For once in his life, Mate Murphy was feeling very lucky.

2

~~~~~~~~~~
⚓

The *Flying Dutchman* of Lake Superior

Captain James McMaugh, of the St. Lawrence & Chicago Steam Navigation Company's steamer *Algonquin*, was not the kind of man to put much stock in premonitions, omens, superstitions, or the supernatural tales so popular in the fo'c'sles of ships. What he saw, he saw. That was all there was to it. What he saw on the afternoon of November 21, 1902, was the 245-foot steamer, *Bannockburn*, plugging along through choppy seas on Lake Superior. At the time both ships were, as Captain McMaugh calculated, about fifty miles southeast of Passage Island and northeast of Keweenaw Point. This was just about where they should be, considering that they were each engaged in the grain trade from Ft. William and Port Arthur to lower lakes ports, the *Algonquin*, upbound, and the *Bannockburn*, downbound.

Peering through his glasses, Captain McMaugh noted that the *Bannockburn*, undoubtedly as a concession to the usual fall weather on Lake Superior, was not towing her two barges, but was making the voyage alone. She was some distance away. The day was hazy, but he recognized her immediately. There were not many vessels out at this time of

the year. The *Bannockburn's* profile and her three masts left
no doubt as to her identity. She, like the *Algonquin*, was
making good weather of it, and he noted nothing unusual
about her.

Aboard the *Bannockburn*, Captain George R. Wood was
probably making the same observations about the *Algonquin*, noting in his log that the weather was gusty and quite
hazy. There has always prevailed a fine line of distinction, as
recorded in ship's logs, between "hazy" and "foggy," a
frustrating question of judgment that has plagued generations of legal minds and investigating boards. Left to his own
inclinations, the shipmaster usually chooses the term "hazy."
Should something unpleasant happen later, an entry of
"foggy" would inspire embarrassing questions as to the ship's
speed in conditions that would normally indicate a drastic
reduction, or perhaps even coming to anchor. The term
"hazy" precludes many of these unpleasantries.

Having duly noted the passing of the *Bannockburn*, Captain McMaugh turned his attention to other matters for,
perhaps, two or three minutes before glancing out the pilothouse window for another look. The *Bannockburn* had disappeared from sight. The haze was confusing, but she should
still be plainly visible. The distance was not that great.

"I must say," Captain McMaugh remarked to his first mate, "that vessel certainly has gotten out of sight remarkably quickly."

Twenty-four hours earlier, on November twentieth, the *Bannockburn*, along with the steamers *Chili* and *Saturn*, had been "under the spouts," loading grain at the Canadian Northern elevator at Port Arthur. The cargo was 85,000 bushels of wheat consigned to another elevator at Midland, Ontario, in Georgian Bay. Captain Wood had indicated to Mr. Sellars, the elevator superintendent, that if he had good weather and prompt unloading at Midland, another trip might be possible. Mr. Sellars, noting that ice was already beginning to build out from shore, doubted it.

The *Bannockburn* was one of a vast armada of sturdy, steel, British-built ships in service all over the globe. She had been built in 1893 at Middlesborough, on the Tees Estuary, taking form in the yard of Sir R. Dixon & Co. Her rivets were set and hammered home by some of the best shipbuilders in the world. Statistically, she boasted a gross tonnage of 1620, an over-all length of 245 feet and a forty-foot beam. Soon after launching she came to Canada to join the steamers, *Glengarry, Rosemount, Westmount,* and *Fairmount,* in the considerable fleet of the Montreal Transportation Company, with headquarters at Kingston, Ontario. Since a major part of the company's business was in the grain trade, which involved frequent transiting of the Welland Canal and the small locks that circumvent the rapids of the St. Lawrence River, their steamers and their tow barges were limited in length. The *Bannockburn*'s 245-foot length was about maximum. Surveyors, going over her from stem to stern upon her arrival, assigned her Lloyds highest rating, A-1. She gave every indication of being as staunch and rugged as those for whom she was named . . . the brave Scots under Robert Bruce at Bannockburn, in 1314, who defeated a larger force of English under Edward II, thereby assuring the continuance of Scotland as an independent kingdom. It was a grand name that she bore with pride.

When she cleared Midland on her upbound trip, the *Bannockburn* had a crew of twenty men. The engineering staff was one short, but this matter had been taken care of by the company's agent at the Soo. When the ship left the Canadian ship canal at 3:40 A.M. on November nineteenth she had a new second-assistant engineer, Joseph Dawson. Charles Selby, her regular second-assistant engineer, advanced to first-assistant status.

The *Bannockburn*'s crew, below officer grade particularly, was typical of many then manning Great Lakes vessels . . . they were young. Ship operators, the Montreal Transportation Company among them, were well aware that jobs were scarce and young men plentiful. The prevailing wage scale reflected this philosophy. Of the twenty-one aboard, as the grain came swishing down into her holds at Port Arthur, eleven were from Kingston, the ship's registered home port. Chief Engineer George Booth was the only married man among the Kingston group, and he was only thirty-three years old. First assistant engineer Charles Selby was twenty-four and Second Mate William Chalkley, twenty-two. They were the senior members. From then on down the line . . . wheelsmen Ernest Rodway and Arthur Callaghan, assistant cook Sidney Smith, oiler Cecil Linton, watchman George Gillespie, and deckhands Edward O'Reilly, James Garvin, and Joseph McDonald, the average age was somewhere between seventeen and twenty. Wheelsman Callaghan, although only sixteen, was the sole support of four orphaned brothers.

Captain George R. Wood, thirty-seven years old, was not from Kingston but had plied the harbor long enough to be looked upon as a native. His home was in Port Dalhousie,

Ontario.[1] It was his first season on the *Bannockburn*. He had spent the previous year on the *Glengarry,* another company vessel, now commanded by his brother, John W. Wood. Another brother, Eugene, lived in Conneaut, Ohio, and was second assistant engineer on the car ferry *Marquette & Bessemer No. 2.*

The *Bannockburn* did not finish loading on the twentieth, but lay snuggled up beside the elevator until early the next morning, when she topped off her cargo, closed her hatches, and departed. It is estimated that she left Port Arthur at about nine o'clock. This would put her about where Captain James McMaugh had reported her in midafternoon of the twenty-first.

The *Algonquin* had encountered a stiff breeze and a making sea all the way into port, but as night fell the weather deteriorated rapidly. The wind blew a whistling gale and sent towering, punishing seas sweeping the length of Lake Superior.

Upbound to Port Arthur that wild night was the passenger steamer, *Huronic,* of the Northern Navigation Company's fleet. Aboard her was Fred Landon,[2] a scholarly young waiter who kept a daily diary of his fresh-water adventures. Two entries are significant:

NOVEMBER 21: At night we had the worst storm of the season.
NOVEMBER 22: During the storm of last night our engines sustained slight damage which they are repairing today.

[1] Port Dalhousie, a marine-oriented community since its founding, was first a village and then a town. In 1960 it was amalgamated with the city of St. Catherines. Early Scottish settlers pronounced it "Port Dalucy."

[2] The *Huronic's* young waiter, Fred Landon, was working to finance his education at Western University, now the University of Western Ontario. It is gratifying to note that he was graduated from that institution with honors in 1906. Forty-two years later he was its vice president. A distinguished and much-honored writer and historian, he is the author of *Lake Huron,* a scholarly contribution to *The American Lakes Series,* Bobbs-Merrill Company, Indianapolis, Indiana, 1944.

Waiting on the officers' table on the morning of the twenty-second, as the pilothouse men came off watch and sat down to breakfast, he heard one say that he believed they had seen the *Bannockburn* during the night.

If so, they were the last to see her, for sometime during that terrible night the *Bannockburn* vanished from the face of the sea!

The *Huronic* completed her voyage to Port Arthur and departed, downbound, on the evening of the twenty-fifth, still unaware of the *Bannockburn*'s disappearance. They probably heard the news at the Soo, but the fact was not confirmed until they arrived back in Sarnia, the *Huronic*'s home port. Landon's diary had this entry on November twenty-eighth:

Heard today of the missing *Bannocknurn*. This boat we passed on the night of the 21st.

When the wheat-laden ship became seriously overdue at the Soo locks, the news inspired a variety of conflicting reports and alleged discoveries that have not been explained to this day. The first, appearing in the Fort William *Times-Journal*, on November twenty-seventh, credited Mr. Sellars, the elevator superintendent, with having received word that the *Bannockburn* was lying behind Slate Island, twenty miles out from Jackfish Bay. Mr. Sellars vehemently denied the story, saying he had no intimation of the whereabouts of the vessel.

"I have heard nothing of her," he stated, "absolutely nothing."

Later, the newspaper carried this story:

The *Bannockburn* was located on the mainland north of Michipicoten Island. This morning J. J. O'Connor, of Port Arthur, received the following telegram from George L. McCurdy, superintendent of Marine Insurance, Chicago. "*Ban-*

nockburn ashore on mainland north of Michipicoten Island. News brought by *Germanic*." The *Germanic* is a freighter owned by the J. T. Hutchinson Co. of Cleveland.

The presumption among experienced mariners, after hearing this news, was that the *Bannockburn*, to ease the pounding she must have been taking, had sought the quieter waters in the lee of the north shore and had somehow run aground along the desolate Ontario coast.

Back in Kingston, where his office had been besieged by worried families, L. L. Henderson, inside manager of the Montreal Transportation Company, also received a wire from the Chicago office of the Underwriter's Association:

THE STEAMER "BANNOCKBURN" HAS BEEN LOCATED ON THE NORTH SHORE OF LAKE SUPERIOR, OPPOSITE MICHIPICOTEN ISLAND. CREW SAFE.

A smiling Mr. Henderson relayed the good word to all concerned. The Kingston newspaper, the *Daily Whig*, advised its readers that although the ship was ashore, its people were apparently unharmed. The atmosphere of worry and distress, the newspaper commented, brought back memories of a time a few years earlier, when one of the company's schooners, the *Glenora*, had been dismasted on Lake Superior, and had drifted around for over a week before being picked up. The *Bannockburn*, it explained, had remained unaccounted for, simply because of the lonely area of the accident and total lack of communications at that point.

Strangely, in Ottawa, the Department of Customs received still another telegram, the source of which was not released, stating that the *Bannockburn* was ashore not on the mainland but on Michipicoten Island itself.

At Sault Ste. Marie (the Soo) these dispatches from Chicago to Ottawa and Kingston were taken with several grains of salt. Veteran mariners there knew Lake Superior well and

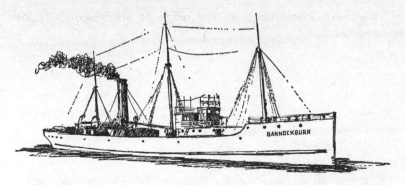

placed no faith in the reports of the *Bannockburn* being ashore. It just didn't add up, they explained. First, they pointed out, the weather since the night of the storm had been fine. There was nothing, therefore, to prevent a boat from the ship from making the trip to Michipicoten Harbor, where there was a telegraph station, or even to the Soo. Moreover, had her boats been damaged in the storm, the trip overland to Michipicoten Harbor would have taken two days at the most. More significantly, the people at Michipicoten had heard or seen nothing of the *Bannockburn*.

However, on the basis of the reported sighting by the *Germanic*, the underwriters ordered the Great Lakes Towing Company's big wrecking tug, *Favorite*, to the scene. The *Favorite*, after steaming around the island and many miles along the bleak shoreline, wirelessed that it could find nothing. Next, Frank Koehler, representing the *Bannockburn*'s insurers, arrived at the Soo and chartered the tug, *Boynton*, to search for the steamer between Caribou Island and Michipicoten Island.

In Chicago, meanwhile, George L. McCurdy, author of the premature telegram reporting the ship aground, admitted, when pressed, that he had had no positive information, but had based his message on the news that the wreck was reported by the steamer *Germanic*.

What ship had the *Germanic* sighted? No wreck was found nor were any other vessels listed as "missing." Later, when the *Germanic* was contacted, her officers disclaimed any knowledge of sighting a grounded vessel and could not account for such a report. Had they sighted a ship in such a position, they insisted, they would have put about and investigated, in the event any lives could be saved. Nor could Mr. McCurdy recall the exact source of his information. It was all distressingly vague.

Captain William Landon, of the tug *Boynton*, made a very thorough search around Caribou Island and Michipicoten Island, and retraced the *Favorite*'s course along the north shore. The weather was no longer fine. When the plunging tug threw spray over the pilothouse windows, obscuring his vision, Captain Landon had himself lashed to the top of the pilothouse. Again, the tug found nothing.

Even before the *Boynton* returned from her fruitless search, the underwriters had already given the *Bannockburn* up for lost. "It is supposed," they stated, "that the steamer stranded on Caribou Island."

Caribou Island is twenty-two miles south of Michipicoten Island and is surrounded by dangerous shoals on its westerly and northerly sides. It takes little imagination to envision the storm-wracked *Bannockburn*, dropping thirty feet in the trough of the seas, disemboweling herself on reefs that extend out a full mile from the island. If Captain Wood had been counting on the lighthouse at Caribou to guide him and to provide the important reference point he needed, on the black and stormy night of November twenty-first, he would have been looking in vain. The light was out!

It was a situation that had already caused some warm words to be exchanged across the border. Captain Wood may have been completely unaware of any controversy, or the fact that the lighthouse, through some quaint custom decreed in Ottawa, had been closed on November fifteenth!

While both American and Canadian vessel operators pointed out that their ships would still be making trips either to the Canadian or American lakeheads for grain throughout the month, and possibly into early December, the light had not been reactivated. Marine columns, particularly in the United States, were quite bitter in denouncing the policy.

The *Bannockburn* lost on Caribou's reefs? This was the popular consensus, until the steamer *Frank Rockefeller*, an American whaleback ore carrier, steamed into the Soo and reported passing through a considerable field of wreckage off Stannard Rock, well to the west and south of Caribou Island. Yet, the area indicated was right in the usual steamer tracks and would have been discovered by any one of a hundred ships, had it been there for any length of time. It could, of course, have been carried there by the prevailing winds, even though the *Bannockburn* might have perished far to the north. There was nothing to identify it as being from the missing ship. Still, she was the only one overdue . . . long overdue.

In Kingston, the *Daily Whig* had the painful task of telling the townspeople that the *Bannockburn*, thought safe only a few days earlier, was, indeed, still missing. But even had she steamed miraculously into Kingston Harbor that very day, it would have been a sad homecoming for Chief Engineer George Booth, the only married Kingstonian aboard. On the day the ship was reported aground, the crew safe, his eleven-year-old daughter died of heart failure. The next day one of the two remaining children, a son, was hospitalized with diptheria.

The more he thought about it, Captain James McMaugh of the *Algonquin* became convinced that the *Bannockburn* had burst her boilers and had blown up in the short interval of time between his first sighting of her, and the time he had looked for her again, two or three minutes later, only to find her gone. Considering the distance between the vessels and that all the pilothouse windows and doors were closed, it is quite likely that the explosion might not have been heard aboard the *Algonquin*. From the position of the two ships as of that moment, the wreckage discovered by the *Frank Rockefeller* was about where the prevailing northwest winds would have carried it in a few days' time. But what about the sighting by the men in the pilothouse of the *Huronic* on the night of November twenty-first, possibly eight or nine hours after Captain McMaugh had commented to his mate that the *Bannockburn* had gotten out of sight remarkably quickly? How could the observers in the *Huronic* be sure it was the *Bannockburn* they had seen? The night was dark and a great storm was raging. But sailors have an instinctive skill in identifying vessels, even at night, by the position of their deck lights and other individual peculiarities a landsman would miss. Then, too, they would be very familiar with the vessels that were likely to be moving to or from the Canadian lakehead in the month of November. Without a question, it was the *Bannockburn* they saw.

The editor of the *Daily Whig*, in announcing that all hope had been abandoned, put it quite poetically:

> It is generally conceded that the missing steamer is not within earthly hailing distance, that she has found an everlasting berth in the unexplored depths of Lake Superior, and that the facts of her foundering will never be known.

The boiler-explosion theory continued to be a lively subject for conversation in marine circles, although the failure of boilers that are regularly inspected and adequately maintained is an extreme rarity. Were the *Bannockburn*'s boilers in good condition? One would assume that they had been thoroughly inspected during fit-out time in the spring, which is customary. Yet, when reporters talked to Captain Gaskin, the veteran Montreal Transportation Company marine superintendent, he made a statement that was strange indeed, coming from a man in his position. "She could not have been in a collision," said Captain Gaskin, "since no other ship is reported missing or damaged. That leaves only three other possibilities . . . she either burst her boilers, hit a rock or shoal, or . . . her machinery went through her bottom!"

Her machinery went through her bottom? On the face of it, this theory sounded preposterous, utterly absurd. The *Bannockburn* was only nine years old. British-built steel tramps have sailed a half century without suffering such a fatal indignity. It is the last thing one would expect. And, yet, Captain Gaskin was the one and only person qualified to judge the seaworthiness of all the company's vessels. Their condition was his responsibility. He would best know the over-all soundness of the *Bannockburn*, although his ability to do anything about it might be another matter. Ship operators, and there is no reason to think his employers were the exceptions, were notoriously loath to spend money on their vessels as long as they floated and their boilers still held steam.

A few weeks after the *Bannockburn* had vanished, when the lock at the Canadian Soo was drained for the winter, a steel plate from the bottom of a ship was discovered. Some were sure it was from the lost vessel. If so, and if the condition of the *Bannockburn*'s bottom were such that she was dropping plates, it is possible that her machinery fell through it later, as she plunged and rolled in the storm on the night of the twenty-first. If her bottom had been so outrageously neglected, would not the same be true of her boilers? The end for ship and crew, in either event, would have been swift and merciful.

Loading experts, earlier, had scotched rumors that the ship was overloaded. Her cargo of 85,000 bushels of wheat, they explained, while completely filling her holds, would still not

put her down within a foot of the allowable draft for that season of the year. The editor of the *Daily Whig*, as it developed, was quite right in his prediction that the facts of the *Bannockburn*'s foundering would probably never be known, for her loss is just as much a mystery now as it was in 1902. The few clues found really told nothing—a single life preserver and a lone oar, found on the south shore of Lake Superior many months later.

Superstitious sailors, and there were still many around in the early years of the century, likened the *Bannockburn* to the legendary *Flying Dutchman* of salt water . . . a vessel that vanished off the Cape of Good Hope in a gale, only to reappear on the seas as a mysterious phantom ship, most frequently sighted during the night watches as she beats to windward on her endless voyage. On stormy nights, several sailors claimed to have seen the *Bannockburn*, buffeting her way down Lake Superior, her lamps blinking in the storm scud, while in the darkened pilothouse her master looked vainly for the welcoming flash of Caribou Island Light.

On the Great Lakes, as on salt water, a vanished ship has her place in the limelight but briefly, while the search for her continues, and those who wait for her grieve. The march of commerce goes on relentlessly, while the men who were once part of it are too soon forgotten. They and their ship live again only in the occasional stories of writers who revive the mystery for other generations of readers to ponder over.

The only lasting memorial for the *Bannockburn,* and it is really for her master, not the ship, hangs today in St. John's Anglican Church, in Port Dalhousie, Ontario, a simple tablet that reads:

> IN MEMORIAM. CAPT. GEORGE RICHARD WOOD,
> BORN MARCH 9, 1865. DIED NOV. 22, 1902.
> ERECTED BY HIS BROTHER, JOHN W. WOOD.

3

⚓

Hard Times for the *Benjamin Noble*

The spring of 1914 was notable for its economic problems. Hundreds of thousands of men were out of work, soup kitchens were doing a rushing business, organized labor was bitter. Down in Massillon, Ohio, "General" Jacob S. Coxey was planning to lead his second great march of the unemployed on Washington.

The year had started out on a hopeful note. On January fourteenth, Henry Ford, creator of what he called "the universal automobile," had made a revolutionary announcement that, beginning immediately and henceforth, all his auto workers would be paid a minimum of five dollars for an eight-hour day. While Ford workers were understandably elated, rival automobile manufacturers and industrialists in general waxed exceedingly wrathful and were inclined to say nasty things about Mr. Ford. The Ford plant was enjoying booming good health, as was its imperturbable founder. Elsewhere, factories were closing. More hopeless men joined the ranks of the idle.

The ills that had plagued the nation's industries for many months were soon reflected in the fleets of ships that transported the basic ingredients of steel—iron ore, coal and limestone—to the blast furnaces of all the lower lakes ports.

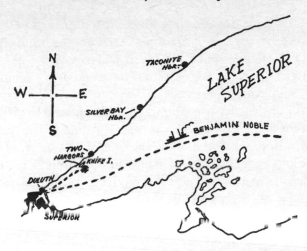

Despite an exceptionally mild winter that left the upper
lakes practically ice-free, many owners did not plan to fit out
their vessels until May, some not at all. A few managers
ordered their ships out early, hoping for an improvement in
economic conditions, but meanwhile comforted because they
could lay them up any time after their modest tonnage commitments had been met. In April, usually a busy fitting-out
period, long ships still lay tethered to their docks all along
the lakes, silent reminders of the evil days that had fallen
upon the country.

An exception was the steamer *Benjamin Noble*. Almost
new, only five years from the ways of the Detroit Shipbuilding Company, she opened the shipping season at Conneaut,
Ohio, by steaming into the harbor on April sixteenth, the
same day "Coxey's Army" of unemployed started out for
Washington.

Built in 1909, she was the only vessel of the Capitol Transportation Company of Detroit, Michigan, of which J. A.
Francombe was president and manager. Obviously designed
with the modest locks of the Welland Canal in mind, she was
just over 239 feet long and slightly more than forty feet of

beam. Her triple-expansion engine of an indicated 800 horse-power and her twelve-foot propeller combined to give her a modest eleven-miles-per-hour speed when loaded. Like many "canallers" she had big hatches to made her "handy" to work, considering that she was likely to load a great variety of cargoes during her life. She was not big enough to carry iron ore profitably, but there were other commodities needing transportation, and the *Benjamin Noble* was ready and capable of carrying them. During the first four years of her existence she had hauled stone, scrap iron, pulpwood, railroad iron, and coal . . . a great deal of coal.

Mr. Francombe had been very energetic during the winter of 1913-14, lining up cargoes for the *Benjamin Noble* to haul during the spring and throughout the summer. The end reult of one contract commitment reposed in a long line of railroad gondola cars "spotted" along Conneaut's Dock Three—railroad rails by the hundreds. They had originated at the mills of the Cambria Steel Company and were consigned to a railroad contractor who would take delivery at Duluth.

Captain John Eisenhardt was appalled. He had no idea of the total weight but confided to a dock worker that the ship could scarcely be expected to take it all on one trip. Mr. Francombe, however, had left no doubt but that this was exactly what he expected. Moreover, he had indicated that the shipment was a rush one, and was important in the light of future cargoes that might be anticipated as a result of prompt dispatch and delivery.

As soon as the ship was securely moored at a point where the gondola cars could be placed directly at her side, the loading began. The canal-size vessels, since they frequently took on and discharged cargoes where shoreside facilities did not exist, carried their own loading and unloading gear. The *Benjamin Noble*'s consisted of lifting and swinging booms on her two masts, serving each of her two holds. The lifting capacity of the booms was not great, but sufficient to handle the rails, one at a time. Each layer of rails had to be separated from the one below it by wooden blocking, which allowed room for the placing of lift slings when loading or unloading. More blocking had to be built up at the sides of each layer to keep the cargo from shifting in a beam sea. It was slow and laborious work.

Poor Captain Eisenhardt must have been at his wits' end. After working up through the ranks for years, the *Benjamin Noble* was his first command. And this was his first trip in her, as master. He obviously didn't like the situation at all. There was too much cargo to take in one voyage, scarcely enough to justify two. He knew that Mr. Francombe had probably figured his costs rather closely in bidding on the business. And he would have been at a distinct disadvantage when competing with other shipping operators who had vessels large enough to take the entire load in one trip without an overloading problem. Yes, Mr. Francombe had probably done a neat bit of manipulating with his pencil, but he was expecting far too much of his ship, to say nothing of what he demanded of a captain who was charged with the safety of his vessel and crew.

Captain Eisenhardt could, of course, resign his position and notify Mr. Francombe of his intention. It would take a lot of courage to quit before he had completed his first voyage as skipper. Economic conditions being what they were, hundreds of men with master's papers were ashore and at liberty. Many would welcome a chance to take over the *Benjamin Noble* and wink at what her draft marks registered. Mr. Francombe could have taken his pick. Captain Eisenhardt would probably never again have an opportunity to command his own ship. The word would be out that he was undependable. The circumstances would never be aired, just the fact that he had quit. There would then be serious doubts in the minds of prospective employers that he could withstand the pressures of command, particularly if his successor in the *Benjamin Noble* made a routine trip to Duluth with the cargo of railroad iron. It was not an enviable position, but Captain Eisenhardt apparently concluded that he would not make a hasty decision that he would regret later. After all, the ship was just beginning to load. Perhaps when she was down to her full draft and much of the cargo still remained in the cars, it would be apparent even to Mr. Francombe that two trips would be necessary. Captain Eisenhardt stayed aboard as the loading continued apace.

The job proceeded smoothly enough, but compared to other cargoes it was painfully slow. Each rail, after it had been lifted and carefully maneuvered into the hold, had to be inched up tight to the previous one, with crowbars. Aware that a vessel of the modest length of his command would be prone to a pitching motion in a seaway, Captain Eisenhardt made sure that plenty of blocking was placed between the ends of the rails and the bulkheads, including the one that separated the two holds. Each layer of rails put the steamer lower in the water. Her normal loaded draft was seventeen feet. When she was down to this mark he gave no indication that he was aware of this information. One at a time, another layer of rails went aboard, and still another. The water lapped up to the eighteen-foot draft mark painted on the ship's stem, and crept upward, inch by inch.

The *Benjamin Noble* had been loading for six days when Captain Eisenhardt ordered his first mate to stop. Two more cars of rails remained on the dock siding, but there they would have to stay. Their weight would have sunk the ship right there in her loading slip. She was outrageously over-loaded. Nor had her condition escaped the notice of the workers on the nearby coal-loading machines. They had been watching the progress of loading and they expressed amazement daily as the rails continued to go aboard. A dock fore-man commented to Captain Eisenhardt that the ship looked dangerously low in the water. The captain's reply had been somewhat evasive. The foreman could only recall that he had said something about following the shore as near as possible all the way up the lakes.

Another worker, when he heard his superior repeat the captain's words, was quick to reply, "Hell, he ain't goin' to get very far up the lakes."

The *Benjamin Noble* finished loading on the evening of April twenty-first. Captain Eisenhardt announced that he would sail on the following morning. The overnight delay was necessary because a big steamer would be loading a coal cargo at the dumping machine most of the night.

Now was the logical time for any of the ship's crew, who had second thoughts about shipping out on an obviously overloaded vessel, to pick up their gear, demand their pay, and find other jobs. But there were no other jobs in the spring of 1914, and they knew it, from Captain Eisenhardt on down to watchman Earle Crawford. Every man aboard who had any steamboating experience at all knew that the ship was in a dangerous condition. Chief Engineer A. C. Coger, of Port Clinton, Ohio, must have been aware of the situation. It was his first job as chief engineer, and he was in no position to make an issue of something that was traditionally the master's responsibility. He must have felt that the *Benjamin Noble* could make the trip without harm; otherwise, he would not have permitted his son, Frank, to ship on as an oiler. Fireman Otto Guntch and William Goullett, both of Toledo, were old hands, as was Paul Bolaraski, the second engineer. Steward John Colnan and Thomas Proud, second cook, had served together on many steamers and were undoubtedly aware of conditions. Perhaps they were, but they were also cognizant of the fact that, if they quit, they would probably not get another job. Not a man left the ship. Captain Eisenhardt did not mail a crew list to Mr. Francombe, but William Ford, shipping master for the

Lake Carriers' Association, attested that the ship left with a full crew of eighteen.

One dock employee, whose name has gone unrecorded, was so impressed by the ship's overloaded condition that he showed up the next morning to take a photograph as she left the harbor. It was not a particularly good snapshop and certainly unsuitable for reproduction. But it does show the *Benjamin Noble* easing out of her slip with her anchor pockets practically submerged and a frightening lack of freeboard aft. Captain Eisenhardt and a wheelsman were on the flying bridge.

Deeply laden as she was, the *Benjamin Noble* would not have been able to maintain her normal loaded speed of eleven miles per hour. She was pushing too much water ahead of her for that. But at least Chief Engineer Coger could not complain that the aft end was not down deep enough for his propeller to get a good "bite."

The departure of the *Benjamin Noble* from Conneaut, unhindered and unchallenged, illustrated the vast changes that have come through the years. Today, the owners would not be likely to find a captain who would take out a vessel so grossly overloaded. Nor would they also be able to muster a crew. The unions would take care of that. But, in the event they did, the United States Coast Guard would "arrest" the ship, preventing it from leaving port. The Coast Guard, however, did not come to the Great Lakes until 1915, when it took over the old U.S. Lifesaving Service, a year too late to help the *Benjamin Noble*. Even the lifesavers would have been helpless to stop her. Their responsibility was saving lives after a disaster occurred. They had no marine safety-enforcement powers to prevent one from happening.

It took the overburdened steamer three days to crawl westward on Lake Erie to Bar Point, snake her way up the Detroit and St. Clair rivers, steam the length of Lake Huron to Detour Passage, and wend a cautious course up the St. Marys

River to the Soo. The fact that she got that far was probably due to the unusually mild weather on Lake Huron.

The *Benjamin Noble* locked through the Soo on Saturday evening, April twenty-fifth, following the steamers *Rosemount* and *Scottish Hero*. At the same time the *Yosemite* was entering an adjoining lock. The *Rufus P. Ranney* had to wait until the other vessels cleared the lock gates before entering at eight o'clock. They made virtually a parade of steamers as they found their way between blinking buoys up the winding channel of the upper St. Marys River to Whitefish Bay and Gros Cap Light.

Shortly after all five vessels had passed beyond sight of the locks and the weather signal tower, northeast gale warnings were hoisted. Captain Eisenhardt could not have been aware of this. Had he known, he probably would have immediately turned his vessel and retreated back down the river to a sheltered anchorage. As it was, he continued, blissfully unaware of the monstrous weather front then developing behind him. For the balance of the night a wet, drippy fog held over most of Lake Superior, inspiring anxious moments and a great hooting of fog signals near Whitefish Bay, where the upbound and downbound courses converge. The wind picked up on the morning of the twenty-sixth and blew fresh all day, dispersing the fog. Later, it began to rain, quietly at first and then in lashing sheets. Through the night the rain changed to sleet, with intermittent flurries of snow. Captain Eisenhardt, since he had no choice now, proceeded on his course to Duluth.

The northeast winds that came whooping across the width of Lake Superior, from Whitefish Point to Michipicoten Harbor, to romp westward the entire length of the lake, began modestly enough, on the morning of the twenty-seventh. By noon it was beginning to give evidence of being the worst spring gale in years. From Coppermine Point to Eagle Harbor and on to the Apostle Islands and beyond, the seas began to build into hostile gray mountains, growing in stature with each passing mile. Fortunately for the *Benjamin Noble*, they were following seas. Even so, breaking rudely over her stern as they surely were, she must have been punished cruelly. Restricted by her heavy load to perhaps eight or nine knots, or less, they would be overtaking and sweeping her with ruthless frequency. Her hatches had obviously been battened down with all the strongbacks she carried. Captain Eisenhardt would have seen to that. He would have been thankful many times for the extra blocking he had ordered between the rails and the bulkheads. She could not have withstood the seas long had they attacked her from another direction.

Magnificently, almost unbelievably, the *Benjamin Noble* staggered on toward Duluth, almost a cork in a maelstrom. Shipping agents, there, had already wired the steamship companies about the severity of the storm. Many managers were advising their masters not to venture out into Lake Superior until the gale had blown itself out. Ore-laden vessels in Duluth harbor either stayed tied up at the ore docks or anchored close in behind the shelter of Minnesota Point, the arm of land that sweeps out from the mainland to give the city its fine, protected harbor.

Seldom had winds of such velocity been experienced. Not far from where a dozen vessels lay swinging at their anchors, with extra fathoms of chain out, a huge coal-unloading machine, with the roar of a hundred buckling beams, collapsed under the force of the gale, crashing down upon a steamer. In Duluth dozens of store windows blew in. Trees were felled. Utility poles came tumbling down. Iron-ore dust, swept from hundreds of loaded hopper cars, rose in red clouds and was driven into the pine-covered hills behind the city. Meanwhile, the *Benjamin Noble*, fighting gallantly, was coming on!

After such a truly heroic battle against overwhelming odds,

and only a couple of miles short of Duluth harbor, the sturdy
"canaller" certainly deserved a better fate than the one that
befell her. The Duluth harbor entrance is through a canal
that bisects Minnesota Point. Concrete walls form its sides.
On the lake end, piers serve day and night as a guide to the
mariner. In 1914 both piers were lighted at night by kerosene
navagational lights. During the height of the gale, early on
the night of the twenty-seventh, seas that were climbing ten
feet over the canal wall put out the south light! The lightkeepers were brave men, but not foolhardy. To attempt to
reach the piers to rekindle the light would have been suicide.
The south light stayed out!

Earlier, before the gale had reached its full-blown status,
the steamer *Minneapolis*, loaded with lumber and shingles,
had steamed out between the piers, downbound for Chicago.
Her master had apparently reached his own conclusion that
the storm would be of short duration, despite warnings to the
contrary. Somewhere off the Apostle Islands he had abruptly
changed his mind. The *Minneapolis* was making almost no
headway against the oncoming graybeards and was in danger
of structural damage. The captain decided to return to
Duluth, a decision easier come by than implemented. He
finally got her turned around but, during the minutes the
vessel was in the trough of the seas, the entire deckload of
shingles was swept away. Pounding back toward the harbor
with as much speed and dignity as he could muster, he was
confounded to see only one pier-head lamp lighted. Was it
the north or south light? The safety of his ship and crew depended upon exact knowledge. To guess wrong would be
fatal. Every shipmaster on the lakes remembered what had
happened to the *Mataafa* in broad daylight, in just such a
gale as was now raging. After striking bottom she took a shear
to starboard, striking the north pier, after which she was
carried away from the pier to go aground and break in
half. Nine men in her after crew had frozen to death a

scant quarter mile from the mainland. Driven onward by the wind and seas battering her from astern, the *Minneapolis* was perilously close to the canal when the bow watchman screamed: "Breakers ahead . . . breakers ahead!" The *Minneapolis* turned just in time to avoid piling on Minnesota Point.

On came the stout-hearted *Benjamin Noble*, with a determined Captain Eisenhardt straining his eyes to see the pierhead lights through the driven scud and spume. What was that? Only one light? Where was the other one? Captain Eisenhardt simply had to know! He guessed what had happened. One of the lights had been knocked out but, unless he knew which one, they might as well both be out. To guess wrong would be the end of the *Benjamin Noble*, and probably most or all of her crew. It was a fearful decision to make. Captain Eisenhardt was unwilling to chance a guess. He took the only alternative open to him: he turned his vessel to starboard, risking losing her in the deadly troughs of the seas he had been avoiding all the way up Lake Superior. Marine men feel that he must have held some faint hope of reaching Two Harbors, an important ore-shipping harbor about twenty-five miles northeast of Duluth. He really did not have a choice.

The *Benjamin Noble* did not make Two Harbors or any other port. Sometime during the night, in the beam seas she would have encountered on her new course, she finally succumbed. Grossly overloaded as she was, rolling heavily in those merciless seas, that deadly cargo must have shifted violently. Under those circumstances the end must have come quickly—very quickly. There was no time to cry out an alarm, to get the crew topsides, or even time for them to don life preservers. Not a single member of the ship's crew was ever found, although the bold shoreline was searched faithfully for a couple of weeks. Walter Murray, patrolman with the United States Lifesaving Service, found two hatch covers on the beach at Minnesota Point, late the next day. Subsequently, after the ship had disappeared, a couple of oars, lifebelts, and small bits of her pilothouse were washed ashore. It was the consensus among the men who searched for her that she struck near Knife Island, not far offshore, where the sandbank terminates, there to capsize and slide off into deep water, trapping her crew within the hull.

Storms and gales are enemies that well-constructed and ably manned vessels should be able to survive many times during their active lifespan. The *Rosemount, Scottish Hero, Yosemite,* and *Rufus P. Ranney*—the *Benjamin Noble*'s lock companions at the Soo—all managed to come through in good shape. For some hours concern was felt for the safety of the steamers, *William H. Truesdale, Willis King, F. T. Heffelfinger,* and the *James Laughlin,* downbound in the same blow. All were accounted for when it was over. But they were not overloaded, had ample freeboard, and could successfully turn, if necessary—all of them blessed with advantages denied the wretchedly overburdened *Benjamin Noble.*

It is unfortunate that monuments are seldom erected to vanished ships. How appropriate if one could be built on that bluff and rugged shore, at a point overlooking the cold blue waters off Knife Island.

A suitable inscription might read:

Out beyond the surf, between the shore and horizon, lies the gallant ship, *Benjamin Noble,* and her people . . . victims not of Lake Superior but of economic ills of a year best forgotten— 1914.

4
〰️〰️〰️
⚓

Eight Bells for the *Clifton*

Captain Emmet D. Gallagher of the steamer *Clifton* was an orderly, methodical, and precise man. Most sailors are. Limited to a bunk and locker as a seaman, he learns to limit his belongings to the bare necessities, adjusting to better things and more expansive quarters when he becomes an officer. Even so, a man can get along aboard ship without some of the things he takes for granted when ashore and at home.

Captain Gallagher had known leaner days and far meaner quarters than were his aboard the *Clifton*. Still, the old habits persist, and in his cabin, which also doubled as his office, there was a place for everything and everything was in its place, to paraphrase an old adage. His desk was always a model of neatness, and woe to the porter should he neglect to make the bed and tidy up while the "old man" was having his breakfast. In the pilothouse, too, every chart was in its proper numerical order, the pencils on the chart table were always sharp, the brass was polished, and the log was kept up to the minute.

He took special pride in the accuracy of the pilothouse clock, insisting that it be wound by wheelsman Peter Burns before he took over his evening eight-bells watch. It was a

thirty-hour Seth Thomas movement and, like most such clocks, performed at maximum efficiency if wound every twenty-four hours, at exactly the same time.

"Somethin' mighty comfortin' when she strikes eight bells," he once philosophized to second mate "Mac" McDonough. "Especially to the men who go off duty then."

There was something special about being a Gallagher, particularly a Gallagher from Beaver Island. They were a singular breed, most of them descendents of the hardy fishermen James Jesse "King" Strang found on the big Lake Michigan island when he made it the "kingdom" of his Mormon followers. From his headquarters in the island village of St. James (named after himself, of course) Strang had ordered every kind of harassment, including physical violence, to drive the Irish fishermen off, but when "King

James," as he liked to be called, was set upon and shot by two of his own disgruntled subjects, the Sullivans and Bradys and Gallaghers were still holding their own.

Later, when the commercial Great Lakes fleets of iron-ore, coal, and grain carriers developed, nearly every able-bodied man on the island who wasn't fishing for a living took to the sailor's way of life.

"Hell," one of them explained, "there wasn't nothin' else to do."

Over the years an uncommonly large number of Gallaghers lived to become masters of Great Lakes ships. Captain Emmet D. Gallagher was neither the first nor by far the last.

"Gallaghers—real Beaver Island Gallaghers—are sort of in a class by themselves," a shipowner once counseled a new aide in the personnel department. "They're tough and sometimes a bit headstrong, but at the same time they're fair and kindly people and by God, they're sailors! If you see one of them sign his home town as St. James, you can be sure he's one of the real Beaver Island Gallaghers."

On September 20, 1924, as the *Clifton* was loading stone at Sturgeon Bay, Wisconsin, Captain Emmet Gallagher, epitomizing the best traits of the Beaver Island Gallaghers, was having his troubles. A combination of circumstances had left him grievously shorthanded, with several fewer than the number of men he should have had to operate his ship efficiently. First, Emil Bonnett, an assistant cook, had quit his job when the *Clifton* was unloading stone at Toledo. Then, when the ship docked at the Leatham D. Smith dock at Sturgeon Bay, coal passer J. L. Shipley and firemen William Anger and Harry Tipler, all local men, had asked for their time. It was common knowledge aboard ship, too, that conveyor operator Pearl Purdy was moving from Sturgeon Bay to Detroit. His family had already gone on ahead to find a house. Captain Gallagher surmised that Purdy, who had two children, was going to try to find a shore job. He expressed a hope to first mate Edward Peck that Purdy would finish out the season on the *Clifton.* The other conveyor operator, George Maples, was a good man, but the loss of Purdy would mean finding still another replacement.

"I hope he stays, too," agreed the mate. "Anyway, with a name like Pearl, he isn't going to have an easy time in Detroit."

Captain Gallagher was not too surprised at the departures. The *Clifton* normally had a considerable turnover in personnel, largely because of the ship herself. She had originally been built in 1892 as the *Samuel Mather,* a whaleback or "pig" boat as the sailors soon dubbed them. She was one of many of the unusual vessels built by Captain Alexander McDougall . . . ships with long cigar-shaped hulls that characterized his theories of streamlining. When loaded, they looked something like surfaced submarines—with pointed bows and sterns and rounded sides.

"Why build high bluff bows and sides to resist the seas?" he asked. "Welcome them aboard and by their very weight they will steady the ship."

The cabins were in big, round steel turrets that rose from the deck, aft, and also supported a second deck of crew's quarters and pilothouse. A single smaller turret on the bow led down to the fo'c'sle where more men were quartered. There were no portholes, and the only light was from oil lamps or a single electric bulb. It was a dark, dank, and smelly place, practically under water when the ship was loaded, and a noisy shuddering hole when the "pig" burrowed herself into big seas. A man could scarcely stay in his bunk, let alone sleep. In any kind of weather the decks were constantly swept by the seas, and passage fore and aft was a matter of hanging onto the ever-present lifelines. Little wonder that the lower ratings of sailors wanted no part of the whalebacks. Even aft, the quarters were small, crowded, and, again, besieged by the seas in any kind of blow. The officers were accommodated on the upper deck in somewhat more spacious quarters. But they were still a far cry from what sailors of a later generation were to know.

The situation on the *Clifton* had been compounded somewhat because, recently, she had been converted into a self-unloader, requiring still more men to operate the machinery and conveyors. The work had been done at Sturgeon Bay by the shipyard owned by Leatham D. Smith. Mr. Smith also owned the dock where the *Clifton* was loading, the quarry from whence came the stone she was to carry, and he had a considerable financial interest in the Progress Steamship Company, the *Clifton*'s owners. From Cleveland, where he was also vessel manager of the Cleveland Cliffs Iron Company, Albert E. R. Schneider directed the affairs of the Progress Steamship Company and its three steamers, the *Clifton*, *Bay State*, and *Fontana*.

Mr. Smith, an engineer by profession, had recently invented a self-unloading system for the three vessels. It consisted of a conveyor at the bottom of hopperlike holds and an endless vertical-bucket arrangement to carry the bulk cargo, usually stone, topsides, where it was delivered to another conveyor. The second conveyor was on a long, swinging boom, supported by a large A-frame built just aft of the forward turret. Thus, the ships could divest themselves of their own cargo almost anywhere, but they were particularly handy in small ports or at docks that did not provide shore-side cranes with clamshell buckets to snatch out whatever bulk cargo was being carried. Mr. Smith's self-unloaders, it developed, were quite successful, although they gave the ships a rather grotesque appearance, compared to the typical bulk carriers.

It was a pity that the inconvenience of a depleted crew list should come upon Captain Gallagher at such a time. The last trip had been a pleasant one, partly because he had shared his cabin with his father, John. The old gentleman had enjoyed his annual outing and was urged to stay aboard for another voyage. But the rigors of fall sailing did not appeal to him, and he declined, preferring to return to Beaver Island, where the fall harvest promised to be a busy one. Most of all he had enjoyed those long, yarning sessions in the pilothouse at night. Captain Gallagher always made a point of providing employment for some of his Beaver Island friends, and John Gallagher had found it most gratifying to spin old yarns of the island to his fellow islanders, although they were of other generations. "Mac" McDonough, the second mate, could remember some of the people and incidents mentioned, but to wheelsmen Joe Scheid and Peter Burns it was all new and fascinating. All three had signed the articles as being from St. James. They would have loved to have him yarn on into the wee hours of the morning, but promptly at midnight, eight bells, John Gallagher would say good night and go to bed.

In accordance with a long-accepted custom, Captain Gallagher left the job of replacing departing engineroom and black-hole crewmen pretty much to Chief Engineer Walter J. Oertling. Those working topsides were his own responsibility. In the large lake cities it would have been a simple matter to put in a call to the hiring hall, specifying the jobs open and what skills were most needed. But Sturgeon Bay had no hiring hall; finding replacement was largely a matter of personal contact with a group of friends and acquaintances. Chief Oertling instructed his men going off duty to see if they could recruit a couple of coal passers. Captain Gallagher was in need of a pair of deckhands. He decided that finding someone to replace Emil Bonnett, the lately departed assistant cook, would be relatively impossible in Sturgeon Bay. Besides, the wife of the head cook, Sam Stevenson, had shown up and offered to help her husband and second cook John Hamilton in return for transportation to Detroit for herself and a nine-year-old daughter, headed home to Benton Harbor, Michigan. He would call the hiring hall in Detroit for another assistant cook. Those of the crew who headed "uptown" while the *Clifton* was loading, were instructed to bring back any likely-looking sailors to round out the crew.

Chief Engineer Oertling was not too hopeful. He had been through the same hunt for help many times. He had been on the *Clifton* less than a year himself. The son of a well-known captain, he had sailed as assistant engineer and chief engineer for over twenty years on the Goodrich Transit boats. His previous job had been that of chief engineer on the passenger and package freight steamer, *Arizona*. Many wondered why he had quit the *Arizona* to take over the *Clifton*'s engine-room and the consequent downgrading of living quarters, responsibility, and working conditions. But it was a personal matter and it could be that living in Sturgeon Bay, the job on the *Clifton* would permit him to see his family more frequently. Jack Sullivan, the first assistant engineer, was from Mitchell, South Dakota, had no local contacts and thus could offer little help. Meanwhile, a steady stream of crushed stone was rattling down chutes into the *Clifton*'s hold.

Altogether, both Captain Gallagher and Chief Engineer Oertling were rather surprised at the quality of the replacements rounded up by the crew. They were accustomed to accepting what came their way from the hiring halls, particularly when they asked for black-gang help. Often, the new men were chronic alcoholics who lasted only until pay-day and frequently had to be sobered up before they could stand their regular watches. This was different.

As coal passers, Mr. Oertling drew twenty-one-year-old Robert Stedman and nineteen-year-old Harold Hart, both clean-cut, alert young fellows. Stedman's father, president of the Door County State Bank, was out of town visiting another son and daughter at the University of Wisconsin when Robert decided to ship out on the *Clifton*. Young Hart, a close friend of Stedman, wanted to be with his chum, and both agreed that it would be good "to see what Detroit is like." They intended to make only the one trip.

Mr. Oertling did not think it necessary to tell them that they were not likely to see much of Detroit in the few hours it would take the *Clifton* to spew out her cargo. They would, in any event, get a splendid view of the city's skyline on the way down the Detroit River. He doubted, however, if this is what they had in mind.

Captain Gallagher was pleased to welcome aboard as deck-hands, Lawrence Haen and George Husak. Haen, nineteen, was a cousin of Bernard Haen, one of the *Clifton*'s oilers. Husak was twenty-one and quite independent by nature. He had been graduated from high school in Milwaukee and turned down an offer from his parents of either joining his father in the tailoring business or attending the University of Wisconsin. He worked a couple of summers in Sturgeon Bay, liked the community, and preferred, as he confided to friends, "to paddle my own canoe."

The *Clifton*'s loading had been completed when the new hands reported for work. Of the thirty souls aboard, thirteen were from Sturgeon Bay. The cargo totaled 2200 tons of crushed stone consigned to the Birmingham Sand & Stone Company in Detroit. Both Lawrence Haen and George Husak began to earn their keep by helping the experienced deckhands, Stanley Guth, Bernard Soderstrom, and Andy Olson, manhandle the hatch-cover sections in place and hammer home the "strongbacks" that held them securely.

It was four o'clock that Saturday afternoon, eight bells again, when Captain Gallagher, gauging the *Clifton*'s turning radius carefully, quietly gave wheelsman Joe Scheid his steering orders: "Steady now . . . a couple points more to port . . . midships . . . steady now . . . come around slowly . . . hold 'er . . . steady as she goes." Slowly and quietly—they were never much for noise and commotion—the thirty-two-year-old whaleback found her channel in the Sturgeon Bay Ship Canal and made a cautious passage to the open water of Lake Michigan. At an average running speed of ten miles per hour it would take her approximately fifteen hours to cover the one hundred and fifty-one miles from the canal piers to Old Point Mackinac, about halfway through the always-dangerous Straits of Mackinac. The actual time would depend somewhat on what weather conditions the *Clifton* encountered during the night.

Outbound from the Sturgeon Bay piers, Captain Gallagher swung his ship to port on an angling upbound course that would keep him well to the east of Fisherman Shoal, Fish Island, St. Martin Island's shoals, Poverty Island, and Summer Island. At the same time he would be considerably west of Gull Island, Trout Island Shoal, and the maze of rocks and shallows extending outward from Whiskey Island and Squaw Island. He had heard enough shipwreck stories from other generations of Gallaghers to have a healthy respect for the northern end of Lake Michigan. It was an area where casualness led to casualties. Captain Gallagher, although he had traveled the route hundreds of times before, probably left no doubt in the minds of mates Peck and McDonough just what compass bearing he wanted them to steer while he was getting his sleep.

The *Clifton*'s immediate objective was Lansing Shoal Light, which stands like a traffic buoy in the main steamer track about midway between Garden Island and Point Patterson, on the south shore of Michigan's upper peninsula. In the meantime, of course, a sharp lookout would be kept for the downbound vessels whose courses would necessarily require them to use Lansing Shoal Light as a point of reference. There would be other ships closing from the port side, package freighters out of Green Bay and ore carriers out of Escanaba taking either Porte Des Morts (door of death) or Rock Island passages. And, of course, there were always big

Ann Arbor Railroad car ferries shuttling back and forth from Frankfort to Manistique. Yes, indeed, it was not the place to be lax in the matter of qualified watchmen and lookouts. If the evening had chanced to turn up a bit of fog, you may be sure that Captain Gallagher would have had all the pilot-house windows open and a man stationed on top of the bow turret. All would be listening intently for bell buoys and steamer whistles and watching for the fog-shrouded mast-head lights of vessels bearing down upon them.

There was no fog that night, however, and in due course of time the *Clifton* came abreast of Lansing Shoal Light, hauled to the starboard in a slightly southeasterly compass bearing, steering directly for Old Mackinac Point. Here, as she passed, at seven o'clock on Sunday morning, the local reporting station dispatched a telegram to the *Clifton*'s owners, verifying her position as of that time. This was a regular service in the days when many ships, the *Clifton* included, were without wireless or any kind of communication once they left port. From the telegrams from the various reporting stations along the lakes, shipowners were thus able to schedule their approximate arrival times at their destinations and arrange for any services they might require.

Just after passing Old Mackinac Point Light, the *Clifton* hauled southeast, heading down the South Channel between the mainland and Bois Blanc Island. Again off Cheboygan, she turned to the east on a course that would take her out into deep Lake Huron and the long haul to Port Huron at its southernmost tip. Here, though it had not been apparent when the *Clifton* was in the straits and in the lee of the mainland, Captain Gallagher found a stiff southwest wind blowing, building seas that marched right over the vessel's rounded sides to spend themselves against the after turrets. This was the kind of weather the old whaleback had been built for, and she accepted it with a minimum of fuss and resistance. She kept well out in the lake on the downbound course recommended by the Lake Carrier's Association.

Off Forty Mile Point at eleven o'clock, that wild and gray Sunday morning, with the mounting seas marching relentlessly northward, the big wrecking and salvage tug *Favorite*, of the Great Lakes Towing Company fleet, upbound to the Soo, hove into sight off the *Clifton*'s starboard bow.

Aboard the tug, homeward bound after releasing a stranded steamer, Captain Alex Cunning, her almost legendary skipper, observed that the *Clifton* was burying her snout in the seas and, while taking a lot of water over her decks, was apparently making good weather of it. A fact he so noted in his log.

The *Favorite*, running before the seas, was taking them over her stern. The deck passageways on both sides were being flooded regularly. Her crew, having no reason to be on deck, kept to their warm and snug quarters.

Captain Cunning wiped the condensation from a porthole glass and peered through the spume and scud once more. The *Clifton* was still in sight and belching black smoke that the wind flattened and spread over a couple of miles of heaving sea.

He leaned against the binnacle and folded his arms comfortably over the lamp housing. "Old Emmet is takin' a pretty good dustin' out there," he observed to wheelsman Jim Lapham. "Before the day is over he'll be wishin' he was back on Beaver Island, all snug for the winter. Never had any hankerin' to ship out on one of them pig boats myself. I'd rather look down on the water than up at it."

Beginning late Sunday afternoon and continuing all that night, a furious gale swept up the lake from the southwest. Some of the largest vessels in the bulk trade fled to harbors of refuge. Those caught far from protection steamed in as close to the lee of the western shoreline as they could get and dropped both anchors. The seas that roamed Lake

Huron that night were the kind that old skippers later like to yarn about around the fireside in their retirement years. They were the kind that disrupted shipping, created monumental scheduling difficulties, and caused no end of trouble for those ashore who were vitally concerned with such matters as contracts, tonnage commitments, fueling, repairs, provisioning, and the endless details that go hand in hand with operating cargo steamers.

The *Clifton*, allowing a full twenty-four hours for the passage down Lake Huron to Port Huron and almost another full day wending her way at reduced speed down the winding St. Clair River, Lake St. Clair, and practically the length of the Detroit River, was due at the Birmingham Sand & Stone Company dock sometime late Monday afternoon or early evening. Having her own unloading gear, she was independent of the shoreside clamshell buckets and could begin to spew out her cargo as soon as she was tied up and her boom had swung out.

No particular concern was felt by those at the sand and stone dock when the *Clifton* had not appeared by Tuesday morning. The news of the storm and subsequent delays to all shipping had become common knowledge. But when she was still not in sight at noon Wednesday, a query to her owners was certainly in order. Had the Progress Steamship Company, the telegram read, had any word of the steamer or her estimated arrival time in Detroit?

In Cleveland, A. E. R. Schneider, consulting a mass of messages from reporting stations as to the position of the many vessels under his management, at once became aware that the *Clifton* had never been reported at Port Huron! Her last known position was when she passed Old Mackinac Point on Sunday morning. It was now late Wednesday.

Concluding that the ship, if she were still afloat, had perhaps experienced mechanical trouble and had been carried by the wind and seas to some remote anchorage, Mr.

Schneider dispatched a wire to Leatham D. Smith in Sturgeon Bay, apprising him of the situation and inquiring if the *Clifton* had any known or suspected engine trouble when she had left that port. More wires were dispatched to reporting station, asking that messages be put aboard all ships upbound or downbound in Lake Huron, requesting that the masters keep a sharp lookout for the *Clifton* or any sign of wreckage. The Coast Guard was notified and was asked to institute an immediate search. From Selfridge Field at Mount Clemens, Michigan, military planes were alerted and began systematic air sweeps up and down the east shore of the lake. The tug *Manistique*, was chartered to search anywhere her master thought it likely the *Clifton* might have come to grief. Both the other Progress Steamship Company vessels, the *Bay State* and *Fontana*, were diverted from their normal courses and ordered to steam up and down the lake, with all hands that could be spared to be on watch, looking for the overdue ship. Being a highly efficient and capable vessel manager, Mr. Schneider did what had to be done with a minimum of dramatics. Still, before the day was over, every sailor on the Great Lakes knew that the old *Clifton* had gone missing.

Up at the Soo, the wireless-equipped *Favorite* heard the news almost at once. Captain Alex Cunning, realizing that he was probably the last mortal to set eyes on the old whaleback, quickly wired Mr. Schneider of the sighting off Forty Mile Point on Sunday morning, adding that in his considered opinion she appeared to be in no trouble at that time, had not indicated that anything was wrong—as she could easily have done—and was, in his judgment, making good weather of it despite some rather considerable seas.

Back at Sturgeon Bay, word that the *Clifton* was missing and presumed, by many, to be lost, plunged the entire community into mourning. Nearly half the ship's crew were friends and neighbors. Crowds gathered at the Leatham D. Smith dock, whence the *Clifton* had departed, feeling that the latest news of the search would undoubtedly come to Mr. Smith who was also vice president of the Progress Steamship Company.

Early in the anguished waiting period a rumor was started that the *Clifton* had been reported safely in shelter at Oscoda, Michigan, far down on the west shoreline of Lake Huron. Spirits lifted among those not knowledgeable in marine matters, but experienced sailors—and there were many in Sturgeon Bay—quietly pointed out that the available depth of water at Oscoda could not possibly accommodate a vessel of the *Clifton*'s draft. On the other hand, they added, had the ship sought shelter in any of the other available harbors—Tawas Bay, Au Sable, Thunder Bay, or Alpena— her owners would have long since been notified.

All around the lakes, on street corners, at the docks, in the ship chandlery stores, the old familiar questions were being asked: "What happened to the *Clifton?*" Skippers who were out on Lake Huron that night and had been unable to run for shelter reported that the gale, while of relatively short duration, was the worst they had ever experienced, reaching a screaming, roaring crescendo between four and five o'clock on Monday morning. Few doubted that the 308-foot *Clifton* could have survived the punishing seas that were running rampant then. Captain Gallagher, they concluded, could not have continued battering his way through the seas on the same course he was steering when sighted by the *Favorite*. He would have had to turn sometime during the night, when the gale intensified, and flee with the wind and seas at his back. But with those seas at the height reported by the unfortunate skippers who experienced them, the *Clifton*, low in the water when loaded, would undoubtedly have been swept from end to end with each rising mountain of black water.

There was some speculation that Mr. Smith's self-unloading gear, while undeniably efficient, was simply too much weight and bulk to be carried on a vessel such as the *Clifton*, already mostly under water when she was fully loaded. There was always the possibility that the big, swinging boom had torn loose from its lashings and had swung far out over the side, rolling the ship, already in the trough of the seas, so far that her cargo had shifted. The combination of a shifted load of stone and a long conveyor boom hanging over the side could easily have capsized her. The self-unloader rigs were fine for a conventional vessel, they argued, but they were bound to alter the metacentric height (center of buoyancy); for a vessel designed with a minimum of freeboard to start with, what else could one expect? Then there was the matter of hatches. The original whaleback design of Alexander McDougall had followed his theory of welcoming the seas aboard by offering as little resistance as possible. Thus, the hatch covers were actually ship's plates that fitted the "skin" of the ship and, when battened or bolted down, offered no more opposition to boarding seas than did the rest of the rounded hull. But the exigencies of the stone, sand, and gravel trade were such that the flush hatch covers were impractical. Conventional hatch openings with protruding combings were more satisfactory in many ways. The hatch covers were those that were still in use on many ships: heavy oak timbers that, once in place, were held secure by long steel bars or "strongbacks." Now, however, the modification of the hatches on the *Clifton* did, indeed, offer resistance to the seas. Many wondered if a hull specifically designed to welcome the seas aboard could be successfully adapted to include protruding hatch combings, without inviting disaster.

Then there was the matter of her engine. Was it, as had been hinted, something short of perfection? There was no basis for such speculation, since the engines Alexander McDougall had specified for his whalebacks had a universal reputation for ruggedness and dependability. Surely, chief engineer Walter Oertling would not have been likely to have quit a good job on the *Arizona* to ship on the *Clifton* if she suffered engineroom infirmities beyond his ability to quickly put to rights. Engineers are dedicated people, and had the *Clifton* been cursed with troublesome engine or ancillary gear the matter would have been common gossip in every engineroom. Even the opportunity of seeing his family oftener would not have justified leaving a job, where he had over twenty years of service and seniority, to sign on with new owners if her power plant had something amiss. No, Walter Oertling must have had every confidence in the *Clifton*'s engine.

Leatham D. Smith, in whose shipyard the *Clifton* had been fitted out with his self-unloading device and from whose stone dock the ship had taken her last cargo, was first and foremost an engineer, having been graduated from the University of Wisconsin in 1909. He was named after his father's partner, John Leatham, who, with the elder Smith, was engaged in the lumbering, marine-salvage, and towing industries for many years. Leatham D. Smith's interests were primarily in shipbuilding and conversions. During World War I, his yard built a substantial fleet of wooden sea-going tugs. It was he who pointed out that during the winter of 1923-24, while the *Clifton* was being converted into a self-unloader, she was also changed and modernized in several ways. It was a matter of record, too, that only three weeks before she had taken her final cargo at Mr. Smith's stone dock, the *Clifton* had been surveyed and inspected at Detroit by the Steamboat Inspection Service and had passed with flying colors. This would preclude any deficiencies in her equipment, boiler, and engine at the time. What might have happened out there on Lake Huron during the night of September twenty-first or the morning of the twenty-second is another matter—one that gave rise to endless speculation.

Mr. Schneider, meanwhile, was staying close to his desk and telephone in Cleveland. The aviators out of Selfridge Field had reported nought but the usual sightings of vessels upbound and downbound going about their normal chores. None that came under surveillance resembled the missing *Clifton*. There were whalebacks, to be sure, but none with the distinctive profile given by the addition of Mr. Smith's self-unloading device. The tug, *Manistique*, wiring from Kincardine, Ontario, reported that she had gone up and down the eastern shoreline, from Point Edward to Port Elgin, several times, at varying distances from the shore, without finding a single clue.

The tug *Falcon*, however, upbound for the straits with a barge in tow, reported finding a welter of unidentifiable wreckage thirty-five miles southeast by east of Alpena, Michigan. Mr. Schneider immediately ordered the *Fontana* to that location. From Captain S. A. West of the steamer *William G. Mather* came word that he had picked up a wireless from the captain of the *Anna C. Minch*, indicating that his ship had passed a ship's tail rack about fourteen miles southeast of Thunder Bay.

Captain H. M. Hansen of the steamer *Clemens A. Reiss* radioed through the Reiss Steamship Company's office that his ship had sighted and passed a small lead-colored raft with four air chambers, some twelve miles north of Yankee Reef in Lake Huron. "No bodies or equipment were on the raft," he concluded.

Mr. Schneider had long since resigned himself to the fact that the *Clifton* had joined the long list of ships "gone missing" on the Great Lakes and was already immersed in all the unpleasant details of insurance claims, affidavits, depositions, and the final determination of the actual makeup of the crew list when the ship had left Sturgeon Bay. It was a grim business—one that comes to every shipowner or manager when one of his vessels has been lost. Beyond the cold, formal forms he was required to fill out by governmental agencies, there were the poignant, personal messages from the parents and relatives of the *Clifton*'s people, asking that the search

be continued and wondering if any attempt would be made
to recover the bodies of their loved ones. Mr. Schneider, in
reply to the latter question, could only assure them that
Richard A. Harrison, traveling commissioner for the Lake
Carriers' Association had already left for Kincardine, Ontario, where, it was felt, the *Clifton*'s lost crewmen, if they
got clear of the foundering ship, would make their unhappy
rendezvous with land. Personally, he was of the opinion that
the end came suddenly, so suddenly that the ship's people,
in their cabins, the engineroom, the firehold, and in the
pilothouse, would have had no opportunity to escape and
were, undoubtedly, still within the ship.

   Captain Dalton Hudson, master of the Great Lakes Transportation Company's steamer, *Glencairn*, out of Midland,
Ontario, had been one of the skippers caught in the fearful
gale that had raged the length and breadth of Lake Huron,
the night the *Clifton* vanished. He had been one of the first
to declare that the whaleback could not possibly have survived the seas he had encountered during those frightening
hours of darkness. He was not surprised then, on the afternoon of September twenty-eighth, when the *Glencairn*, downbound with grain, to Goderich, Ontario, began to encounter
wooden hatch covers practically in the center of the lake.
They were the usual oak timbers, bolted together in groups
of four. They could have come from any ship, except that
none but the *Clifton* was missing. Captain Hudson was a
compassionate man, in addition to being an extraordinarily
capable skipper. He knew that the "find" of the hatch covers
was really the only significant clue discovered thus far, and
that a compilation of statistics on wind direction and velocity
over a period covering the last week could pretty much
determine the drift of the wreckage and thus reveal the approximate location of the ship when it foundered.

   Despite the pressures of his schedule and the inevitable
"chin music" he would get from the front office over the

delay, Captain Hudson ordered his wheelsman to steer a search pattern around the area of the floating hatch covers. For two hours, as the eager crew lined the rails with pike poles in hand, ready to hook anything of importance, the *Glencairn* circled and probed.

A cry from a crewman on the port side brought Captain Hudson and one of the mates to the deck. A group of men were clustered around one man who pointed excitedly and clawed with his pike pole at something that was still out of reach.

There, alternately submerged and revealed by the modest chop of the seas, staring up like the eye of Cyclops, was a searchlight! Quickly, a grapling hook was thrown over the wreckage that supported it and strong arms drew it to the side of the *Glencairn*. It was the top and part of the front of a pilothouse, or the shattered remains of what had once been one. More crewmen arrived with ropes and the entire section of wreckage was lifted to the deck. Several held it on end so the inside could be searched for clues to the identity of the vessel it once graced. And there, above the center window frame, was the *Clifton*'s pilothouse clock! The hands apparently stopped when the ship went down, pointed, as Captain Hudson later communicated to Mr. Schneider, to exactly four o'clock.

It was eight bells again . . . again and forever for Captain Gallagher and the *Clifton*.

5

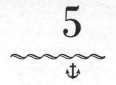

Soft and Brown ... with a Touch of Green ....

The *Andaste* viewed from any angle was scarcely a thing of beauty.

Even after she disappeared on Lake Michigan on the night of September 9, 1929, there were few charitable enough to recall any graceful features about her, probably because she had none. She was a working ship, pure and simple, too small for her times and trying to make amends for it by accommodating on her deck a grotesque maze of machinery. Big, round, hopperlike loading hatches accepted her cargo; a clanking, continuous scraper-type device, and a long, mobile conveyor boom unloaded it. The boom was supported, in action, by a tall steel tripod A-frame just aft of her fo'c'sle house. Altogether they comprised the latest in an efficient self-discharging system, particularly adapted for what had become her standard burden—sand, stone, and gravel. It was supposed to add years to her useful life. Perhaps it did, for the *Andaste* was still plugging along at her normal nine miles per hour in her thirty-seventh year when the end came. Her charterers and managers pointed out that it was her new self-unloading system, the epitome of proficiency, that made it economically possible to operate her. Others, recalling that a similar rig had been installed on the whaleback steamer *Clifton*, missing on Lake Huron now for five years, hinted that it was the heavy topsides gear that killed her.

The *Andaste* was launched from the yard of the Cleveland Ship Building Company in 1892, a few days ahead of her sister ship, the *Choctaw*. As their Hull No. 16, she slid into the brackish Cuyahoga River, 266 feet long between perpendiculars, with a beam of thirty-eight feet and a molded depth of a little over twenty-two feet. With a gross tonnage of 1573, she had a cargo capacity of 3000 tons and seven hatches for loading and unloading it. Both vessels were built for and accepted by the Lake Superior Iron Company.

At the *Andaste*'s launching ceremonies her builders furnished marine writers with all the details of her fine engine, a triple-expansion masterpiece with a thirty-six-inch stroke that supplied an indicated 900 horsepower at 90 revolutions. Scotch boilers, eleven feet in diameter and twelve feet in length, each with two furnaces, produced a working steam pressure of 160 pounds per square inch.

These were imposing statistics but they did nothing to alter her outward appearance, which was not designed to appeal to the aesthetic senses. She was a "straightback" ship with none of the graceful hull sheer of the conventional vessel. From about the waterline, when she was loaded, her sides sloped inboard. "Tumble-home" the sailors call it, a design characteristic more often used on small tankers. They usually have a high "trunk" running between the after houses and the fo'c'sle house, an arrangement that encloses a myriad of pipes and valves, but also serves to fend off the seas. The *Andaste* had a flat deck with hatches almost flush with the plating. At the bow her pie-shaped fo'c'sle house, enclosing the anchor windlass among other things, was set back from her spar deck, allowing seamen to walk around it to reach the mooring bitts. Engine, navigating house, and

crew's quarters were all aft. From afar, if one discounted her
unusual bow and noted her extremely modest freeboard, she
somewhat resembled one of Alexander McDougall's "pig"
boats or whaleback vessels. She also had all the whaleback's
wet-deck characteristics in any kind of seaway.

Physical appearance was not a factor in the ships operated
by the Lake Superior Iron Company; efficiency and dura-
bility were the desired features. For six years the *Andaste* and
Choctaw were the epitome of these virtues, regularly carrying
capacity cargoes of iron ore, pig iron, and coal with a minimum of fuss or trouble. In 1898 the company liquidated its
marine properties. The sister ships were then acquired by the
Cleveland-Cliffs Iron Company, operators of a vast Great
Lakes fleet. Spring of 1899 found them bedecked in the traditional colors of their new owners, black hull with deckhouses
in Cliffs' distinctive green. The combination didn't last long
on either ship. The Cleveland-Cliffs people were, and still
are, fastidious owners and take great pride in the appearance
of their vessels. The tumble-home design of the *Andaste* and
Choctaw led to disturbing problems. Large chunks of iron
ore that fell from the unloading buckets crashed down on
her sloping sides, leaving scabrous red stains and scars. This
could not be tolerated in the Cliffs line, so the hulls were then
painted an iron ore red so the stains would not be so objec-
tionable. The *Andaste* and *Choctaw* were the the only exceptions in history to the Cleveland-Cliffs color scheme.

Coal, iron ore, and grain, the mainstays of upper lakes
shipping, were the lot of the *Andaste* for a long time and,
more frequently as the years wore on, cargoes of pig iron.
Each season, however, the ship's profits dwindled as newer,
bigger, and faster vessels entered the bulk trade. Then, too,
by 1920 the pig-iron volume had declined alarmingly. But
by now the *Choctaw* had been gone for four years, rammed
and sunk in 275 feet of water by the Canadian steamer
Wacondah in the summer of 1916, on Lake Huron.

In an effort to prolong her life by diversifying her port of call potentials, the *Andaste* went to the shipyards of the Great Lakes Engineering Company at River Rouge, Michigan, in the winter of 1920-21, to be shortened by twenty-four feet. Her new over-all length would permit her to transit the Welland Canal and the small St. Lawrence River canals. For approximately five years she was a familiar sight at Port Colborne, Port Weller, and a score of towns and villages along the St. Lawrence, carrying grain from Buffalo to Montreal. Occasionally, when the need demanded, she loaded coal at Buffalo for delivery at Marquette, Michigan, bringing back pig iron for the Buffalo mills. Whatever the cargo, it was loaded and unloaded under the watchful eyes of her able commander, Captain Milton J. Brown.

Despite her new measurements and steady employment, the *Andaste*'s role as a straightback bulk-cargo carrier working in a highly competitive field was but a respite from what appeared to be an inevitable rendezvous with a ship-breaker's yard. In 1925 she was sold to the Cliffs-L. D. Smith Steamship Company, managed and operated by Leatham D. Smith of Sturgeon Bay, Wisconsin. Albert E. R. Schneider, vessel manager for the Cleveland-Cliffs Iron Company, also had a substantial share of the investment and her management.

Mr. Smith, a shipyard owner, quarry operator, and a yachtsman of vast experience, had designed a self-unloading system for ships, a device that would, theoretically at least, prolong the lives of older and smaller vessels by making them the ultimate in efficiency. Its primary function, as in the case of the giant self-unloaders that ply the lakes today, was that of enabling any such ship to spew out its own cargo anywhere the vessel could moor, thus eliminating the need for expensive shoreside unloading equipment.

Apparently for tax purposes, the *Andaste* was registered in 1928 as belonging to the Andaste Steamship Company of Cleveland, but still with Leatham Smith and Albert E. R.

Schneider as principle shareholders. In the same year, offered as a self-sufficient and going vessel, she was chartered out to the Construction Materials Company of Chicago. They, under the terms of the charter, took over as managers and operators. The *Andaste*'s function, in the Construction Materials Company's formula of operation, was to supply their yard, far up the Calumet River, in South Chicago, with a continuous supply of sand, gravel, and crushed stone, obtained at several Lake Michigan ports, including Mr. Smith's quarry dock at Sturgeon Bay.

Not included in any official charter papers, agreements, or conversations was "Queenie," a somewhat forlorn-looking, mostly Airedale dog that had become a recent fixture at the riverside dock in South Chicago. She had wandered in unannounced one day, timid and obviously in need of food and friends. Softened at first by lunchbox handouts and, as the days wore on, by kindly treatment and more nourishing fare, she had adopted the men and machines as her very own.

Almost as soon as the *Andaste* became a regular caller at the dock a strong bond of friendship developed between Queenie and Captain Albert L. Anderson, the ship's new skipper. He had wanted to make her the *Andaste*'s mascot, but Queenie turned out not to be a seafaring dog, being afflicted with almost instant seasickness when the deck began to roll in Lake Michigan's chop. From then on she restricted her visits aboard ship to times when it was securely moored to the dock. The shoreside workers claimed that from a half-dozen different hoots and blasts along the busy river, Queenie could recognize the *Andaste*'s whistle, clamoring for the attention of bridge tenders and careless tug skippers while wending her way upstream. Long before the ship herself hove into view she was at the dock, registering utter joy in the only way a dog knows—excited barking and a great wagging of the tail.

Captain Anderson, as befits the skipper of a working boat,

was no fashion plate; he wore what felt comfortable, regardless of the accepted seasons. In mid-August he accompanied Frank Barnett of the Construction Materials Company on a business trip to downtown Chicago. On the way back Captain Anderson was struck by the appearance and feel of a straw hat he had spotted in a store window. Despite the lateness of the season he had bought it on the spot, discarding his former attire and donning the new skimmer for the trip back to the boat. Queenie met him at the yard gate, whimpering happily, her adoring eyes expressing complete approval.

"It was a damned fine hat," Barnett recalled later, "sort of soft and brown . . . with a touch of green on the band."

On the afternoon of September 9, 1929, the *Andaste* was at Ferrysburg, Michigan, on the eastern shore of Lake Michigan, moored a considerable distance up the Grand River, directly across from Grand Haven, taking on a load of gravel. While the shore staff at the Construction Materials Company's dock directed streams of two-inch gravel down the loading spouts into the ship's holds, the *Andaste*'s crew was pretty much scattered.

Grand Haven and Ferrysburg had always been sailors' towns, in the sense that many of their men were employed on the Great Lakes fleets. Grand Haven was the eastern Lake Michigan terminus of the Grand Trunk & Western Railroads' big car ferries, really huge ships that transported railroad cars across the lake to Milwaukee, Wisconsin. Many local men spent their entire working lives in some capacity or other on the car ferries, which operated the year round. Others shipped out on the ships of many fleets during the duration of the coal, iron ore, and grain season, usually from early April until late November or early December. Some of the *Andaste*'s people were from Grand Haven and Ferrysburg. Like most sailors when their ship touches home port, they beat a path to their own doors, leaving the ship in the care of others with no local ties or responsibilities. The area was also well represented aboard the other vessels supplying the Construction Materials Company with its basic raw-materials requirements—the *Sandmaster, Sandcraft,* the *Fred W. Green,* and the tugs *Liberty* and *Freedom.*

That afternoon Captain Anderson had gone ashore to attend to ship's business, mail a letter to his wife in Sturgeon Bay, Wisconsin, and "stretch his legs a bit." During his hours uptown he had encountered and passed the time of day with many friends, some of whom had admired and commented on his new straw hat.

"It was," some later remembered: "sort of soft and brown with a touch of green on the band."

The *Andaste's* departure time from the upriver Ferrysburg dock that night was not noted, but George Van Arkel of the Grand Haven Coast Guard Station logged her as passing outbound between the harbor piers at 9:03 P.M. He watched her gradually fade from sight on her normal west-southwest course. It is recorded fact, however, that from the time of Van Arkel's last sighting, the *Andaste* was never seen again! She just disappeared . . . utterly and completely.

The crew list of the *Andaste* varied considerably during the season, ranging from twenty-two to twenty-nine. It was at twenty-five this trip and, but for some strange quirks of fate, would have been twenty-eight.

Wheelsman Joseph Collins had chosen this lovely September season to lay off for a two-week vacation. Ernie Kasperson, brother of Frank Kasperson, another wheelsman, planned to ship out as steward on the *Andaste,* but personal business prevented his reaching the ship before it sailed. Albert Boyink intended to join his close friend, Second Mate Joseph J. McCadde, as a member of the crew, but could not terminate his previous employment in time to get aboard.

On the other hand, fate was outrageously unkind to young Earl Zietlow, who shouldn't have been on the ship in any capacity. Only fourteen, but big for his age, he was shipping out for the first time, courtesy of a recommendation by Wheelsman Collins. Collins saw him later, before the *Andaste* sailed, sitting on a stool in the galley, peeling potatoes.

"He seemed happy," said Collins.

The *Andaste*, making four trips a week from Ferrysburg to South Chicago, normally should have tied up at her Construction Materials Company dock sometime late Tuesday morning. Queenie was watching for her, but the day and all Tuesday night passed without the sound of the gravel carrier's somber whistle hooting its usual challenges to the bridge tenders. By Wednesday morning Queenie was pacing the dock nervously, whining and whimpering, despite assuring words from the yard workers.

A sudden shift of wind, followed by a severe northwest gale, developed after the *Andaste* departed. It had been predicted at the weather-bureau headquarters, but the information did not reach A. E. Heyer, the local meteorologist, until long after the *Andaste* had departed the piers, far too late to warn her by posting the gale-warning signals at the Coast Guard station. The Grand Haven *Daily Tribune* had carried only a notice of small-craft warnings in its afternoon edition.

The night watch at the Coast Guard station at Holland, Michigan, south of Grand Haven, reported the lights of a ship between two and four A.M., but saw no flares or signals of distress. Residents of beach cottages just south of Grand Haven, a Mr. and Mrs. R. C. Meech and John Koliker, told of seeing ship lights about five miles offshore between two and four A.M. on Tuesday. Shortly after one A.M. on the morning of Tuesday the tenth, Captain Crawford of the Goodrich Line steamer, *Alabama*, was awakened when his ship took four bad rolls. He immediately went to the bridge and ordered Second Mate Henry Erbe to hold her into the wind, then blowing at sixty miles per hour. Both the captain and mate saw the lights of another ship to the west and north of the *Alabama*. The head and range lights told them the distant vessel was westbound but she did not seem to be moving. There was no indication that she was in trouble or needed help.

When the Construction Materials people finally became aware that one of their ships was missing they overlooked no avenue of search. They had delayed, understandably, when ill-founded reports from various sources indicated that the *Andaste* had been sighted in shelter at several places, and one actually said she was on her way up the Calumet River. When it became apparent that none of the reports was based on fact, planes were chartered to augment search aircraft from the Great Lakes Naval Training Station, assigned to scour the southern end of Lake Michigan. A fleet of yachts, a regular flotilla organized by the Chicago Yacht Club to aid seamen in distress, left their moorings on Thursday morning, sweeping east and northeast on the *Andaste*'s course. All ships with wireless were notified to be on the lookout for the gravel carrier or her wreckage. Similar instructions were given to the ships not equipped with wireless at docks all along the lake. From the east shore of Lake Michigan an armada of Coast Guard craft, fish tugs, and private boats from Grand Haven, Holland, and Muskegon joined the hunt. The Construction Materials Company's two tugs, *Liberty* and *Freedom*, had long since been steaming back and forth, crisscrossing the missing *Andaste*'s usual course.

By now the Grand Haven *Daily Tribune* had concluded the vessel was lost and announced it with a Thursday-afternoon banner headline: *ANDASTE* ABOUT GIVEN UP FOR LOST. Later that day the paper published an extra with an even more sensational banner head: *ANDASTE* WRECKAGE IS FOUND TODAY!

The grim news resulted from a trip Captain George Van Hall, a commercial fisherman from Holland, had made to lift his nets. Eleven miles south and west of Holland his tug, the *Bertha G.*, encountered a vast floating field of wreckage, some of it entwined in his nets. With his crew of Vernon King, John Anderson, Henry Swatosh, and George Ziel, he managed to recover a cabin door, part of a stairway, a section of railing, and a water tank support. Around them, in the welter of debris, four-by-ten-foot strongbacks, used to secure the *Andaste*'s hatches, tossed in the morning chop of Lake Michigan. They searched diligently, but they could find no bodies. Back at the Holland Coast Guard dock, company representatives and men who had previously sailed on the *Andaste* identified the door and strongbacks, as being from the ill-fated ship.

The people of the *Andaste* took their time coming ashore. Fittingly enough, Captain Anderson's body was among the first to be found, without a lifebelt or his new hat but with $479 in his wallet. The others followed, choosing various points along the beach to make their reunion with the land they had left so recently. Altogether, over a period of days, fourteen of the *Andaste*'s twenty-five people were found. Eleven wore life preservers.

One of them was Fred Nienhouse, who had been a sailor less than a year. Prior to signing on the *Andaste* he had helped his father operate the family farm, on the shore of the lake, three miles north of Ferrysburg. They found him on the beach, arms outstretched toward the farm home in which he had been born.

"Poor Fred," said one of the recovery team, with a sigh, "a couple of hundred feet more and he would have made it all the way back home."

Back in Grand Haven, wheelsman Joseph Collins cele-brated his decision to take a vacation as the wisest he had ever made. The subject of newspaper interviews and con-gratulations from his fellow townspeople, more attention than he had ever had in his life, he celebrated so gloriously, apparently with help from the juice of fermented grapes, that he was jailed.

Hailed before Justice C. F. Burr, he admitted his guilt and was given a choice of a thirty-dollar fine or fifteen days in the calaboose. With all his belongings aboard the sunken *Andaste* and his current resources strained by the celebrating, he spent one night in jail while friends raised funds for his release. Contrite and subdued, he made amends for his conduct by testifying knowledgeably and freely in the investigation that followed.

Nearly always, when a ship sinks or disappears, there are ugly and often unfounded rumors of inadequacies of equipment or dangerous characteristics of the ship itself. With the *Andaste*, word somehow got about that she was seriously overloaded and that her lifeboat davits were so badly rusted they were unusuable in case of an emergency. Someone suggested that engine failure might have left her helpless in the trough of high seas, where she would have been quickly overwhelmed. This, apparently, was the result of a remark First Mate Charles Brown was said to have made to his wife, relative to some engine trouble the *Andaste* had encountered recently. Another wild tale hinted that sailors had sometimes referred to her as "the black coffin."

In Chicago, Louis Broucek, a former crewman, when queried by reporters, said that the vessel had always had difficulty recruiting a full crew.

"She used to pitch and roll so much," he said, "that it was hard to get a crew for her. Seaworthy and all that, but still the boys were afraid of her.

"There's another thing about that boat. She used to shift her cargo. That means that when she rolled about, the gravel or stone would slide to one side. Many times the crew would have to go down and trim the load even."

The rumors started almost as soon as it was known definitely that the *Andaste* was no more. Nor was there any slackening of gossip when, after the ship had been gone a week, Henry Strabbing and Bartel Hemkes of Holland made a dramatic discovery while searching for bodies along the Holland beach. They picked up a splintered white board, apparently from a pilothouse or cabin. Penciled on it was a message:

> Worst storm I have ever been in. Can't hold up much longer. Hope we're saved.

It was signed with the initials: A.L.A.—those of Captain Albert L. Anderson!

"I have no doubt the message was penciled by the *Andaste*'s skipper," said Gilbert Vande Water, coroner of Ottawa County.

Others, however, did have doubts, including the local federal steamboat inspectors, Captain Bernard J. Gellick, inspector of hulls, and Hugh P. Mulligan, inspector of boilers. With Bert Gale, vice president of the State Bank, William Phillips, deputy customs collector, and E. C. Hurless, clerk of the inspections office, they conducted an investigation into the matter.

"It just doesn't make sense," said Captain Gillick, "a professional seaman such as Captain Anderson would have written in ship's-log style, giving the approximate location, time, and the cause of the sinking."

Inspector Mulligan agreed.

And why, the inspectors asked, had not Captain Anderson, had he wished to leave a message, used the ship's gear provided for just such occasions? Every ship, they pointed out, carries in its pilothouse or chartroom, a copper cylinder that is supposed to contain at all times (but never does) a list of all crewmen aboard. To this, a ship's officer, preferably the skipper, is supposed to add the nature of the disaster, the supposed location, and other pertinent information. Cork-lined and with a watertight screw-on lid, it is meant to be thrown into the sea as the ship goes down. Eventually, then,

Photo from Richard J. Wright collection

Steamer *Kaliyuga,* loaded with iron ore, disappeared on Lake Huron, October 19, 1905. BELOW: The *Benjamin Noble* in happier days. Shown with a heaping cargo of coal, she was later lost with all hands off Knife Island, Lake Superior, with a load of railroad rails.

Photo courtesy Robert J. MacDonald

Photo courtesy Richard J. Wright

Ill-fated car ferry *Milwaukee,* vanished with all hands on Lake Michigan, October 22, 1929. BELOW: The gallant old *Wisconsin,* a favorite on Lake Michigan for years, foundered off Kenosha, Wisconsin, on the morning of October 29, 1929.

Photo courtesy Walter Remick

Photo courtesy Milton J. Brown

Her decks cluttered with self-unloading machinery, the *Andaste* divests herself of a stone cargo. She and her crew sailed into the unknown on Lake Michigan on the night of September 9, 1929. BELOW: Sturdy Canadian package freighter *Kamloops*, loaded with wire and paper-making machinery, vanished in the vicinity of Isle Royale, Lake Superior, December 7, 1927.

Photo courtesy Richard J. Wright

From an oil painting, courtesy of James Oag

Composite steamer *John Owen* went down with all hands on November 12, 1919, on Lake Superior, while loaded with grain. BELOW: Last seen off Long Point, on Lake Erie, the Canadian ore carrier *Merida* disappeared with all hands in October, 1916.

Photo from the author's collection

Photo from the author's collection

Lumber steamer *C. F. Curtis* was towing the barges *Seldon E. Marvin* and the *Peterson* when all were lost with all hands on Lake Superior in 1914. BELOW: The *L. R. Doty*, a fine big steamer loaded with corn, mysteriously disappeared on Lake Michigan in October of 1898. She is shown here a year earlier as she passed through the Soo locks.

Photo courtesy Richard J. Wright

Photo from the author's collection

Twenty-five-day-old steamer *Cyprus,* on her second voyage, was
lost in a modest Lake Superior blow because of leaking hatch
covers. Inset, Charles Pitz, the only survivor. BELOW: Steamer
William B. Davock, shown here heavy with iron ore, vanished
with all hands in the "Armistice Day Storm" of November 11,
1940.

Photo from the author's collection

Photo courtesy Parry Sound Historical Society

The *Lambton*, a Canadian government steamer, "went missing" with her entire crew in 1922. It is thought she was lost somewhere in the vicinity of Caribou Island. BELOW: The *Daniel J. Morrell*, a 580-foot steamer, broke up and sank in a furious Lake Huron gale on November 29, 1966. Of the crew of twenty-nine, only one man, Dennis Hale, survived.

Photo by Thomas A. Sykora, courtesy Great Lakes Historical Society

Photo courtesy Walter Remick

Big wooden steamer *Dean Richmond* had a valuable cargo of zinc ingots aboard when she foundered with all hands on Lake Erie in 1893. BELOW: Wooden steamer *Adella Shores,* bound from Ludington, Michigan, to Duluth, Minnesota, with a cargo of salt, was lost with all hands on Lake Superior, May, 1909.

Photo from the author's collection

should none survive, the cause of the disaster would become known.

The *Andaste* had such a message case, as testified by Edward Roberts, a workman who had laid linoleum on the ship earlier in the year. He related that he had seen it in the Captain's cabin and that Captain Anderson had explained its use, telling him that it was a captain's duty to record the names an addresses of the crew and, if possible, the cause of the ship's foundering, should occasion demand. The message case was never found, although parts of the captain's cabin had been washed ashore. It was considered highly unlikely that Captain Anderson could have written the message on the board in the dead of night, with the seas running high and while the *Andaste*'s crew were thrashing about in the water. Without a life preserver, apparently, since none was on him when his body was discovered, he would have been too busy staying alive to take pen in hand, so to speak, to enlighten others via a message written on a board. The board itself bore no evidence of having been in the water for a week, or of being battered by the winds, seas, and sand on the beach. The unusual clarity of the writing precluded that.

The inspectors concluded that it was a cruel hoax, perpetrated by parties unknown, imposters who sought only to create a sensation.

The inquest into the loss of the *Andaste* began at 9:30 A.M., about two weeks after the disaster, in the supervisor's room at the Ottawa County Courthouse, in Holland. It was conducted by coroner Gilbert Vande Water and prosecuting attorney Clarence A. Lokker. As is customary, all persons having knowledge of the ship, her cargo, her loading, or her seaworthiness were served subpoenas. They were a goodly number, with ranks swelled by attorneys, the ship's owners, their employees, and marine men from near and far. The testimony was heard by a coroner's jury of six Holland businessmen. Specifically, the inquest was conducted in connection with the deaths of Ralph Wiley of Benton Harbor, second engineer of the *Andaste*, and Captain Charles Brown of Grand Haven, serving as first mate, whose bodies were the first to be recovered.

For several hours the jury listened as representatives of the Construction Materials Company, captains of lake vessels, federal inspectors, and local men, who were sailors or had served on the missing ship, related all they knew about her—her cargo, the life preservers, the lifeboats, her machinery, her handling characteristics, her conduct in a seaway, and the lake's weather conditions on the night of September ninth.

Captain Crawford and Second Mate Erbe of the passenger and package freight ship, *Alabama*, repeated and corroborated earlier statements as to the severity of the gale that lashed Lake Michigan on the night of September ninth. Captain Crawford also stated that he had sought shelter in Grand Haven harbor, considering it too dangerous to try to make the piers at Holland or Muskegon, and had arrived in Grand Haven at 4:43 A.M.

Meteorologist H. E. Heyer testified to weather conditions that night. A small-craft warning had been issued previous to the *Andaste*'s sailing, the northwest storm warning arriving two hours after she left port, he said. The barometer had registered 29.04 at nine P.M. on Monday, the ninth, indicating a storm but nothing undue.

Peter Boet, assistant manager of the Construction Materials Company, told of the cargo and how the 1900-odd tons were loaded by spouts and trimmed. The *Andaste*'s draft, when loading was completed, was 17.6 feet forward and eighteen feet aft. "It was her lightest load of the season," said Mr. Boet.

Anxious to put at rest the rumors of the poor condition of the the lifeboat davits, or at least to get to the bottom of the matter, Prosecutor Lokker queried those in charge of the regular inspections of steamships.

Mr. Mulligan pointed out that earlier in the year, when the *Andaste* was being towed from her berth, the tug, *Liberty*, had overturned, throwing her crew into the water. At that time, he stated, the *Andaste*'s lifeboats were quickly swung out in their davits and lowered several feet as the ship's crew sought to effect a rescue. However, small craft in the vicinity pulled the tugmen out of the water before the *Andaste*'s boats could be launched.

Captain Gellick, inspector of hulls, carefully explained his spring inspection of the life-saving equipment, the destruction of three life preservers he had condemned, and the renewal of at least three more that were not up to standard. "When she sailed," he said, "the *Andaste* had thirty-seven first-class life preservers."

The lifeboats were personally inspected by Captain Gellick's assistant, Peter Thompson, who found them equipped with twelve Coston lights in an air-tight compartment. The lifeboats themselves were almost new, of a type built in Brooklyn, New York, in 1926. They were steel, with air bulkheads and regulation rudders and steering oars. It was the considered opinion of many present, including Captain Gellick and Peter Thompson, that had the ship been laboring in the trough of the seas, it would have been almost impossible to launch the lifeboats.

Conscious of the engine-trouble rumor, Prosecutor Lokker sought enlightenment. Before fitting out for her last season, the *Andaste* had been the subject of a $28,000 mechanical refit at the Johnson Boiler Works in Ferrysburg, at which time she was inspected several times by Mr. Mulligan, as required by federal law. The specific dates were March first, fifth, and twelfth. In April he inspected her on the twenty-third and twenty-fifth.

"What were your observations on those dates?" asked Lokker.

"I do not know of a more able boat," replied Mulligan.

Further inspections of the *Andaste* were made later in the season, after she was placed in drydock in Chicago, on June first, for a couple of new hull plates, a refill of the stern bearings, and the replacement of one blade of her propeller. In addition to these repairs the Chicago steamboat inspectors checked her entire hull, rudder, and seacocks before reporting her to be in A-1 condition.

John Swift, owner of a cottage nine miles north of the Holland harbor and south of Grand Haven, told the jurymen he was awakened about one A.M. by a terrific wind. He noticed lights of a ship, seemingly close to shore. He dressed and attended to things about the cottage, and retired at about four A.M., at which time he still saw the lights. Arising at six o'clock, he found no trace of a ship, he said.

Questioned as to why he did not notify the Coast Guard station at Holland, he said he thought it would have been ridiculous as the lights would have been as clearly visible to the Coast Guard lookout as himself. He felt, however, that there was trouble of some kind.

Asked as to how long a man could live in heavy seas with a life preserver, Captain Gellick said it depended upon the physical condition of the man and his endurance. He gave fourteen hours as the usual limit and cited the experience of a man he knew, the only survivor of a freighter disaster. With unusual endurance, he estimated, a man might remain alive for twenty-four hours.

The Construction Materials Company had been the subject of some harsh criticism early in the hunt for survivors for not reporting their ship overdue sooner. It was felt that perhaps some lives might have been saved had the intensive search been organized as soon as the ship became overdue instead of waiting almost two days.

At the time the company was being roundly castigated for its tardiness in reporting the *Andaste* overdue, R. C. Yeomans, a vice president of the firm, explained to reporters that it was not unusual for the *Andaste* to be late, especially if she encountered severe weather. They had every confidence in Captain Anderson, he stated emphatically. He cited from memory several occasions when the ship had sought shelter, delaying her arrival at South Chicago and causing some concern to her charterers. The captain, he said, rarely bothered to notify his office. He was content to bring his ship in when weather conditions again were favorable. Such an incident, he related, had taken place the previous fall, in November of 1928. The *Andaste* had cleared Muskegon for Milwaukee, loaded. Shortly thereafter she ran into a stiff blow and was missing for about twenty-four hours; considerable apprehension was felt for her safety. During that period, unfounded reports placed her as far north as Sturgeon Bay.

Another official of the Construction Materials Company, R. C. Brinkman, told the jury that he had telephoned the Grand Haven Coast Guard Station Tuesday afternoon to see if the *Andaste* had cleared the port Monday night, as he wished to meet her in South Chicago; his calls to his office there revealed that she had not arrived. Wednesday morning he conferred with other officials in the Chicago office; they agreed that the boat was lying in somewhere for weather. He had then endeavored to charter a seaplane but was not successful. Both he and Mr. Yeomans, he testified, made calls to the several Coast Guard stations on both sides of Lake Michigan, inquiring as to the whereabouts of the *Andaste*. Conflicting reports came in on Wednesday night, he said, that the boat had been sighted. However, on Wednesday afternoon he chartered a plane and circled the lower lake shoreline, at times going out some distance into the lake and landing at Grand Haven at five thirty that afternoon.

Mr. Brinkman said that at no time did he or his associates have any real concern as Captain Anderson had frequently been overdue; he cited instances of twenty-five and even thirty hours, when the captain had laid in at some place, without reporting to the Grand Haven or Chicago offices. Hence, it was not until Thursday morning that the officers began to be really worried. He told of getting into communication with the Great Lakes Naval Training Station to get the search planes out. He did not, however, make an appeal to the Coast Guard stations.

Earlier, while the search for the missing ship and her people was still underway, Joseph Dunlevy, first officer of the steamer, *City of Grand Rapids*, stated that he had seen a ship in midlake on Tuesday night, September tenth, with lights resembling those of the *Andaste*. This was not a subject for discussion at the inquest since it was considered unlikely that the *Andaste* would have been afloat in or near the main steamer lanes for a full twenty-four hours without communicating some kind of distress signal to the many vessels that would have undoubtedly passed near her. True, she had no wireless, but as the inspectors indicated, she had plenty of Coston flares. And since the vessel sighted by First Officer Dunlevy had lights, she was certainly in possession of electrical power and could have signaled with her searchlight.

An oar, found on the beach, was produced and shown to Joseph Collins, the vacationing wheelsman of the vanished ship. He identified it as being a steering oar from one of the lifeboats. Nor did he think it significant that the body of First Mate Charles Brown had been found wearing high rubber boots.

There had been some speculation during the period of many rumors that the boots might indicate that at the time of the foundering, First Mate Brown might have been down in the hold with some of the crew trying to trim a shifted cargo. Working in wet gravel, rubber boots would have been the logical attire.

"He used to wear them all the time," Collins asserted, "even on watch in the pilothouse, if he felt like it."

Collins agreed with Captain Gellick and others that should

the *Andaste* have had the misfortune to fall off into the trough of the seas, from whatever cause, it would have been practically impossible to launch the lifeboats.

Captain George Van Hall, who had an accurate log of the currents on the day following the disaster and whose fishing tug, the *Bertha G.*, had discovered the first wreckage from the ship, testified it was his opinion that the *Andaste* sank twenty or thirty miles from shore.

Coast Guard officers and Captain Crawford of the *Alabama* also agreed that the ship did not go down near shore between Grand Haven and Holland. The lights seen and siren whistles that were claimed to have been heard by some on shore, they concurred, were from some other boat.

Altogether, twenty-two witnesses were heard. And although the jurors themselves interjected questions, along with those of Prosecutor Lokker and his assistant, Jay Den Herder, not a witness could give any opinion as to what had happened to the *Andaste*. She was simply gone and that was all there was to it.

Mayor E. C. Brooks of Holland, foreman of the jury that consisted of Wynand Wychers, Henry Winters, Fred Beeukes, E. B. Stephan, and William Vissers, deliberated somewhat more than an hour before announcing their verdict. It was pretty much what had been expected:

> That upon the basis of the testimony heard at the inquest, the deceased came to their death by reason of the sinking of the steamer *Andaste* at an unknown place in Lake Michigan, considerably west of the port of Holland on September 9th, 1929.
>
> We are convinced that the steamer *Andaste* was a staunch and seaworthy vessel carefully loaded and prepared for the voyage from Grand Haven to Chicago. The vessel had been carefully inspected by the proper authorities and was fully equipped with lifeboats and life preservers and other apparatus for the safety of human life at sea.
>
> We are convinced that officers and men of the Coast Guard

stations at Grand Haven and Holland were tireless and unremitting in their efforts to locate men and ship from the moment that the possibility of disaster was communicated from Chicago. We are unable to locate the place of the disaster, the reason for it, nor can we find any trace of laxity on the part of those in charge.

The full report was of some length, but more significant than the formal wording—absolving all concerned of blame—were the three recommendations of the jurymen, all prominent Holland businessmen:

1. That ships the size and nature of the *Andaste,* even though not carrying passengers, should be equipped with wireless.

2. That the proper authorities should establish on each of the Great Lakes some central marine office where delay in the arrival of vessels at scheduled ports should be reported.

3. That proper facilities be maintained on each of the lakes for immediate search for and rescue of vessels probably in distress.

Even before the inquest was called and while the hunt for the people and wreckage of the *Andaste* was still underway all along the eastern shoreline of Lake Michigan, the Grand Haven *Daily Tribune* was announcing her successor, the 6000-ton steamer, *Fontana,* from Cleveland:

The ship had been chartered before the accident, to help take care of the unusually heavy demand for building products. "She has been secured by the officers of the Construction Materials Company to replace the lost *Andaste* and is expected in here Thursday.

Another little news item, almost lost in the massive coverage of the disaster, would have been of particular interest to

"Queenie," still whimpering occasionally and uneasily pacing the South Chicago dock, as if hopeful of at last hearing the hooting of the *Andaste*'s whistle.

A yacht, searching on the course normally followed by the *Andaste,* had recovered a couple of men's hats thirty miles out in the lake.

One was sort of soft and brown . . . with a touch of green on the band.

6

~~~~~~~~
⚓

A Matter of Professional Pride

As the final days of 1929 ticked relentlessly toward the end of another calendar milestone, a somewhat harassed gentleman, Dickerson N. Hoover, was spending long hours at his desk in Washington. Mr. Hoover, Supervising Inspector General of the Steamboat Inspection Service, was making out reports. A few blocks away, Mr. Hoover's brother, J. Edgar Hoover, director of the United States Department of Justice, was probably making out reports, too. His were of other matters and far more likely to arouse comment in the newspapers.

Mr. Dickerson N. Hoover's reports were directed to the Hon. Robert P. Lamont, Secretary of Commerce, under whose department the Steamboat Inspection Service functioned. It was the continuing task of Mr. Hoover's many men in the several districts of the service regularly to inspect all United States flag commercial vessels as to their general seaworthiness, machinery, boilers, and safety-at-sea requirements as specified by federal law. Theirs was the responsibility of verifying that every such vessel was in proper condition to meet and survive whatever came in the way of hazards at sea, and to avoid as many as possible by holding to inflexible standards of maintenance and repair. When a ship came to grief, despite their meticulous examinations, their subsequent investigations were as thorough and painstaking as the periodic inspections of the ship had been.

Altogether, 1929 had been a rather deplorable year, particularly the months of September and October on Lake Michigan. First, there had been the poor old *Andaste* and her luckless crew, missing over three months now, with not a soul to tell where or why she had gone down. Then came the case of the Grand Trunk Western Railroad's big car ferry, *Milwaukee*, lost with her entire crew of forty-seven, on the wild night of October twenty-second. Only a few nights later came the strange bit of business of the passenger and package freighter, *Wisconsin*, Chicago to Milwaukee, foundering off Kenosha. Like the *Milwaukee* she had departed her berth in northeast gale warnings and when only fifteen miles from Kenosha began to transmit wireless signals for help. The *Wisconsin* was scarcely on the bottom, when the *Senator*, a long steamer loaded with automobiles, groping through fog off Port Washington, was rammed and sunk by a big bulk carrier, the *Marquette*.

Mr. Hoover would undoubtedly have given a pretty penny to have had Captain Robert McKay of the *Milwaukee* and Captain Dougal Morrison of the *Wisconsin* on hand to answer some rather embarrassing questions. But both had gone down with their ships and he could do little but ponder on the reasons and, perhaps, the tensions and pressures that had influenced their decisions to leave port when every factor of weather, let alone common sense, should have ruled against it. This was particularly true in the case of the *Milwaukee* and the man who ruled her pilothouse. Beginning the report on the *Milwaukee* was simple:

Investigated and find that the steamer *Milwaukee* left the port of Milwaukee at 3 P.M. October 22, 1929, and has never returned to this or any other port. . . .

Like most marine men of responsibility and authority Mr. Hoover was familiar with the car-ferry and package-freight business and the necessity for maintaining schedules whenever possible. Still, there are times when the line of distinction between courage and foolhardiness is a thin and tenuous one. Perhaps men in his position may have felt that both skippers had gone beyond that line, far beyond.

The car-ferry operations on Lake Michigan were, in 1929, as they are today, a unique phase of American rail transportation. Between loading and unloading terminals on each side of the lake, three great railroads employed fleets of car ferries to shuttle freight cars across the lake. They were special ships—big, powerful, and broad-beamed. It is a demanding service for both ships and crews, and the result is a sort of *esprit de corps* that sets the car-ferry men apart. Unlike the iron-ore, coal, grain, and package-freight vessels, the sturdy car ferries operate the year round. Often beset by fields of wind-driven ice and lashed by wintry gales, they carry on in what approximates Arctic navigation. Obviously, too, the cargoes of railroad rolling stock require special safety measures to hold the cars immobile, even while the ships themselves are pitching and rolling atrociously. A system of big jacks, clamps, blocks, and heavy chains lock the cars securely on the four sets of tracks. These restraining devices are carefully attended to during each voyage because the mental picture of what could happen if the cars broke loose is forever in the minds of the car-ferry men.

Captain Robert McKay was a somewhat unusual individual. "Captain Bob"—or "Heavy Weather" McKay, as he was known in Grand Haven—had arrived in that city as a youthful emigrant from the Orkney Islands, with a Scots burr that he never lost. He sailed for years with Captain George Robertson and Captain Thomas Trail, two veteran Scottish skippers who treated him as a son. Under their tutelage and with his own resolute determination he held every rank but that of captain. Although obviously qualified he was reluctant to take out his master's papers, because he felt a vague premonition of evil and tragedy he could not overcome. This he once confided to a friend who later remembered the great pride he had exhibited when he finally passed the examination. Once, when first mate on the old *Naomi*, he was a hero. When the ship caught fire far out on the lake, it was Robert McKay whose calm orders prevented panic and soothed the passengers while the lifeboats were being launched. He was definitely a man of dual personality. Ashore in his favorite haunt, William Grunst's cigar store in Grand Haven, he was the picture of affability, yarning by the hour with old sailors and friends. Aboard his ship with the manifold responsibilities of his office he was another person. "Rough, tough, and gruff," was the way a one-time shipmate put it. And although all the mates on the *Milwaukee* had their master's papers, the captain was not the kind of man to welcome advice or counsel. Publicity was a thing he abhorred. On the occasion of his promotion and transfer to the *Milwaukee*, when the officers and crew of his former command presented him with a watch at an impromptu festive gathering, he stormed out of his cabin in a rage, driving off a woman reporter who had assumed she was about to chronicle a pleasant and touching presentation.

This was the man who, at noon on October twenty-second, had brought his ship into Milwaukee after a wild crossing from Grand Haven. Lake Michigan was being churned by a gale from the north that was to break all local records for continuity and velocity of wind. The enormous seas marched the length of the lake to their inevitable destiny with land and when they found it they left a trail of wreckage unparalleled even by the "big blow" of 1913. At South Haven, St. Joseph, and Benton Harbor, Michigan, piers and docks were swept away, small craft by the score were demolished, and beach cottages reduced to kindling. At Gary and Michigan City, Indiana, luxury beach homes along the dunes were swept away, and hundreds of families fled inland. Chicago's expansive shoreline boulevard was under water, adjacent parks were obliterated, and as far north as Milwaukee, along the Wisconsin shore, boathouses were dashed to pieces, roads were washed away, trees were ripped up and several 1300-ton sections of a new concrete breakwater broke up under the pounding of the seas. C. H. Hubbard, superintendent of the 12th Lighthouse District, was kept busy tabulating telephoned reports of damage to the district's installations. It was apparent that several lighthouses and Coast Guard stations, undermined by water and buffeted by wind and seas, would have to be rebuilt.

Under these conditions Captain McKay brought his ship smartly into its dock as a matter of course. Headed the other way, the Grand Trunk car ferry, *Grand Haven*, left Milwaukee at two A.M. on the twenty-second and arrived safely at Grand Haven at five P.M. the same day, taking fifteen hours for a trip which, under normal sailing conditions, took only six. Her captain reported a very hard passage with mountainous seas . . . seas that grew in height as the gale winds held from the north.

By three o'clock on the afternoon of the twenty-second the *Milwaukee*'s car deck had been cleared of its inbound cargo, and a string of twenty-five eastbound cars, carefully broken up into "cuts" of two or three cars, was shunted into her cavernous four-track hold or car deck. There, while the experienced crew applied the restraining jacks, clamps, and chains, Purser A. R. Sadon checked the identifying numbers on the cars loaded and noted their contents on his manifest. It was broken down as two cars of lumber, three cars of barley, seven cars of feed, two cars of canned peas, one car of grits, one car of corn, three cars of salt, one car of butter, one car of veneer, two cars of bathtubs, one car of cheese, and one car of automobiles. For insurance purposes the contents were valued at $100,000, the box cars at $63,500.

The gale had reached such a crest of fury by the time loading was completed and the car-ferry's stern gate lowered that many of the crew and all of the shore gang assumed, without giving the matter a second thought, that the *Milwaukee* would stay at her dock until the weather moderated. Three of the crew were so sure of this that they had taken a streetcar to downtown Milwaukee to attend a movie.

In the pilothouse it was another matter. Captain McKay had given no indication of reluctance to sail, nor had any of the mates ventured to offer an opinion or ascertain his intentions. It may have been that he considered his ship to be more than equal to the storm then raging and growing in intensity. On the other hand he had been ignoring weather conditions for so long, or at least paying slight heed to them, that he may never have considered waiting for the wind and seas to abate. Or it may be, as was later rumored, that the choice was not altogether his, even though in the final analysis it is the captain's prerogative to make the decision, or should be, since he bears the ultimate responsibility. In any event, promptly at three o'clock that fateful afternoon he signaled the engineroom to "stand by," ordered the hawsers cast off, rang for "half speed ahead" and maneuvered his ship from the dock. To some of the people in the railroad's trackside office and others working nearby, the ship's departure whistle brought incredulous expressions . . . complete disbelief in what their ears told them was happening. Yet, there it was, the big, black bulk of the *Milwaukee* lining up on a course that would take her through the harbor piers in a matter of minutes!

Many noted, significantly, that in their adjacent loading slips neither of the car ferries of the Pere Marquette line, one of which had arrived before the *Milwaukee* and another that had docked later, were making any attempt to leave port. Both had suffered hard passages inbound and wanted no more of Lake Michigan in her present mood.

Besides the three light-hearted crewmen who had seen fit to take in a movie, there were others, who, for one reason or another, were not at their appointed posts when the *Milwaukee*'s engine-order telegraph jumped to "stand by." Thomas McNello, an oiler, was in Grand Haven taking a three-day relief break; his father, Philip, was aboard as a coal passer. Second Mate Elmer Hahn and his fiancée, Miss Nellie Gould, had chosen that date for their wedding. Both were in Milwaukee receiving the congratulations of friends and relatives when the ship sailed. In Milwaukee, too, safely abed in St. Mary's Hospital, was Joseph Shuntick, second assistant engineer.

The *Milwaukee*, already wallowing in the chop just inside the piers, passed within five hundred feet of the Coast Guard tower, where the Weather Bureau's northeast storm-signal flags had been stretched taut in the wind since early morning. Intermittent rain squalls were being recorded all along the Wisconsin's shoreline. The last person to see her was the captain of the *U.S. Lightship 95*, stationed three miles due east of the Milwaukee harbor entrance. He logged her as passing to the north of the lightship, "pitching and rolling heavily." He noted, too, that she remained in view for about ten minutes until a combination of rain, mist, and sea took her forever from the sight of mortal man. At that time she was still on a typical "Heavy Weather" McKay course—due east instead of holding a little to the north, where his ship would have met the seas at a more favorable angle instead of exposing her high profile to them and sliding into successive troughs.

The hours following the *Milwaukee*'s last sighting were among the most tempestuous in the lake's history, something that had to be experienced to be believed. In the dark of night the wind tore the crests from the tops of malevolent seas that had been abuilding for a full day. Masthead lights of the unfortunate vessels sore beset in the storm described horrifying arcs. Black mountains of water climbed aboard to do their mischief every few seconds, pounding at hatches and thundering against deckhouses and cabin bulkheads. Down below the firemen were hard put to maintain footing in the fireholds. Loose coal, carpets of it, slid back and forth on the steel floor with every roll of the ship. This they disregarded although it was a constant peril, working desperately in the full knowledge that steam and steam alone would give their vessel enough power to keep out of the troughs of those murderous seas.

The package freighter *Delos W. Cooke* had unwittingly left Chicago before the storm warnings were hoisted, expecting nothing more than the usual nasty seas that are so typical of Lake Michigan in the fall. Twenty-seven hours later she was back in Chicago, badly battered after a fruitless attempt to beat her way up the lake.

"We just took a long, terrible ride for nothing," recalls Willis A. Bruso, the *Cooke*'s wheelsman and now a captain in the United States Coast Guard.

Interlake Steamship's 600-foot steamer, *Robert Hobson*, only two years out of her builder's yard, left Indiana Harbor at 9:10 P.M. on the twenty-first. She had bucked the seas up the lake to a point about fourteen miles abreast of Ludington and was making relatively good progress when her master discovered that she was "working" so much that rivets were loosening and shearing, and deck plates were beginning to crack. He ordered her turned immediately and finally put in at South Chicago, almost in sinking condition. A survey showed 25,500 rivets to be renewed and several plates to be replaced. The bill was estimated at $35,000.

Not far away when the *Hobson* swung around was another big steamer, the *Amasa Stone*, downbound and running before the wind and sea with 10,000 tons of coal in her holds. Even so, she suffered heavy damage from seas that the master reported equal to those he had experienced in the big 1913 storm.

No particular apprehension or fear was felt for the safety of the *Milwaukee*, even when she became many hours over-due at Grand Haven. It is customary in severe weather for the car ferries to beat back and forth or up and down the lake, waiting for a lessening of the winds and seas to make their often tricky approaches to the harbor piers. Oiler McNello, on his three-day break, recalled a storm in which the *Milwaukee* steamed for thirty-eight hours in a full gale while the seas boarded her directly over the bow and shot spray over her twin smokestacks.

Only when the ship became thirty-six hours overdue was serious alarm expressed and this partly because another Grand Trunk car ferry, the *Grand Rapids*, departing Mil-waukee four hours after the missing vessel, had safely arrived at her dock but had seen nothing of the *Milwaukee*. This could be accounted for, marine men said, because the *Grand Rapids* was newer, larger, and faster than the *Milwaukee* and would not have to make as many concessions to the gale. Captain McKay, they concluded, had finally altered his course and had steamed far up the lake, meeting the seas head on while waiting for them to abate. In fact, a report that a vessel had been sighted in shelter behind Beaver Island was accepted as evidence that "Heavy Weather" Mc-Kay had at last sought some measure of relief from his old adversary, the storm.

The seas had subsided to a gentle chop by the morning of the twenty-fourth. Captain Ray Hayward of the steamer, *Colonel,* downbound off Racine, was walking aft to the galley with nothing more important on his mind than breakfast when he was hailed from the bridge.

"Something in the water over there, Captain," called the second mate, pointing toward the distant Wisconsin shore.

Hayward and the mate looked through their binoculars at a wide field of flotsam that danced in the sea.

"Hard starboard, take us closer," Captain Hayward ordered the wheelsman.

When the *Colonel* eased slowly up to the wreckage they found mattresses, furniture, and quantities of wood that had apparently once been part of a deckhouse or cabin. It was painted white, but this meant little since it was a common color on ships. But the *Milwaukee* was missing and her upperworks were white. With ropes and pike poles, the *Colonel*'s crewmen recovered much of the wood but could find no identifying marks linking it positively to the car ferry.

It was grim news at Milwaukee. Captain Charles McLaren, Grand Trunk Western Railroad's marine superintendent, though he had protested optimism all along, immediately appealed to the Kohler Aircraft Corporation to have one of their planes fly over the wreckage to see if the pilots could make out anything that would establish the wreckage as that of the car ferry.

The Kohler pilots did more than that. Although they could not find the wreckage Captain Hayward had reported, they crisscrossed the lake on a search pattern, going far to the north where Captain McKay would most likely have taken his vessel, assuming that he had finally bowed to the gale's will.

Out from the harbors of Racine, Milwaukee, South Haven, Holland, Grand Haven, and St. Joseph, fleets of Coast Guard search boats, alerted after the *Colonel*'s find, began a systematic scouring of the lake. The three other Grand Trunk ferries continued their normal sailings, but mounted extra watchmen to look for wreckage. Superintendent McLaren was still hopeful, even though the vessel sighted off Beaver

Island proved not to be the missing *Milwaukee*. The ship was aground and identified as a package freighter with a similar profile.

All doubts as to the big car-ferry's fate vanished the next morning with the finding of the bodies of two of her crew off Kenosha. Both had on life preservers marked "S.S. MIL-WAUKEE." The watch of one had stopped at 9:45, a fact that was later deemed important. Later in the day the *Steel Chemist*, out of Chicago discovered two more dead sailors, while the *Albert Gary* picked up one farther out in the lake. At dusk a Coast Guard boat recovered another pair. The next day a Coast Guard crew from St. Joseph, Michigan, under Captain Samuel Carlson, found one of the *Milwaukee*'s lifeboats bobbing in a welter of wreckage. It contained four dead crewmen. Three were wearing life preservers, and the fourth, wheelsman Arnold Moran, was huddled under a canvas tarpaulin. All had apparently died of exposure and exhaustion. Off Holland, Michigan, floating serenely near near the shore, the Coast Guardsmen found another lifeboat. It was empty, and its canvas covering was still secured and taut, indicating that none of the crew had attempted to launch it. Inside, all the required equipment was safely stowed . . . flares, rudder, food, water, and oars.

Still later, on October twenty-seventh, as the search continued, surfman Francis R. Deto of the South Haven station was among a group investigating wreckage washed ashore. Another lifeboat, No. 3, was resting on the beach intact and obviously unused by the *Milwaukee*'s crew. Also floating nearby was a pike pole and three life preservers. Surfman Deto spotted another object tumbling in the light surf. It was the ship's message case and inside was a note! It said:

S. S. Milwaukee, October 22, '29 8:30 P.M. The ship is making water fast. We have turned around and headed for Milwaukee. Pumps are working but sea gate is bent in and can't keep the

water out. Flicker is flooded. Seas are tremendous. Things
look bad. Crew roll is about the same as on the last pay day.

                        [signed] A. R. SADON, Purser

The message was written on the official printed stationery
of the Grand Trunk car ferries; the handwriting, according
to Grand Haven people who knew him, was definitely that
of Sadon.

The "flicker," mentioned by the purser, is seaman's language for their sleeping and living-quarters compartment.
On the *Milwaukee*, it was under the car deck just aft of the
boiler- and enginerooms.

Tragedy often brings to the surface the unaccountable
mental quirks that drive sensation seekers to strange and
cruel actions. In the wake of the discovery of Purser Sadon's
message came two more, both in bottles found on the beach.
The first, found not far from Muskegon, said:

This is the worst storm I have ever seen. Can't stay up much
longer. Hole in the side of the boat.

                        [signed] McKAY

Mrs. McKay examined the note carefully but could not
verify it as the captain's writing or signature. Neither could
Marine Superintendent Captain McLaren who was familiar
with the handwriting of the *Milwaukee*'s commander.

Another note, picked up near Holland, read:

Whoever finds this be sure and write. It is rather rough today.
It keeps me busy hanging on, let alone trying to write.

Unsigned, it was dated September 10, 1929. Coast Guard
officials classified it as a belated hoax relating to the disappearance of the *Andaste*.

Back in Milwaukee, when it became certain that a major
Great Lakes disaster had taken place, Captain William A.

Collins, head of the local Steamboat Inspection Service, announced that a complete investigation of the car-ferry's loss would get underway immediately.

Like most marine men, and even those who had no direct connection with the lake shipping industry, Captain Collins had noted that the Grand Trunk vessels continued to sail, even when the weather "outside" became so boisterous other ships stayed in port.

The masters of the Pere Marquette ships who had wisely stayed in port were interviewed and questioned about their reasons; their replies were almost identical: "On account of the weather" . . . "Too rough for us out there."

"We want to find out," Captain Collins told reporters, "if the sinking of the vessel was due to negligence of those who ordered the ship to clear port in the face of strong warnings, or if the manner of handling the ship was contributory to the tragedy."

The Grand Trunk commodore and marine superintendent, Captain McLaren, said his company welcomed any investigation that might be made into the unfortunate affair. "My company," he stated, "would not knowingly take any risks, either with the lives of its employees or with its property."

The task of the inspectors was not an easy one. It was tedious, time-consuming, and involved delving into personal and unpleasant areas. Still, their own reputations, in a sense, were at stake. They were the ones who had attested to the vessel's fitness for sea. But the certificate of seaworthiness was granted only after they had prowled through the dank double bottoms, crawled around her boiler casings, sounded her hull plates, tapped her rivets, observed her engines, tested the boiler tubes, operated her steering engine and rudder, and checked all her life-saving gear. They were, in effect, judge and jury in determining whether or not a vessel met the stringent requirements as set by federal law.

Many things could have happened to the *Milwaukee* as she
pitched and rolled, and many of these contingencies came to
the minds of the inspectors. First was her cargo. Had all the
restraining gear failed under punishment it had never been
subjected to before? Had the cars broken loose to plunge
to and fro, and becoming derailed, piled up on one side of
the ship? It was not beyond supposition to picture them
crashing against the side of the ship, tearing her plates or
even plunging through the hull into the sea. And there was
always the question of a boiler failure or engine breakdown
that would cause the ship to lose all motive power and thus
fall, helpless, into the troughs of towering seas that would
crash over her stern gate and quickly overwhelm her. Perhaps
the steering engine had failed at a crucial time. It would
obviously have been under great stress. And how about the
flooded flicker mentioned by Purser Sadon? Only a thin bulkhead separated the flicker, which was above and just aft of
the boiler and enginerooms. It was not difficult to imagine
that bulkhead giving way to flood both. Either dread event,
or a combination of several, could have sent her down. Or
had the difficult Captain McKay simply expected of his ship
what she could not give?

In their own office the Inspectors hauled out the complete
dossier on the vanished ship and poured over it with the
attention to detail a doctor might give the case history of a
seriously ill patient. In this case the patient was *in absentia*,
so to speak, although various documents attested that her
history began with her "birth" in 1903, in Cleveland, as a
twin-screw vessel of 338 feet and a gross tonnage of 2933.

The *Milwaukee*'s record showed that she had been inspected and certificated on June 8, 1929, by Captain Henry
Erichsen, assistant inspector of hulls, and Abraham Auld,
assistant inspector of boilers. She was reinspected by the
Grand Haven inspectors on August 14, the report of which
showed that the vessel and her equipment had been in good

condition, with the exception of one broken deadlight glass on the starboard side of the flicker. This was ordered renewed. Captain McKay later told the inspectors that this had been done, and they, apparently, took his word for it. Prior to the 1929 inspections the records showed that she had been drydocked at Manitowoc, Wisconsin, on three separate occasions: in June of 1926, in May of 1927, and in March of 1928. During these periods the Grand Trunk people had expended $33,532.65 for necessary repairs to hull, rudder, steering gear, and propellers.

The message signed by Purser Sadon, and further checked with samples of his handwriting in the Grand Trunk offices, has already established that the flicker was filled with water from an undetermined leakage, that the vessel had turned around and that the stern or sea gate had been bent in, allowing the seas to roam the car deck. Since his tragic account was written at 8:30 P.M., and the watch on the first body found had stopped at 9:45, it was concluded that the *Milwaukee* must have been afloat for approximately an hour and fifteen minutes after the purser had thrown the message case overboard.

Captain Owen D. Gallagher of the car ferry *Grand Haven*, when questioned, had his own theory. "Well, of course, my opinion is that, heading into that awful sea, she was filling herself over the stern. Captain McKay, probably knowing that he had to do something to avoid this, ventured to turn around. The stern swinging around against a heavy sea probably carried the sea gate away."

The inspectors agreed that Captain Gallagher's statement, in view of his long experience, was a reasonable one.

There had been ugly but persistent rumors that Captain McKay was overly fond of spirits. The inspectors, after talking to many of his friends and associates, found this to be absolutely untrue.

The inspectors were interested, too, in the vague implica-

tions that the masters of the Grand Trunk car ferries sometimes did not sail of their own free will and accord, and that
there was an indirect desire on the part of the marine
superintendent to have them go out in all kinds of weather.
This was vehemently denied by Captain McLaren and could
not be proved by the inspectors. Indeed, the shipmasters interviewed indicated their resentment of Captain McLaren's
wiring and telephoning them about the weather and the
movement of other steamers. The inspectors, however, felt
it within the duties of a prudent and conscientious manager
to keep his captains advised as to weather and other pertinent
conditions.

It was the unanimous feeling of the *Milwaukee* inspectors
that "stress of weather" was the cause of the car ferry's
foundering and not any particular structural weakness that
might have escaped notice. In this they had ample proof of
the severity of the gale in damage and casualty records from
other ships that had been at sea that terrible night. The
captains of the steamers *Neptune, J. J. Block, James E. Davidson,* and the *W. D. Calverly Jr.*—the smallest 346 feet in
length and the largest 604 feet—all reported heavy storm
damage. The *William F. Snyder Jr.,* a 590-foot vessel had to
go into drydock immediately for renewal of 50,000 rivets in
deck stringers and shear strakes.

Of particular concern, although the car ferries were known
to be rugged, well-constructed boats, was the evidence contained in Purser Sadon's note, particularly the three-word
sentence, "Flicker is flooded."

How did the flicker become flooded? There were watertight closures to keep any seas that reached her car deck from
finding their way into the ship's compartments. Sometime
during the storm, as the hull was bent and twisted in the
pitching and rolling, something had happened to destroy the
watertight integrity of the lower compartments, particularly
the flicker. The inspectors and others were inclined to place

the blame on the scuttle hatches. They were round, manhole-like openings that permitted access to the after spaces of the *Milwaukee* for inspection of her shaft couplings and bearings. The coverings were of steel as was the deck itself and were held secure by wedging-action "dogs" that supposedly and under ordinary conditions would have sealed off any water that might wash over the stern. But conditions on the night of October 22 were far from ordinary. It took little imagination to envision the tormented car deck twisting in the throes of more stress and strain than it had ever before been subjected to. Flexing and bending as the seas mauled the car ferry, the scuttle hatches probably popped loose only to be swept away by succeeding seas; this could have been the *coup de grâce* that finished her.

Those with long memories could recall the somewhat mysterious circumstances under which the *Milwaukee*'s sister ship, the *Pere Marquette No. 18*, was lost in a storm on September 9, 1910. Like the vanished *Milwaukee*, she had gone down far out in the lake after filling from the stern. The owners of the *Pere Marquette No. 18*, however, had wisely equipped her with wireless, and a distress call quickly brought help from another vessel of the same line. Even so, there was a heavy loss of life, although none of those rescued could explain by what means the water had gained access to the after compartments. Unlike the *Milwaukee*, the *Pere Marquette No. 18* had no stern gate, but with the *Milwaukee*'s bent in, as Purser Sadon reported, she would have been in much the same position. In fact, after the last tragic message was written, there was every possibility that it had been carried away altogether.

One inspector commented in writing to a superior:

It is to be borne in mind in the use of the car ferries that they are probably being loaded more deeply than years ago when they first came out, due to the fact that the cars are bigger and heavier than they were then. There is less freeboard and there is no law or authority that this service possesses with reference to indicating what the freeboard shall be on the Great Lakes. The sea gate is provided for the purpose of breaking the force of the sea as it comes on board the stern in rough weather, but there is some question in my mind as to whether the sea gate as at present used on vessels of this type is properly located. Here we have a case of the sea gate bent in and undoubtedly the water that came aboard made its way forward and got down below through the hatches. This would explain what the purser meant by stating that the flicker, which is aft, was flooded. If the sea gate, instead of being so far aft, was constructed farther inboard, it is possible that even though the seas boarded the vessel on the stern, the water would not be able to make its way forward upon the car deck . . . this could be done with the stern end of car ferries closed in by a full gate of strength equal to the ship's superstructure and no openings in the car deck aft of this enclosure.

These and many more things were being considered by Mr. Hoover in his report to the Secretary of Commerce, the Hon. Robert P. Lamont. Among his recommendations to prevent a repetition of the tragic loss of a ship and its entire crew, he wrote:

I recommend that consideration (insofar as the authority of the board of supervising inspectors will permit) be given to the matter of the requirements of the Wireless Ship Act.

Of the lessons to be learned from this disaster, one stands out clear, and that is the value of radio communication . . . we do believe that had radio communication been available from the *Milwaukee*, earlier search could have been made with the possibility of saving life . . . as it was, the first signs of wreckage was not discovered until the morning of October twenty-fourth, approximately 30 to 36 hours after the *Milwaukee* sank, and even then it was not known that the wreckage was from the *Milwaukee* . . . the loss of this boat shows the necessity of radio and particularly of the ability of sending messages from the ship.

Mr. Hoover was quite critical of Captain McKay and was obviously not completely convinced that the matter of whether to sail or not to sail was entirely in the hands of the car-ferry skippers.

It is evident that Captain McKay of the *Milwaukee* knew full well the weather conditions when he started out on his last trip, having just crossed the lake a few hours previously, with the storm and sea of equal severity as when he left. Whether he went out of his own free will and accord we cannot positively state. The fact stands out quite clearly that each of the four Grand Trunk Ferries had left port and were out in the big storm of October 22, while car ferries of the other lines remained in port or did not venture out again until the storm abated. We have evidence of where the superintendent of one of the car-ferry lines even wired one of his masters during the time of the storm, to "take no chances." Perhaps if there had been such advice extended to Captain McKay, there would be a different story to tell today.

Of course, we all know that the *Milwaukee* should never have gone out, but it seems to us that from his past experience, the criticism of eyewitnesses to the *Milwaukee*'s departure, all experienced sailor men, and the condition of the weather, that it was a foolhardy thing to do, and showed poor judgment on the part of Captain McKay . . . whether or not this sort of moral urge, as stated by the other Grand Trunk Masters, predominated in his mind over his better judgment, thinking that if the other fellow can go, I can too, influenced him to go out, we cannot say . . . it may have been a matter of professional pride.

... With the Best of Intentions

In Chicago, late on the afternoon of October 28, 1929, Captain Dougal Morrison of the Goodrich Line's old passenger and package-freight steamer, *Wisconsin*, sat with his feet propped up on his desk, contemplating the woes of command. Outside, the second great storm in a week was buffeting the city and the entire west shore of Lake Michigan. Towering graybeards came romping nearly the length of the lake, climbed gleefully over the Lincoln Park seawall and swept on over the already undermined and washed-out sections of the Outer Drive. The two storms, back to back, had in hours wiped out years of work by the city's park crews.

Aboard the *Wisconsin* the fierce wind rattled the windows on the passenger decks, hammered unsuccessfully on the captain's office door, and swept spitefully on to torment whatever else it could find. Captain Morrison could hear it whistling overhead on the boat deck, strumming the taut canvas on the lifeboats, making a hollow sound as it encountered the ventilators, and quickly changing to a high-pitched whine as it encircled the shrouds, stays, and wireless antenna. Down below he could hear vague bumping noises as the freight crew trundled cargo aboard. Intermittent hammering sounds told him that others were nailing down blocking to keep heavy packing crates from shifting. Idly, he wondered if they were doing a good job. It was now raining, too, sheets of it slashing furiously the length of the ship and sluicing the office windows. He wondered if that persistent leak at the top of the starboard window would show up again. It did.

Captain Morrison was feeling rather introspective and could be forgiven if the events of the past week were such as to make a shipmaster mentally review some past decisions and wonder what part luck had played in proving them right. He meditated on the fate of his friend, Captain Robert McKay of the *Milwaukee*. Only a week ago Captain McKay had been an emminently respected commander. Now, some rather important people were saying harsh things about him. He wondered, too, whether the old saying that familiarity breeds contempt could be applied to Captain McKay's decision to sail despite the terrible seas. Anyway, he concluded, the decision was made with the best of intentions.

In the next few hours Captain Morrison would be making some decisions, some of which would be questionable, but the important one for the time being was whether or not to sail in the face of gale warnings that had been flying all day. Not far away another Goodrich steamer, the *Alabama*, was loading and apparently intended to sail. The decision was really not so difficult for Captain Crawford of the *Alabama*. He would be taking a quartering course across the lake to Grand Haven, Michigan. The gale, sweeping from the northeast, was building its big seas over the lake, punishing the western coast of Lake Michigan but leaving the eastern shoreline waters relatively calm. In any event, the *Alabama* would endure the worst of the seas but a short time. Captain Morrison, however, would have to beat his way up the west shore for the entire voyage, taking the full brunt of the gale and brutal seas that were cresting over twenty feet a mile offshore.

Somewhere along the line, if all went well, the *Wisconsin*

would meet another Goodrich steamer, the *Illinois*, which shared the Chicago-Milwaukee night shuttle run with the *Wisconsin*. Even now, the *Illinois* was loading cargo at Milwaukee and Captain Morrison wondered if her skipper, Captain Fred J. Delletre, was going to cancel his scheduled sailing. As a matter of fact, Captain Delletre, a prudent man, without wondering about what the captain of the *Wisconsin* was going to do, did just that.

Painful memories of the previous week must have stirred the fires of caution in Captain Charles McLaren, the Grand Trunk's marine superintendent, for the car ferries *Grand Haven* and *Grand Rapids* were ordered not to sail from Milwaukee. Every harbor along the west shore of Lake Michigan was plugged with ships of all kinds and sizes, "waiting for weather."

A faint shouting, muffled by the torrents of rain, told Captain Morrison that the dock crew was trying to maneuver an automobile through the freight gangway. Somehow, this always caused a great hubbub—a general raising of voices and a spirited exchanged of compliments with the ship's cargo handlers.

Being of a practical nature the captain knew that the once-great era of passenger and package-freight ships on the Great Lakes was drawing to a close. He could recall the time when twoscore or more were kept busy on Lake Michigan alone. But the automobile and a growing network of all weather highways was putting an end to it. Each year found a couple more vessels being retired from service with none to take their places. "Retired" was a kind word, he mused, since what the owners really meant was that they were headed for the boneyard. It was easy to reminisce on such an afternoon, and how could one dwell upon a fading era without paying homage to this very ship, the *Wisconsin*. She had known the best and the worst of those historic days.

When the famed Captain Goodrich was awarded a prize

contract by the Detroit, Grand Haven and Milwaukee Railway, in 1880, he at once ordered the building of three iron ships at the Detroit Drydock Company. One was a side-wheel steamer, *City of Milwaukee*, to be used for summer passenger service. The other two, sister ships, were the *Michigan* and *Wisconsin*, both propellers. Designed by Frank E. Kirby, foremost naval architect on the Great Lakes, the *Michigan* and *Wisconsin*, launched in 1881, were to provide year-round freight service between the ports of Milwaukee and Grand Haven. Mr. Kirby, aware of the rigors of winter navigation on the lakes, designed them with special ice-breaking capabilities. Their rounded forefoot and full entrance enabled them to slide right up on the ice, crushing it down with their weight.

Captain Goodrich announced that the two freight boats had cost him $160,000 each, a staggering sum at the time, although they were considered the finest vessels on the lakes. They had been in operation for the Goodrich Transit Company for only two years when the loss of one of his most lucrative railroad contracts forced the captain to retrench. The three ships were offered to and were purchased by the Detroit, Grand Haven and Milwaukee Railway, which immediately set about operating its own steamship line.

The *Michigan* lasted only two years. She was lost in the bitter winter of 1885, foundering off Grand Haven after being locked in a massive, grinding ice field for over three weeks. The *Wisconsin* barely survived the ice war, suffering structural damage that required extensive repairs. She continued to serve as the railroad's night boat for another year, before being sold in 1896 to the E. G. Crosby interests, a group that had taken over the railroad's water route, adding regular service at Muskegon. Renamed *Naomi* in 1898 she ran her course steadily until one night in May 1907, when she caught fire far from either shore.

Captain Morrison could picture the blaze that made a

reluctant hero out of his friend Captain Robert McKay, first mate on the *Naomi* at the time. With the frightened passengers milling around in near panic, McKay had calmly supervised the loading and launching of the lifeboats. His ringing voice of command with its pronounced Scottish burr had efficiently directed the entire operation. Some passengers on the after end had been trapped there by flames. While First Mate McKay was managing the rescue of the others, the freighter *S. S. Curry* arrived on the scene. Her captain, seeing that no time was to be lost, pushed his ship's nose into the *Naomi*'s stern, where the imperiled souls jumped to the *Curry*'s foredeck. Altogether, Morrison mused, it must have been quite a night.

Her superstructure a mass of twisted rails, stanchions, and beams, the *Naomi* was completely rebuilt in the winter of 1908-09 and renamed the *E. G. Crosby*. She now carried a hundred cabins on two decks, with parlors and social halls for passenger recreation. The cabins and parlors were finished in curly birch, with de-luxe furnishings and every convenience the shipbuilding industry offered. The rebuild was said to have cost $200,000, or $40,000 more than the original construction figure. Back on her old Milwaukee to Grand Haven run, the *E. G. Crosby* ran faultlessly.

During the hectic years of World War I she was purchased by the United States Shipping Board for use as a hospital and convalescent ship in New York Harbor. She was renamed the *General Robert M. O'Reilly*. In less than two years, sold by the Government to the Seymour interests, she was back on Lake Michigan as the *Pilgrim*, running between Chicago, Racine, and Milwaukee. Sold again, this time to the reorganized Goodrich Transit Company, her first owners, she stayed on the west-shore run. In 1924, Goodrich, probably as a sentimental gesture, gave her back her original name, *Wisconsin*.

All in all, Captain Morrison philosophized, the old girl

had spent a busy forty-eight years. Her few infirmities were minor affairs. He had no doubt that if the night-boat trade warranted it, she could plug along for another decade, with little trouble. Only last month, he recalled, September seventeenth to be specific, she had passed inspection by the Seamboat Inspection Service, with flying colors.

The noises from below had stopped now, except for some pronounced thumpings on the port side. They were sounds he had grown to recognize as that of the gangways being closed and the strongbacks being hammered into place and wedged tight. Beyond the cabin partition he could hear First Mate Henry Halverson tramping around, divesting himself of his rain gear, kicking off his boots, and hanging his wet coat over the steam radiator. Faintly, the ring of the steward's bell found its way aloft, reminding all the crew that dinner was being served. Distant sounds of doors opening and heavy feet shuffling down the companionways told him that the call was being answered. All of which reminded Captain Morrison that it was time to sail.

It may be that his mental review of the old *Wisconsin*'s past and his knowledge of her present state of good health, as attested to by the Steamboat Inspection Service, were subconscious factors in the decision to sail, regardless of weather. At least no indecision on the part of Captain Morrison was apparent to the first mate, the wheelsman, or the steward who brought a steaming pot of coffee to the pilothouse. The routine of casting off the lines, backing slightly to get some room between the ship and the dock, and finally the "slow ahead" on the telegraph came with the well-regulated order of a thousand departures handled by capable seamen. The *Alabama*, mate Halvorson noted, had already sailed. He could still faintly see her lights in the dusk.

Down below, steward Tom Lange was in bad humor. Mrs. Davidson, the stewardess had missed the boat. Some of her duties would, consequently, fall upon him. His only consolation was that on this trip, which promised to be a grim one, only four passengers, all men, had availed themselves of the opportunity of riding the night boat to Milwaukee. He hoped none of them would get seasick.

The *Wisconsin* began to roll heavily as soon as she left the shelter of the seawall. Not the easy roll of a ship gradually adjusting herself to a brisk blow, but desperate, sickening rolls as she tried to quarter seas that were now cresting well over twenty feet. The pitching began, too, as she dug her nose into them, which pitching green water up over her bow, some of it going clear over the pilothouse. And it was only the beginning.

Down below, Chief Engineer Julius Buschmann watched his machinery and listened to the clamor and cursing in the firehold. There, on the rolling and pitching steel deck, loose coal, slice bars, coal-passers' wheelbarrows, and the firemen themselves slid from side to side. Somehow, it reminded Buschmann of a humorous version of Dante's *Inferno*. The big fire-grate doors swung back and forth with a steady clanging. Shovels, tools, and lanterns slammed in unison against the bulkheads. Ash buckets ran amok, rolling and banging with a fearful clatter. Dodging the sliding gear, the black gang sought gamely to fire their boilers and maintain steam. It was, the chief opined, going to be a long night.

At one A.M., as Buschmann was entering the engine-revolutions count in the log, a sweating, perturbed fireman came hurrying to his desk. The engineer could sense incipient panic in the man's voice.

"Chief, for God's sake come and take a look. There's water coming in the firehold, lots of it!"

There was, indeed, water in the firehold, Buschmann discovered, and it was rising by the minute. A quick check failed to reveal the source, but by any standards it was a serious leak. Already it was ankle-deep and washing back and forth with the roll of the ship.

Back in the engineroom he alerted those on watch by banging a wrench on the brass rail around the oiler's walkway. "Forget what you're doing," he yelled, "and let's get the pumps going, all of them."

While this was being done he got Captain Morrison on the voice pipe, requesting that he personally take stock of the situation. The captain was aware that some of the cargo had shifted, resulting in a pronounced list to port, but he was appalled at the still-rising tide of water in the firehold. With the engineer and a couple of oilers he tried to find the source. On the cargo deck he found a shambles. Tons of freight were loose and roaring from side to side with each roll of the *Wisconsin*. Supporting beams had been bent, packing cases had broken open, and a wide assortment of products constituted a tidal wave of destruction that swept from side to side with each tilt of the deck. Far over on the port side, however, was a jumble of barrels filled with steel castings. When loaded they had been placed in the center of the deck and surrounded by four-inch blocking to keep them from shifting. There was no sign of the blocking now, and while the source of the leak could still not be pinpointed, the search crew was of the opinion that the tons of castings, breaking loose and smashing violently against the port side, had pushed out some plates.

The water in the firehold was gaining rapidly, despite the pumps. At the captain's orders Buschmann cut down the engine revolutions to provide more steam for the pumps. The extra steam had no effect on the water building up in the firehold. Already it had surged into the ash pits, filling the area with acrid fumes. The firemen were now working in water up to their knees and wondering how long it would be before the water reached the grates and gradually extinguished the fires. Deprived of steam pressure, the old *Wisconsin* would not be long for this world.

Captain Morrison, meanwhile, beat a path to the wireless

room, where young Kenneth Carlson, the *Milwaukee*'s Sparks, was keeping his nightly vigil.

At midnight, Elmer Webster had taken over the late watch at the Chicago Radiomarine Station and for an hour and a half had been handling routine messages, mostly to owners from ships in shelter from the storm.

At 1:30 A.M. the *Milwaukee*'s Kenneth Carlson flashed his first message from the imperiled ship:

"We are four miles off Kenosha. Fireholds all flooded. In immediate danger. Please stay with us. May need your help soon.
[Signed] *"Wisconsin"*

1:40 "Please get captain of steamer *Illinois*. Tell him we need help."

1:43 Operator Webster relayed message to Captain Delletre of the *Illinois*, in harbor at Milwaukee.

1:50 "My chain has parted. Tug *Butterfield* trying to turn me around. Will come soon.
[Signed] "Capt. Delletre"

1:52 Operator Webster relayed Delletre's message to the *Wisconsin*, adding, "Am sending you Racine and Kenosha Coast Guards."

2:15 "Due to sink any time now. For God's sake send help."

2:17 "Hold on, help on way."
[Signed] "Webster"

2:25 Webster phoned *Wisconsin*'s message to Captain Taylor, superintendent of transportation for the Goodrich Line, at his Chicago home.

2:30 Webster flashed *Wisconsin* at direction of Captain Taylor. "Have captain of *Wisconsin* send me message under his signature."

2:35 "Fires out. No steam. Rush boats for tow before it is too late. We may save her.
[Signed] "Captain Morrison"

2:50 Captain Morrison repeated message.

3:00 SOS SOS SOS

3:30 "Am drifting in toward Kenosha."

3:40 "Can stay up half hour longer, is help coming?"

3:50 "Can see Coast Guard coming to us. They are about half-way out from Kenosha."

4:00 "Kenosha Coast Guard here. Have attached two of their lines."

4:05 "Coast Guard can do nothing. Is standing by to take off our crew. Are larger boats coming?"

4:08 "Tugboats and other Coast Guard on way. We'll make it yet."

> [Signed] "Webster"

4:30 "We have received SOS. We are just outside Milwaukee. It will take us two hours to get there. We are starting now.
> [Signed] "Pere Marquette car ferry"

4:31 "Rush it.

> [Signed] "Webster"

4:32 "Abandoning ship. Leaving boat now. Can't stay longer. Thanks. Won't forget you.

> [Signed] "Wisconsin"

4:34 "Not enough boats for us all.

> [Signed] "Wisconsin"

4:35 Webster tried to reach Wisconsin but could not. He concluded that the power had gone dead or that the ship's wireless operator had left his post to take to the boats.

5:20 Kenosha Coast Guard Station telephoned Goodrich dock at Chicago: "Understand tug Butterfield can't make it. She is turning back."

Kenneth Carlson had, indeed, left his post. The main power plant had been out of service for some time, blinking

out when the water in the engineroom reached the genera-
tors. The water in the firehold had reached a depth of fifteen
feet when the gasoline-powered auxiliary plant, mounted over
the boilers, also sputtered to a stop. Carlson didn't know
whether the water had stopped it or if it had simply run out
of fuel. In any event, he was about to investigate when Mate
Halvorson came into the wireless room carrying a flashlight
and what appeared to be a sturdy police nightstick.

"Get up on deck right away," he said. "And that's an order
from the Old Man!"

Up on the boat deck the last of the emergency lights had
winked out with the loss of the auxiliary power plant. In total
darkness, while the cold wind shrieked insanely and the old
Wisconsin wallowed and rolled in seas that ran as high as
her passenger deck, the crew sought to launch the boats. The
seas assaulting the ship on her weather side rendered the
starboard boats useless. Captain Morrison, in a decision that
was questioned later, ordered both anchors dropped, supposedly to ease the task of launching the boats. It was a deci
sion born of desperation, for he must have known that he
had no steam to raise them again. Even so, the ship continued
to drift shoreward, dragging her anchors. It was pandemo-
nium now. Since it was apparent that only the port boats
could be lowered and they could take only part of the crew,
some of the men went overboard. Others threw over life
rafts and jumped after them. Somehow the four passengers
found their way into the boats, two of them in No. 5 boat
with wireless operator Carlson. The *Wisconsin* was rolling
her deck stanchions under now and recovering more slowly
with each roll. From inside, great thunderings could be heard
as her freight cargo rolled and tumbled from side to side.
Loud cracking noises told of bulkheads giving way. In the
eerie darkness and cold some of the crewmen went under
almost immediately. Others swam to the Coast Guard boats
that were circling the sinking *Wisconsin*.

Chief Engineer Julius Buschmann, a calm, methodical man in his engineroom, was quite the reverse in the water. Crazed with fear, he clung to the side of a life raft, fighting off rescuers and shrieking incoherently. Finally, exhausted by his efforts, he lost his grip and disappeared.

By word of mouth and telephone the news of the *Wisconsin*'s plight had been passed around in Kenosha. When the gray light of dawn arrived, hundreds of the city's citizens were watching from the modest bluff at the foot of Seventy-fifth Street. The ship was little more than a mile offshore now, and they could see her lying almost on her portside, the seas climbing over her.

Clinton Young and his father were at the Kenosha piers, unaware of the tragedy until they saw a Coast Guard boat creep in from the open lake; it was jammed to the gunnels with survivors, yet barely making steerageway because of a heaving line from the *Wisconsin* fouled in her propeller.

"That Coast Guard lifeboat was so overloaded it was almost sinking," Young recalls. "Since the weather was absolutely lousy I knew the boat hadn't been out for a drill."

The helmsman on the crippled rescue boat yelled to Young that the *Wisconsin* had gone down and that there were men still in the water.

Sensing something amiss, Clarence Ferris, a crewman on the Chambers brothers' fishing tug, hurried to the pier. "Come on," said Young, "Let's go get those poor guys." Borrowing one of the Coast Guard station's small boats, they rowed across the slip to the fishing tug. While Ferris lighted the heating torches to fire up the semidiesel engine, Young began throwing extra lines and nets off the deck. Just then the Chambers brothers, Cliff and Lloyd, along with several other fishermen—Julian Ellison, Captain Roland Hill, Pete Adelson, Mike Valentine, Adam Korvaliski, Bernard Deveny, and Ed Einison—arrived. They were all unaware of the offshore drama.

"It was the Chambers brothers' tug but I yelled to get aboard and I'd explain later," Young remembers. "A Kenosha policeman, Ray Gleason, was there and he jumped aboard, too. As we headed out of the harbor I told them about the *Wisconsin* going down and the men still in the water."

Within minutes the tug was rising on the crests of the big seas and falling off into the valleys between them. It began to encounter wreckage, not much at first but soon a great heaving mass of flotsam. Calls for help came from all directions.

Young recalls the scene as if it were yesterday. "There were men all over. Some were praying, some crying, and some who just couldn't even make a noise any more. We spotted twelve men on an eight-man life raft, some so cold they couldn't move. I remember that we kept going after the live ones. Finally, we couldn't see any more, so we pulled out of the wreckage and hurried back to the harbor."

Lloyd Chambers, still a sailor, has vivid memories of the morning the *Wisconsin* went down. "I always thought the Coast Guard was wrong in taking the men from the ship's lifeboats," he explains. "The boats were being blown toward shore and were in no danger of sinking. But by the time they were pulled aboard the Coast Guard boats, there was no room for the poor devils still in the water. And they were the ones who needed help. We pulled right into the wreckage and got as many men as we could. When the Coast Guard boat returned, the man in charge wouldn't go into the mess for fear of fouling his propeller. Nearly everybody they picked up was dead or, like the captain, they died of exposure before they could get back to shore. We pushed everybody we rescued down below, where we had a fire going in the steam boiler we used to lift the nets. Most of them were good as new by the time we got back to the fish dock."

The official list of crew and passengers went down with the

ship, but Purser Harvey Lyons, who survived, was positive that there were seventy-four persons aboard. Nineteen were rushed to hospitals and forty were taken to the police station, where scores of generous citizens brought warm food and dry clothing. A count of heads revealed that sixteen had perished, including Captain Dougal Morrison.

In the three-way investigation launched by the Federal Government, Kenosha County, and the *Wisconsin*'s owners, several questions were posed that might have been embarrassing to Captain Morrison. On the other hand he might have had a logical answer for all of them. But Captain Morrison was dead and could not answer the questions that would have been put to him by his superiors in the Goodrich Transit Company, the Kenosha County coroner, or by Fred J. Meno, supervising inspector of the Steamboat Inspection Service.

The most elementary point of seamanship being discussed was why Captain Morrison, instead of dropping anchors he could not retrieve, had not, as a logical alternative, beached the *Wisconsin*. Many thought this could have been done on the sandy beach off Kenosha with no loss of life. But there were others who pointed out that drawing perhaps an extra fifteen or twenty feet of water as the result of the unexplained leak, the ship would probably have grounded far from shore. There, the *Wisconsin*, literally anchored to the bottom, would have been quickly dismembered by the seas that were running that night. Under those conditions it is doubtful that any of the lifeboats could have been launched. Nearly every community along the Wisconsin shore is rich with stories of beached ships whose crews were lost before rescuers could get to them. Again, at the time he made his decision, Captain Morrison was still under the impression that the tug *Butterfield* was en route to take him in tow. The message saying she had turned back had been sent after the wireless operator, Carlson, had been ordered to the boat deck.

The captain, obviously, still had some faint hope of saving his ship.

Better yet, it was suggested, why, since the *Wisconsin* was only an hour out of Kenosha when she first began radioing distress signals, had not Captain Morrison immediately headed for that port, instead of dawdling about, beseeching others to come to his assistance? Sore beset as he was, he must have at least considered such action. But there is more than meets the landlubber's eye when a skipper attempts to make the harbor piers with the wind and sea at his back, his ship listing badly to port and drawing far more than her accustomed draft. Dropping down between the seas, the *Wisconsin* would quite likely have struck bottom before she reached the piers, perhaps throwing her out of control and into the piers themselves. It had happened before. Every shipmaster remembered the *Mataafa* fleeing for shelter at the Duluth harbor piers, only to hit bottom, shear off into the piers, and then strand herself offshore, where the after crew perished. Yes, Captain Morrison was thinking of his people as well as his ship.

It is one thing to pose questions in a warm courthouse hearing room, quite another matter to conclude what one should have done on that terrible black and cold night when his ship was dying, the wind shrieking, the crew laboring to launch the boats, and the seas breaking completely over her— quite another matter, indeed.

Captain Morrison had made one decision none of the officials could dispute. Within seconds after he had ascertained that his ship was in peril, he had instructed wireless operator Kenneth Carlson to call for help. With the events of the previous week in mind, some wondered how many sailors would still be alive had the *Milwaukee* been wireless-equipped. But, of course, none of these speculations could explain the measured reasoning behind the decisions of the

Wisconsin's skipper during her protracted death throes. Only her master could supply the answers, and he was dead.

"One thing for sure," one official concluded. "Right or wrong, Captain Morrison made his decision with the best of intentions."

8

~~~~~~~~
⚓

A Very Determined Man

It was one of those times when a shipmaster gets no rest
and sometimes wonders why he didn't stay ashore to become
a machinist, a salesman, or a mail carrier. It was the morning
of October 31, 1929, the last day of the most disastrous month
Lake Michigan had ever known. September, with the old
Andaste vanishing with all hands, had been bad enough.
Then, on the night of October twenty-second, the car ferry,
Milwaukee, had foundered, again with her entire crew. Seven
days later, on the morning of the twenty-ninth, the gallant
old *Wisconsin*, after a long and desperate fight to stay afloat,
laid over on her port side and sought out her eternal resting
place. Souvenir hunters were still combing the beach at
Kenosha, Wisconsin, looking for mementoes of the historic
night boat.

Now, it was fog, the worst in many years, blanketing Lake
Michigan like a layer of cotton candy. It lay heavy and wet
from Big Bay de Noc, off the upper peninsula of Michigan,
to Buffington Harbor, Indiana, south and east of Chicago. It
had developed quite suddenly during the evening of the
thirtieth, after masters of many ships had committed themselves to one or the other of the two accepted upbound or

downbound courses to and from the wreck-strewn Straits of Mackinac.

Westbound through the straits and headed for a west-shore Lake Michigan port, the shipmaster of a lakes vessel has a choice of two courses. He can steer 278 degrees, WNW, for forty-one miles beyond Old Mackinac Point Light, until abeam of Lansing Shoal Light and then haul SW by W until safely clear of Gull Island and Boulder Reef. Hauling to port again, he has a southerly course to all the west-shore ports, relatively clear of hazards, if one excepts upbound vessels and the car ferries that steam directly across the lake with great regularity. This is the longer course. It is obviously time and fuel consuming.

The shorter course is the east-shore route. It involves taking a 270-degree heading from Old Mackinac for only twenty miles, before turning hard to port off White Shoal. This is Grays Reef Passage, a rather confined course between Middle Shoal and East Shoal. To the west, of a summer's twilight, rise the low profiles of Hog and Garden islands, sparkling like jewels on an azure sea. Then comes Beaver Island, ominous-looking as darkness descends, seemingly haunted by the ghosts of a thousand tough Irishmen—a fabled island that was once the only "kingdom" within the continental United States. The self-proclaimed Mormon monarch, James Jesse Strang, lived here in the village of St. James, named after himself. Here he issued his lordly directives and boasted of his kingdom's River Jordan, Mount Pisgah, and Lake Genesareth. One can almost hear him now in the blue of dusk, up to his knees in the surf of Beaver Harbor, calling down the curses of the Almighty on a boatload of fleeing dissidents: "Woe, ye sinners . . . woe . . . woe . . . woe."

After Beaver Island all is clear for sixty-five miles, until the North Manitou Shoal Light blinks slightly to starboard. This heralds the dangerous Manitou Passage, between North

and South Manitou Islands and the mainland. Jutting out
from the Michigan shore, Pyramid Point Shoal narrows the
shipping lanes opposite North Manitou. Sleeping Bear Point
and its outlying rocks and shoals does the same disservice to
mariners across the passage from South Manitou. Once beyond both islands, the way is clear. Here the master bound
for Sturgeon Bay or any of the west-shore ports steers his
appropriate course.

Shipmasters caught in fog or foul weather while navigating
Manitou Passage breathe a sigh of relief when South Manitou
is astern. Her rocky shores and offshore reefs hold the bones
of many sail and steam vessels that came upon her in fog or
snow, or sought her lee for shelter. Ronald Rosio, who tended
the South Manitou Light for many years, by combing the
logbooks of former lightkeepers, totaled ninety-six wrecks.
Each left its own legend of disaster: the *J. Y. Scannon,
Charles H. Hurd, Annie Veight, Margaret Dall, H. D. Moore,*
and the *Lonie A. Burton*—all schooners. But steamers had a
habit of "finding" South Manitou, too—sturdy vessels like the
Walter L. Frost, Westmoreland, Three Brothers, and the
Francisco Morazan, the latter a Liberian flag freighter, which
disembowled herself there in 1960. She still lies there, a
grim, gray reminder of South Manitou's infamous heritage of
tragedy.

In a field opposite the South Manitou Island cemetery,
another burial plot holds the remains of an estimated two
hundred unidentified sailors lost in wrecks. More bodies,
victims of a single wreck, are at another location on the
island. Oars and woodwork, fashioned into crude monuments, were still visible in the 1930s.

It is small wonder then, that when the fog descended during the night of October 30, 1929, vessels transiting the
Straits of Mackinac or the hazardous east-shore route, pru-
dently dropped anchor. From Vienna Shoal to Point Betsie
on Lake Michigan, and all along the steamer tracks through

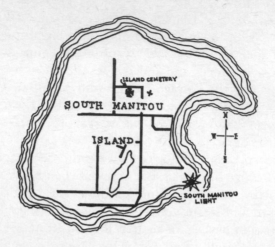

the straits, from McGulpin Point and St. Helena Island to Poe Reef and Lime Kiln Point, a hundred freighters lay tethered to the bottom by their anchor chains, bleating out their dismal fog signals with the regularity of lovesick frogs.

Over off the west shore of Lake Michigan, far from the hazards of the straits or Manitou Passage, dawn of October thirty-first found the 420-foot steamer, *Marquette*, cautiously hooting her way, downbound for Indiana Harbor. Early on the previous evening she had loaded seven thousand tons of iron ore at Escanaba, at the northerly end of Green Bay. The weather had been relatively fair in Little Bay de Noc. Captain Walter S. Ainsbery had hoped for a routine voyage. However, when the *Marquette* came abreast of Minneapolis Shoal, the first patches of fog were encountered. It was a spasmodic affair at first, alternate areas of fog and fair visibility with occasionally a glimpse of Boyer Bluff Light, winking coquettishly from the northernmost tip of Washington Island. But the fog was persistent enough to justify keeping a lookout at the bow and the ship's whistle snoring out its three blasts at one-minute intervals, the standard fog signal. Abreast of Washington Island's West Harbor the fog thickened abruptly. Captain Ainsbery promptly checked his ship down to half speed. The *Marquette* was immersed in its own little world of sight and sound, each distorted and blurred by the wraithlike vapors of the fog. At the bow the lookout stood on tiptoes, tense and watchful. The pilothouse windows were lowered into their wells. All was silent. Distant whistles could be heard as the ship approached the Porte des Morts (Door of Death) Passage. Those who strained to hear them hoped others could hear and correctly interpret the *Marquette*'s throaty sobs. Porte des Morts is a rather narrow strait through which the bulk of deep-draft traffic between Green Bay and Lake Michigan must find its way. In the cold pilothouse every nerve was keyed to the sounds of the night.

"Fog signal dead ahead," the bow lookout called out.

"Fog signal dead ahead," Captain Ainsbery acknowledged, swinging the telegraph indicator to dead-slow.

The nearing vessel was proceeding cautiously, too. Her skipper, once he saw the *Marquette*'s masthead light through the fog, blew one prolonged blast on his whistle, the signal for a normal port-to-port passing.

Captain Ainsbery responded with the same signal. All was well.

Cautiously, when past Plum Island Light, the *Marquette* made her swing to port and steered the prescribed course that would take her between Pilot Island Light and the Waverly Shoal bell buoy. Four miles beyond this bottleneck, safely out on Lake Michigan, Captain Ainsbery hauled his vessel to starboard on his normal, southbound course, assured that the shoal waters were astern.

The fog was worse after daylight than it had been throughout the night. There was a nasty bit of sea running, too. The captain, at his post all night, held out hope that the fog would "burn off" as the morning temperatures rose. At ten A.M. he estimated that his ship was about twenty miles off Port Washington, still checked down to half-speed.

About the time the *Marquette* was off Washington Island, in Green Bay, slowly groping her way toward Porte des Morts Passage, the automobile carrier, *Senator*, was departing Kenosha, bound for Detroit, Toledo, and Buffalo. She was skippered by Captain George Kinch of Ogdensburg, New York, a master of unquestioned ability, but known by former shipmates to be a bit on the "determined" side.

Aside from her midships elevator, the *Senator* resembled any of the long bulk freighters. She had once hauled iron ore, coal, and grain—lots of it. Now in the service of the Nicholson-Universal Steamship Company, she had been altered and converted to carry automobiles from cities of manufacture to distribution points. Her present voyage had started off with a full load of automobiles at Detroit. She had discharged some of them at Milwaukee and the balance at Chicago. She then steamed, light, to Kenosha. On the afternoon and evening of October 30, the elevator had lowered 241 new Nash automobiles into the hold. The *Senator* had two lower decks. Both were full when Captain Kinch signaled his engineroom to stand by. If there was any surprise at the skipper's decision to sail, it was not apparent in the answering signal from below. It was the kind of night when a prudent shipmaster, if already moored safely to a dock, would undoubtedly choose to stay there until better visibility warranted his departure. But Captain Kinch was familiar with facets of responsibility unappreciated by those not in command. There were contract commitments his owners must meet. With November just over the calendar horizon, there was, in his estimation, little justification in lying at the dock just because of a little fog. At 10:30 P.M. the *Senator*'s searchlight pointed an eerie finger along the fog-shrouded dock to aid the shoreside people in casting off her lines. Then, after one long, sonorous blast of her whistle, she steamed slowly out between the harbor piers. The fog enveloped her almost at once. Her lights disappeared as though a blanket had been drawn

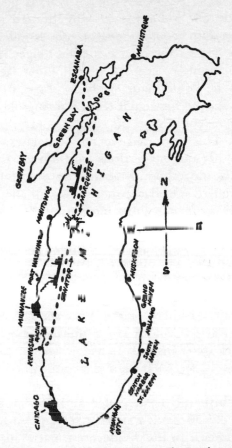

around her. Once a minute, the three impatient hoots of her whistle, distorted by the fog, found their way back to shore. Gradually, they faded away to join the distant symphony of steamer whistles out on the lake, each with its own tone and urgent warning. Captain Kinch was, indeed, a determined man.

The captain had long since abandoned any thought of steaming across the lake on a northeasterly course to utilize the shorter route up the east shore. This would involve navigating both Manitou Passage and Grays Reef Passage.

This he would not attempt, even with limited visibility, let alone the pea-soup fog the *Senator* was prodding with her steering pole. He set the course for the longer route up the west shore, planning to keep well off Boulder Reef and Gull Island, until he could haul safely to starboard. Then, in good time, with the fog signal from Lansing Shoal Light off the port side, he could steer his regular course for the Straits of Mackinac. This he would worry about later. His present concern was his rather perilous position at the moment. Assuming that downbound vessels were on their correct tracks and well to starboard, there was still the chance that one of the big car ferries, shuttling constantly across the lake, could cross his bow at any minute or, worse yet, cut him down. As on the *Marquette*, the windows had been lowered and a strict silence was observed. Any noise coming out of the fog could be significant, even fatal. So it went all night, eyes and ears straining, nerves taut.

Like Captain Ainsbery of the *Marquette*, Captain Kinch thought that daylight and a rising thermometer would soon put the fog to rout. Instead, it had worsened. At times the wheelsman could see no farther than the tip of the steering pole, never more than a couple of hundred feet beyond it. The porter, bringing fresh coffee and collecting the dirty cups, walked on tiptoes. It was ten A.M. Captain Kinch, working on his charts with his dividers, estimated his position as being about twenty miles off Port Washington.

At twenty minutes after ten, lookouts on both vessels reported hearing fog signals from another ship. They could be heard in the pilothouses, too—the chilling, muted throbs, three in quick succession, followed by an eerie silence of one minute. Fog does strange things to sounds at sea. One moment they seem to come from far away and to the right, the next instant close and, perhaps, to the left. On that fateful morning of October thirty-first, although the whistles seemed confused in direction and distance, they were actually coming from dead ahead.

They saw each other at the same time, both steering a stem-to-stem collision course! After tense hours of anticipating just such a dread apparition, the immediate reaction was one of utter disbelief, of paralyzing shock that robbed one, for an instant, of cohesive physical action. Both captains then frantically threw their engine telegraphs to "full astern" and shouted for their wheelsmen to turn. It was an instinctive order, and the only one, in the final analysis, that could be given. It was proper procedure, in any event. Unfortunately, they both turned in the same, intercepting direction. Her engines still throbbing astern, the whole hull trembling and her whistle shrieking, the *Marquette* punched her bow a full twenty feet into the side of the *Senator*, opening a gash so large that the auto carrier began to list immediately.

Captain Kinch knew his ship was doomed. The quick list told him that she had been opened wide below the waterline by the heavily-laden *Marquette*. In addition to being determined, he was also a realist. Wheelsman Herbert Petting, of Fredonia, New York, still stood at his post, awaiting steering orders.

"Can you swim?" asked the captain.

Petting nodded in the affirmative.

"Then you'd better get to hell out of here!"

When Petting took his hasty departure the captain was still in the pilothouse, leaning on one of the windowsills and looking somewhat disconsolately at the fog-shrouded ship that had cut him down.

Ralph Ellis, the *Senator*'s wireless operator, had begun to transmit SOS signals an instant after the collision. He, too, feeling the deck begin to cant over, and having no desire to become a dead hero, joined Petting in the rush aft to the boats.

Shouts of confusion rent the air as the ship's black-gang and engineroom crew clambered to the boat deck. It was at once apparent that the quickening list would prevent any of the boats from being launched. Several manhandled the life rafts overboard and leaped after them. On the spar deck, coal passer William Harris encountered Minnie Gormley, the ship's cook and wife of the steward, Matthew Gormley. She was frantic with fear and screaming hysterically. He helped her to the rail and pulled her off with him. Both managed to reach a raft, but the choppy seas kept rolling it over.

"The cold just turned you blue," Harris later told investigators. "A couple of times I thought it was useless and had almost made up my mind to give up and let go. We were in the water for about fifteen minutes when Mrs. Gormley, who had been calling for help all along, just let go and went down."

The *Senator* had preceded her to the bottom by five minutes.

Wireless operator Ellis was a long way from the rafts when he jumped over the side. The *Marquette* was much nearer. He made for her. Fortunately for him, the collision had released her anchors and had ripped a big hole in her bow at the windlass deck. Hand over hand he went up one of the big anchor chains and through the hole to safety.

The ore carrier herself was taking water, a serious leak by any standards. On orders from the skipper her wireless operator had been sending SOS signals since the crash. Coast Guard boats, under the direction of Captain William Kincaide, and commercial tugs put out from Milwaukee and Sheboygan moments after the first distress flash. Captain Ainsbery had then instructed his operator to tell all concerned that he would attempt to beach his vessel at Port Washington.

Meanwhile, the fishing tug *Delos H. Smith*, by good fortune, was groping her way through the fog when her captain heard the frantic danger whistles and, seconds later, the fog-distorted rumble as the ships came together. With that instinctive judgment that comes with living the life of a commercial fisherman for years, he managed to find the *Senator*'s wreckage and survivors, some of them nearly dead from exposure. Counting wireless operator Ellis and two others picked up by the *Marquette*, the total of those rescued was twenty-one. Seven were missing or had gone down with the ship, including Captain Kinch, the "determined" skipper.

After a more intensive examination of the bow damage and twisted bulkheads, Captain Ainsbery changed his mind about beaching his ship. He wired his owners, the Cleveland Cliffs Iron Company, with that brevity peculiar to shipmasters:

In collision with *Senator*. *Senator* sunk. Am headed for Milwaukee. Bow stove in. Think can make it if bulkhead holds.

The bulkheads held. Late that afternoon the *Marquette*, assisted by tugs, tied up to a Milwaukee pier. Waiting there, were the inspectors of the Steamboat Inspection Service.

Two weeks later, after hundreds of questions had been put to the *Senator*'s survivors, the crew of the *Marquette*, and Captain Ainsbery, the inspectors' reports joined those of the *Andaste*, *Milwaukee*, and *Wisconsin*, on the desk of Supervising Inspector General Dickerson N. Hoover in Washington.

All in all, it was a voluminous and imposing file of testimony, leading Mr. Hoover to sigh and conclude that it had been a deplorable year on Lake Michigan, a deplorable year, indeed.

9

~~~~~~
⚓

Where Is the *Kamloops*...?

Along the east coast of Britain, where at night the mariner accepts the red glow of the blast furnaces as his beacon long before he sees the red and white flash of South Gare lighthouse at its mouth, the Tees estuary, separating Durham and York counties, finds its way to the North Sea, midway between the coastal cities of Hartlepool and Middlebrough. Here, at Haverton Hill, although it was by no means one of the major shipbuilding centers of Great Britain, the steamer *Kamloops*, 2302 gross tons, took shape in 1924. One suspects that on her builder's trials she inspired a great wagging of tongues and lifting of eyebrows among the mariners who viewed her, whether from the fleets of trawlers inbound to Aberdeen, Shields, Hull, and Grimsby or the lumbering old well-deckers hauling pit props from the Scandinavian countries to Britain's collieries. In any event, to the salt-water sailors of a nation famous for its big, world-girdling, three-island tramp ships, and great liners, the *Kamloops*, with its pilothouse forward-engines-aft design, a typical Great Lakes profile, was unmistakably a stranger on the North Sea.

Built on contract for Canada Steamship Lines in the yards of the Furness Ship Building Company Ltd., the *Kamloops*, named for a town in British Columbia, was two hundred

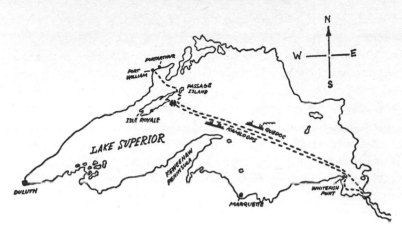

and fifty feet long and forty-two feet of beam, strictly a
utilitarian canaller. She was restricted in length by the trade
she was intended for and because her usual voyages would
carry her through the canal and small locks that then comprised the only access to the Great Lakes by circumventing
the shallows and rapids on the St. Lawrence River, between
Montreal and Lake Ontario.

The canallers, and there were many in operation for
various owners, were literally the tramp freighters of the
Great Lakes . . . unique in their ability to carry diversified
cargoes. In the main, they hauled package freight west and
north to the Canadian twin city ports of Ft. William and
Port Arthur, both busy terminals for the Canadian National
Railway and the Canadian Pacific Railway, at the northernmost tip of Lake Superior. Their cargoes might include
everything from railroad rails, barn lanterns, and crockery,
to machinery and Scotch whisky. Having unburdened themselves of such a wide range of crated, boxed, or bagged commodities, they then usually steamed over to the elevators
along Thunder Bay or the Kaministikwia River to take
aboard a bulk cargo of grain for Toronto, Montreal, or
Quebec City. Much of the grain would eventually be re-

loaded into deep-draft salt-water vessels for overseas shipment.

The *Kamloops* had two pairs of king posts with swinging booms to handle her package freight. When this was disposed of, the booms could be raised to a vertical position, clearing the way for the elevator chutes and simplifying the grain-loading operation.

One of the advantages of having a Great Lakes ship built abroad is that she can begin to earn money immediately by carrying a cargo across the Atlantic to her new home. This the *Kamloops* did, arriving in Montreal with a load of structural steel, wire, and machinery after an eminently satisfactory voyage.

With a considerable investment in a new vessel, Canada Steamship Lines wanted only the best of skippers to command her. From their rather considerable fleet they selected Captain Bill Brian who hailed from Garden Island, near Kingston, Ontario. For years he had been captain of the *Kenora*, another canaller, built in Scotland for the Plummer interests of Toronto and later absorbed by Canada Steamship Lines. Captain Brian though young was intimately acquainted with every one of the twenty-two locks between Montreal and Lake Ontario and the twenty-seven in the Welland Canal, between Lake Ontario and Lake Erie. But despite the long, monotonous trips through the canals at the beginning and end of every voyage, he ran a "happy" ship. The crew lived and worked like a big, harmonious family.

The exigencies of the canaller's economic existence sometimes demanded that she call at ports inaccessible to larger craft. The *Kamloops* knew them all, from the quaint towns flanking the St. Clair River to those along the shores of pine-scented Georgian Bay and the North Channel. And the people living in them knew the *Kamloops*, Captain Bill Brian and most of the crew. At one port a friend presented the captain with "Ginger," an affectionate, rust-colored puppy.

Obviously, of undistinguished lineage but possessing the disposition of a happy Irishman, Ginger quickly adapted to shipboard life, accepting with pride, as she grew, her role of ship's mascot. She was pampered and petted by the crew, but it was to Captain Brian she gave full measure of devotion—at his heels on shoreside excursions to care for ship's business, curling up under his bunk at night, and always sharing his watch in the pilothouse.

On Thursday, December 1, 1927, upbound for Ft. William, with a considerable tonnage of coiled wire and machinery for the Thunder Bay Paper Company already in her holds, the *Kamloops* moored at Courtright, Ontario, on the St. Clair River, to take on a few tiers of bagged salt. While the cargo was being loaded and stowed, Captain Brian, with Ginger at his side, went ashore to see old friends. The wind was fresh and carried a reminder that winter was almost upon the stage. Captain Brian pulled up his coat collar and walked briskly up the road from the dock. Ginger, stopping occasionally to sniff the gusts that came swishing down the length of Lake Huron to stir the piles of fallen leaves, was not in her usual effervescent mood. Strangely, too, when they returned to the ship at midnight, she absolutely refused to cross the gangplank, although she had gleefully raced across it hundreds of times before. Despite an hour of coaxing and bribing with morsels from the galley, she stubbornly kept her distance, outwitting those who attempted to catch her. Reluctantly then, Captain Brian ordered the gangplank drawn aboard, saw the lines cast off, and then directed his ship away from the dock and into the upbound river channel. It was the first pilothouse watch with her master that Ginger had missed in two years.

It took the *Kamloops* a full twenty-four hours to go up Lake Huron, passing Detour and entering confined waters at midnight on December second. All night she steered by the range lights and buoys, up the old and familiar twisting channel, hooting a hundred passing signals to downbound vessels as she maintained her modest pace past Pipe Island, Squaw Island, Lime Island, Round Island, Hay Point, and into Lake Munuscong. Then more of the same careful, watch-ful, and expert navigation along the serpentine course until she reached the West Neebish Channel and, finally, the lower St. Marys River. The *Kamloops* arrived at the Soo and locked through at noon on Saturday, December third.

Late that afternoon as Captain Brian noted the passing of Gros Cap Light in his log, the *Kamloops* left the broadening upper St. Marys and steamed out into Whitefish Bay, where she first felt the full sweep of the northwest wind and rather nasty seas rolling the length of Lake Superior. The pitching and rolling began almost immediately. It was nothing new to the *Kamloops*, for she had encountered similar situations a hundred times in her three years of service. But this trip was different—different simply because of the special im-ported paper-making machinery that accounted for a goodly share of her cargo. It was consigned to the Thunder Bay Paper Company and consisted of vital machine components for an expansion program already underway. If badly dam-aged, it would require a full year, possibly longer, for replace-ment. Considering all eventualities, and this took in his personal position as captain, damage reports, investigations, insurance claims, hearings, and a dozen other painful ex-periences, Captain Brian, apparently concluding that it would be foolish to risk such dread potentials, hauled his vessel to port and steamed close up the south shore, dropping anchor in twenty fathoms of water behind the sheltering arm of Whitefish Point. Others skippers were of the same mind. A full dozen ships, all of them larger than the *Kamloops*, were already at anchor and facing the wind while "waiting for weather." Like Captain Brian, each commander was confident that the gale winds would diminish at daybreak.

Sunday, however, brought no improvement. All day, under

lowering skies and strong winds, the weather-bound fleet lay
behind the point, their numbers increasing as upbound skippers, gauging the wind, sea, and sky, put caution before valor.
On Monday there came a noticeable change for the better.
The wind velocity had dropped considerably and with it a
gradual "leveling off" of the seas. It was what the impatient
steamboat captains had been predicting and hoping for. Not
all of them left the shelter of Whitefish Point, but Captain
Brian (ever conscious that the unloading of his cargo, particularly the machinery, would be a time-consuming operation that would delay his turn under the grain chutes)
ordered the *Kamloops'* anchors hoisted in late afternoon. He
had many unpleasant memories of waiting for days for a
grain cargo and then being forced to load only in the lulls
between blizzards of snow. Particularly vivid was the time he
had brought the *Kenora* to the elevators for a load of flax
only to have an early freeze hit the Thunder Bay area. The
"break" in the temperature never came and the *Kenora* spent
the winter still tied up to the elevator's dockside bollards. He
did not want a repeat performance.

As the *Kamloops* steamed from behind the point and into
deeper water she swung in behind the steamer, *Quedoc*, of
the firm of Paterson Steamships, Limited; Captain Roy
Simpson, master. Both vessels were steering 300 degrees, well
south of Caribou Island and on a NW by W, ⅜ W course
that would carry them almost two hundred miles to the
channel between Blake Point Light, on the northeasternmost
tip of Isle Royale and Passage Island Light. It was the normal
Ft. William steamer track. Captain Simpson had brought the
Quedoc through the upper St. Marys without any undue
concern with the weather and was well abreast of Ile
Parisienne before he gave the matter of seeking shelter a
second thought. Downbound vessels passing to his port
showed no signs of undue stress. Ahead of him he could see
the smoke smudges of upbound ships that had apparently

forsaken the shelter of Whitefish Point to resume their courses. Even then, the *Kamloops* was steaming out from behind the point. Captain Simpson knew the *Kamloops*, her skipper, and he knew, too, that she would be bound for Ft. William. All things considered, he felt perfectly justified in continuing. It was comforting to see the *Kamloops* following along in his wake. They were like a pair of old drayhorses plodding in from the cold pasture, heading for comfortable quarters in the barn for the winter.

Unbeknownst to either Captain Brian, his counterpart on the *Quedoc*, or the masters of other vessels that had left secure anchorages behind Whitefish Point, the most massive cold front in many years was even then starting its move the full length and breadth of Lake Superior. Born in the Arctic wastes of the Northwest Territories it swept down over the great grain prairies of Alberta and Saskatchewan, bringing with it stunning winds, a horrifying drop in temperature, and the heaviest snowfall many of the grain farmers could recall. The tornadolike blizzard spread out over a front of several hundred miles. Barns were flattened, wires came down, and countless travelers were stranded between towns. Nearly every community in its path recorded deaths attributed directly to the storm.

The full force of the calamitous combination of wind, snow, and sub-zero temperatures boomed over Thunder Bay and headed down Lake Superior. At Ft. William the ships, huddled under the elevator chutes up the Mission and Kaministikwia river channels, put out extra lines and closed their hatches. Out in the bay a dozen vessels, waiting patiently for their grain cargoes, dropped a second anchor and kept their engines churning "slow ahead" to keep from being driven into shoal water or across the bay. At adjacent Port Arthur more lay at anchor, biding their time for dockage at the Superior, Thunder Bay, Reliance, Dominion Government, and Saskatchewan Pool elevators. Heading his train

Where Is the Kamloops . . . ? 133

of empties away from the Canadian Pacific Railway elevator
at Ft. William, engineer James Blake watched incredulously
as the wind rocked the cars back and forth. Then, before his
startled eyes, one of the cars was blown completely free of its
coupling to topple over on its side. This was the wind that
hit Lake Superior on Tuesday, December sixth, finding, in
due time, the wallowing *Quedoc, Kamloops,* and a score of
other vessels. What happened out there on the lake was a
matter of history to be related days later, for it was an era
when only passenger ships and the status-conscious flagships
of the various lines—particularly in the Canadian fleets—afforded themselves the luxury of wireless. Each ship was a tiny
island on a monstrous sea of disaster, a theater of conflict
without spectators, and an orchestra composed only of the
shrieking wind, the wracking jolts of the attacking seas, and
the groans and creakings of ships sore beset.

For two days ship traffic into Thunder Bay and the cities of
Ft. William and Port Arthur came to a standstill. The Port
Arthur *News-Chronicle* reported on December eighth:

No steamers have arrived from the east in thirty-six hours, the
ice is forming rapidly and the outlook is very uncertain.

In the same issue, on a somewhat more optimistic vein, the
newspaper said:

No accident has been reported up to the noon hour, and all
ships carrying wireless are reported safe in shelter. The only
hope shipping men have for a continuance of navigation is
warmer weather, but their hopes are dimmed by reports from
the western provinces that a decidedly cold wave still held the
west in its grip.

On December ninth reports from all over the lakes began
to come in of ships that had lost their battles with the gale.
The big steamer, *Altadoc,* of Paterson Steamships Ltd.,

skippered by Dick Simpson, brother of the *Quedoc*'s master, had piled up on Keweenaw Point. Badly holed, her rudder gone, and the whole ship encased in ice, she was a total loss. Other ships were wrecked, too, but locations and conditions were somewhat uncertain.

Later the same day the Canada Steamship Company reported the following vessels of its fleet and their approximate positions as of nine o'clock that morning: The *Donacona* was downbound near Whitefish Point, the *Hamonic* was at the Soo, and the *Westmount, Sarnian, Winnipeg*, and *Kamloops* were in Thunder Bay, all waiting to reach dock.

There was obviously an error, since on the very next day, December tenth, the *News-Chronicle* columns said:

> The steamer *Kamloops* has not yet been reported by any of the vessels arriving at the Head of the Lakes. The steamer, *Winnipeg*, which docked last night, reported the *Kamloops* in shelter at Whitefish early on Tuesday, but nothing has been heard of her since. It is believed she is still in shelter.

Where, indeed, was the *Kamloops*?

By the twelfth, a note of genuine concern was being expressed along the waterfront, mainly because messages to skippers that had been involved in the storm and who had later docked at Superior, Duluth, and the Soo, asking for news of the *Kamloops*, had brought no hopeful replies. The *Kamloops*' owners, according to the newspaper, were of the opinion that the ship might have gotten into difficulties and was staying in shelter behind one of the islands. Acting on this belief, two of the company's vessels, the *Islet Prince* and *Midland Prince*, were sent out to search. Later in the day it was announced that the Canadian Government was sending a tug from Sault Ste. Marie to steam around Whitefish Point in quest of the *Kamloops*. Another tug, the *James Whalen*, chartered by the overdue-ship's owners, left Port Arthur with a roving commission to search for the *Kamloops* in the vicinity of Manitou and Battle islands. Ice-encrusted, she returned days later without having sighted the *Kamloops* or any wreckage.

On December thirteenth, Brock Batten, general agent for Canada Steamship Lines at the head of the lakes, received a message from the main office in Montreal, stating that it had received a report to the effect that the missing package freighter was aground on Keweenaw Point. This was only one of several instances where a ship resembling the *Kamloops* had been sighted, everywhere from the Apostle Island group to lonely Michipicoten Island off the rugged and inhospitable north shore. The sources were vague, unreliable, and particularly difficult to evaluate since word that the ship was overdue did not become general knowledge for the better part of a week. The Keweenaw Point report was considered highly unlikely because numerous rescue and salvage vessels had been in the area as a result of the *Altadoc*'s grounding. Then, too, the U. S. Coast Guard's cutter, *Crawford*, assisting at the scene of the *Altadoc* wreck, searched specifically for the *Kamloops*, covering Keweenaw Point without finding a trace of the missing canaller.

The thoroughness of the search on the part of the Coast Guard was demonstrated by the men of the Eagle Harbor Station under Captain A. F. Glaza. With the possibility that the ship had foundered somewhere off the point and that some crewmen might conceivably have reached Manitou Island, a couple of miles east of Keweenaw Point, Captain Glaza enlisted the help of local fishermen. In the small, shallow-draft fish tugs, the Guardsmen completely encircled the island, shouting and firing off guns at frequent intervals. They found no wreckage and left only after satisfying themselves that there was no life on the island.

"Back on Keweenaw Point we then took a sixteen-mile snowshoe hike," Captain Glaza recounted. "We went across the point and covered the shoreline to the end of the north side and the entire south shore to Mendota Light Station. But we never found a sliver of her, so we gave up hopes of any of her crew having survived."

By now the mystery of a ship and its entire crew disappearing without trace had become an important story in the lower lakes cities. Grizzled captains, long retired, were interviewed and their theories duly recorded. It little mattered that they could rattle off the names of a half-dozen other vessels that had vanished in the years gone by; the story now was the *Kamloops* and the twenty-two people that were aboard her. What had happened to the *Kamloops*?

The most logical place for a storm-driven ship to go aground, particularly if it was on the Ft. William-Port Arthur track, is Isle Royale, a rocky and irregular island, forty-four miles long and lying athwart the entrance to Thunder Bay and a few miles off the Canadian mainland but in United States waters. Running southwest to northeast, it is ringed by a cul de sac of reefs, rocks, and shoals that still hold the bones of a score of ships that found them in fog, snow, or gale—ships that have become legends all over the Great Lakes.

Mariners avoid Isle Royale as they would the plague, and those who have unfortunately "fetched up" there, have left a grim heritage of disaster that seems to hang like a pall over the dark, uninhabited and tortuous shoreline. Cumberland Point commemorates the steamer, *Cumberland*, disemboweled and sunk after striking a submerged reef angling out to the west from Rock of Ages, at the extreme southwest point of the island. Greenstone Rock, off the island's southeast shore, was the final grave for the Canadian Pacific Railway's passenger and freight steamer, *Algoma*, lost with forty-eight souls in a gale of wind, snow, and sleet. Off the south shore the package freighter *Harlem* went "hard on" at Menagerie Island, at a point still known and marked on the charts as Harlem Reef. There were others . . . the *Monarch*, wrecked on Blake Point;

the *Dunelm* and *Chester A. Congdon*, stranded at Canoe Rock; and the *Glenlyon*, gutted on Menagerie Island. These were steamers, and it is any sailor's guess as to how many sailing craft, missing for years, found their final port of call along the shores of Isle Royale.

The south side of the island affords good protection from northwest gales, but the northerly end tapers off into a series of rugged and detached formations of islands, peninsulas, and offshore rocks and shoals. Since the Ft. William and Port Arthur steamer track lies immediately to the north of the island, between Blake Point and Passage Island, the course is adequately marked with lights and buoys, all of which are of help only when the shipmaster can see them. The gale-driven snow and scud on that grim December day in 1927 denied both Captain Simpson of the *Quedoc* and Captain Brian of the *Kamloops* that advantage.

So it was to Isle Royale that the *Midland Prince* turned her attention on December twelfth, steaming slowly the length of the island on both sides, scanning every inlet, bay, and reef. If there were stranded mariners huddled in whatever shelter they could find on shore, the *Midland Prince* sought to arouse them by sonorous blasts of her whistle. But the whistle served only to send aloft thousands of gulls, their petulant cries of protest at the unseemly intrusion of their domain, drowning out any answering hails that might have come from the desolate shores of Isle Royale.

To the north and east cruised the *Islet Prince*, although it would take a dozen ships to inspect all the coves, bays, and islands along that inhospitable north shore from Porphyry Light to Bread Rock, the Slate Islands, and desolate Heron Bay. It is a bleak and lonely shore where, in any of a thousand places, a vessel such as the *Kamloops* could make her final meeting with land without leaving any evidence of having been there.

Both the *Midland Prince* and the *Islet Prince* returned to port well iced-up but without sighting the *Kamloops*. On the other hand they had found no wreckage around the shoals, reefs, or rocks, where a tormented ship, lost in the snow on the Ft. William steamer track might have come to grief. An airplane chartered by the owners flew low over many of the islands the search ships could not safely approach. It, too, returned with negative results.

By now the radio newsmen in the upper lakes cities, aware of the grisly drama such a mystery holds and loath to part with a sure-fire topic, began nearly every news program with the solemn, chilling question: "Where is the *Kamloops*?"

Back at the Canadian Soo, where his ship was being prepared for winter layup, a meditative Captain Roy Simpson of the *Quedoc* was perusing the newspaper accounts of the search for the *Kamloops*. He was recalling to mind that terrible night and day he and Captain Brian had spent as their vessels labored up Lake Superior, speculating if perhaps he should have spoken up sooner, such as the night he had brought the battered *Quedoc* into port. But he wondered, even now, if it really would have made any difference.

The weather, as the *Kamloops* left the shelter of Whitefish Bay and found her path in the *Quedoc*'s wake, a quarter mile astern, had indeed moderated. But the lessening of the wind and quieting of the seas had been a lull of remarkably short duration. By dusk the wind was blowing a northwest gale and the billowing black seas were growing in stature, rearing up as high as the *Quedoc*'s steering pole and striding the length of her hull. All night long both ships plugged into monumental head seas that exploded over their bows and dashed spray as high as the masthead lights. Great seas roamed their decks almost continuously, ruling out any access by the crews. In effect, the forward and after-end crews were virtually marooned. Captain Simpson recalled, somewhat wistfully, how he had yearned most earnestly for a cup of hot tea but had of necessity settled for a glass of water from the pilothouse jug.

Dawn of Tuesday, December sixth, had brought no respite but rather had added to the dangers. The temperature dropped most precipitously to eighteen degrees below zero in the early morning hours, and a rather considerable coating of ice had quickly built up on the superstructure of both vessels. The *Kamloops'* king posts, iced to twice their normal girth, stood up like white monuments, swaying ominously as the ship rolled and pitched. Since there was really no choice, both skippers had held to what they assumed was still their normal course, although just where they were at any particular moment was a matter for some conjecture. Ice had long since carried away the taffrail logs that both ships trailed astern to record the miles traveled, but even had they still been available, no man could have gone on deck to read them. Both commanders had allowed somewhat for a southward drift due to the northwest wind, but the correction needed was also an unknown quantity at the moment. Visibility was a major concern, too, for all day intermittent blizzards of snow had descended upon them. The furious wind carried away the foaming crests of the seas in the form of spray and scud that, already half frozen, rattled against the pilothouses like buckshot. There were times when Captain Simpson could not see half the length of his deck. And during the lulls there were only those dark and terrible seas assaulting his ship. Off to the south and roughly a quarter mile astern, blotted out most of the time by the spume and scud, came the *Kamloops*, similarly beset by the vengeful seas and a growing burden of ice.

Aboard the *Kamloops*, pitching and rolling abominably, Captain Brian was undoubtedly sharing Captain Simpson's worries about the ice building up on the hull and stewing about his utter inability to do anything about it. He would be wondering about his after-end crew, too, knowing that life in the firehold and engineroom must be sheer hell under the circumstances. And probably he was concerned about the ship's two women cooks, Nettie Grafton and Alice Betteridge. During the shipping season they labored in the *Kamloops'* galley, keeping the crew of twenty men supplied with better-than-average shipboard fare. The winter months they spent taking their ease, at home in Southampton, Ontario. It was a hard, seven-days-a-week job on the *Kamloops*, with little time for pleasure or excursions ashore. At the moment they were most certainly wishing they were back in Southampton, attending the Tuesday-afternoon sewing circle at the church.

It was late afternoon, almost dusk, when Captain Simpson was startled almost out of his wits. The lookout, up in the pilothouse, since the deck was untenable and had been for twenty-four hours, was shouting frenziedly: "Rocks . . . rocks . . . dead ahead!"

Now, Captain Simpson knew where he was . . . approaching one of the deadly rock formations at the northerly end of Isle Royale . . . the jagged, ship-destroying outcroppings that have given generations of shipmasters nightmares!

"Starboard . . . starboard," the captain yelled, lunging for the wheel himself and spinning it wildly to the right.

Slowly, ever so slowly—it seemed like an eternity to Captain Simpson—the ice-encrusted *Quedoc* began to respond. Of necessity she slid into the trough between the great seas, rolling villainously, showing her rusty bottom and creating near panic. Seamen were sent flying from their bunks, dishes cascaded from their racks, and the galley coal box went adrift. Down below, the firemen were thrown from their feet, joining fallen coal passers, wheelbarrows, coal and fire tools in a jumbled avalanche that slid from side to side with every roll of the ship. In the engineroom the engineers and oilers grabbed the brass railings and prayed.

Sliding into the trough of a seemingly endless succession of seas was a fearful experience, but it was decidedly better than steaming into that lather of spume and white water booming over the rocks. Captain Simpson, his every effort given to clawing away from that terrible death trap and saving his ship, thought again of the *Kamloops*, now that the immediate danger was past. Between the swirling curtains of snow he saw her again, steaming directly as before, the *Quedoc*'s violent maneuver to starboard apparently having gone undetected. Captain Simpson caught himself yelling: "Turn her . . . turn her!" But the *Kamloops*, probably because her pilothouse was lower and offered a more limited range of visibility, plowed on like a demolition ship intent on penetrating the enemy's protective harbor boom.

In utter frustration Captain Simpson grabbed his whistle pull and blew an impatient series of short blasts, the standard steamboat warning of danger or imminent disaster.

"Hell," he told a friend sometime later, "it was blowing such a gale of wind and snow that I couldn't hear it myself. The *Kamloops* people obviously didn't hear it, either. But if the lookout had been awake and tending to business, he would have seen us turn, and the puffs of steam would have told him we were trying to signal them. There wasn't anybody else around to whistle at, was there?"

There was the possibility, considering that visibility was practically zero during the intermittent blankets of snow, that the *Kamloops* had, indeed, sighted the desperate puff of steam from the *Quedoc*'s whistle, but had disappeared in the snow before any evasive action she might have taken became apparent. She certainly did not haul sharply to starboard as the *Quedoc* had done. She could have taken a sudden turn to port, and if she hadn't capsized because of the tremendous load of ice on her superstructure, there was just a bare chance that she, too, might have steamed out of danger. Others in the same storm, the *Martian*, for example, had reached as far as Isle Royale, only to turn and run a hundred miles back down the lake for shelter.

All things considered, being aware of the *Kamloops'* last known position and witnessing her apparent destruction course, Captain Simpson's lack of interest for a full week was curious behaviour indeed. One would think that after arriving safely in port he would have reported the incident or made inquiries as to her safety. The harbor master could have verified that she had not been sighted, and a word to her owners might have set a search mission underway at once. Even though the *Kamloops* might have sailed directly into the rocks, there was always the chance of survivors huddled on the bleak shore trying to stay alive. Yet, once the belated search program was organized, neither the *Midland Prince* nor the chartered plane sighted any debris. Impaled on the rocks the ship would have easily been visible. And if, while in that position, she had been torn apart and shredded by the seas, wreckage would have been plentiful for a day or two, before it was covered by snow and ice.

One must remember, however, that Captain Simpson would have had no inkling until he reported to his own owners, that the *Altadoc*, his brother's ship, had been wrecked at Keweenaw Point. Communications were slow in 1927, and he would undoubtedly have spent his time at the headquarters office of Paterson Steamships, waiting for the latest word of the *Altadoc* and his brother. Probably he had spent many hours there at the office, waiting for the latest news from Keweenaw.

Yes, under the circumstances, the *Kamloops* might indeed have clawed her way to safety, continuing to the south for many miles, searching for shelter that was not to be hers. Carrying her unwelcome but inescapable encumbrance of ice, hundreds of tons of it, she might have suffered structural damage in her port turn if she had made it without capsizing—damage that would later manifest itself in cracked plates, a broken shaft, or some kind of mechanical or steering failure. She may have even grazed a rock, breaking off propeller blades or bending her rudder. All were within the realm of possibility. And then, without wireless, she would have been alone in the dark of night, driven along in the shrieking wind, driving snow, and mauling seas. Sometime that night, wearying of the unequal struggle, she must have gone down.

Five hundred miles away, at the Courtright home where Captain Brian's friends were caring for his ship's mascot, the lashing winds flapped the shingles and drove volleys of sleet and snow against the windows. Under the dining-room table Ginger huddled, shivering and whining. One wonders if, through that wonderful and mysterious instinct God gives dogs, she already knew where the *Kamloops* was.

10

〰〰〰
⚓

Knives in the Lifeboat!

Ships are among man's most complicated and expensive creations, and they achieve their ultimate purpose when they are at sea, making money for their owners and efficiently performing the tasks for which they were designed. Involved as they are, structurally and mechanically, they are rather simple compared to the people who serve aboard them, from their commanders to their oilers, wipers, and stewards.

A peculiar breed of men are drawn to the seafarer's life, but beyond this common affinity for ships and the lonely life, they are probably very much like a cross section of any group of men drawn to a particular calling. They embrace the full spectrum of mortal man and his infinite psychological dissimilarities—his strengths, frailties, ambitions, loves, fears, hates, and the individual idiosyncrasies that are sometimes his delight, often his burden.

The ship steams on, imperturbably, because its engine and myriad mechanical auxiliary gear is made of iron, steel, copper, or brass, none of which is prey to anger, suspicion, jealousy, pettiness, fears, love affairs, or the other uncounted personal stresses with which man has encumbered himself.

Let us, at Conneaut, Ohio, turn back and stop the clock on the Tuesday morning of December 7, 1909, for a human

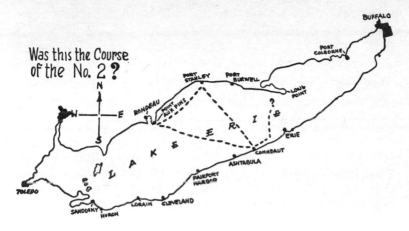

Was this the Course of the No. 2?

inventory of the people who made up the operating personnel of the big car ferry, *Marquette & Bessemer No. 2*, then completing loading for her daily shuttle across Lake Erie to Port Stanley, Ontario.

First there was Captain Robert McLeod, a master of unquestioned ability. He attended his church and lodge frequently, and participated in civic affairs whenever his uncertain schedule permitted. He was one of seven brothers, all born at Kincardine, Ontario. Six became sailors and the seventh, James, stayed ashore to farm. Hugh and Duncan were ship captains, Stuart became a first mate, and Angus, after sailing for a few years, gave up the sailor's life.

Oldest of the clan was Captain John McLeod who, instead of accepting proffered opportunities to command his own ship, chose to stay on the *Marquette & Bessemer No. 2* as brother Robert's first mate. His reasons were personal. Like brothers Robert and Hugh, he had established a home in Conneaut but had recently changed his residence to Courtright, Ontario, after marrying a girl from nearby Sarnia and acquiring rural property there. What's more, as he had confided to Robert, he was worried about the many chores left undone. And, more important, there was still a matter of property taxes to be paid. He had asked brother Hugh—then skipper of a Pittsburgh Steamship Company steamer, laying up his ship in Chicago—to relieve him for a trip or two so he could attend to these details.

Hugh had agreed, but his company was unwilling, preferring that he stay with his ship through the winter layup program. John had been quite unhappy about it.

The majority of the car-ferry's crew of thirty-three were from Conneaut. One of the advantages of the ship's shuttle run was that it was possible for a man to establish a home, with every assurance that he would be able to spend some time there. It was decidedly pleasanter than shipping out on an ore carrier in the spring, with little likelihood of seeing the familiar fireside again until December. Traditionally, the car ferries were the first vessels out in the spring and ran until ice made navigation impractical, sometimes operating until late January. So, they were laid up for a comparatively short time, and even then the annual winter maintenance provided jobs for many of the crew. Still, the very nature of the work and its particular appeal to those who had no family ties or were trying to forget them, usually resulted in a crew roster that included a few with no listed home addresses. The car ferry had three such men: "Paddy" Hart and Ed Harvey, both able seamen, and watchman Fred Walker.

Second Mate Frank Stone, only twenty-five, had been aboard slightly over three months, succeeding Charles Myers who had left to take over the same job on the car ferry *Ashtabula*. He had an unusual background. After two years of high school he had quit to work in his father's jewelry store, where he served enough time to qualify as a master jeweler. He had left the store to take a job as purser on the car ferry. During the winter of 1907-08, he took his examination for mate's and pilot's papers, passing with an unusually high grade to become the youngest man on the lakes holding a full commission as a pilot. When the opportunity for advancement came, he was ready.

The ship boasted no third mate. Captain McLeod stood a regular watch as did his brother, John, and Second Mate Stone. The sixty-mile run across the lake, and quick turn-around, did not justify a third officer.

Chief Engineer Eugene Wood was also a former Canadian, transferring his residency from Port Dalhousie, Ontario, to Conneaut, in 1897, to accept a job as first assistant engineer under the veteran, George Collinge. Two years later, when Collinge resigned, Wood became chief engineer. He was forty years old and usually managed an hour or two at his home at 681 Harbor Street when his ship was in port. Often, his two children would be at the dock, waiting for him. Like Captain McLeod, Wood came from a family of marine men. His brother, George Wood, was master of the steamer, *Bannock-burn*, lost with all hands on Lake Superior in 1902. His assistants were young—Edward Buckler, thirty-three, and Thomas Kennedy, thirty-one. Both had been aboard since the car ferry made its first trip. Buckler had four children and was a close neighbor of Chief Engineer Wood.

The galley department was notable for the physical disparities of its staff. Steward George R. Smith, a sailor since he was thirteen, was exceptionally tall, raw-boned, and husky. Second Cook Harry Thomas, from Port Stanley, was of medium height and thin. But, rounding out the trio was the porter, diminutive but exuberant Manuel Souars, twenty years old. The brunt of many pranks and jokes, all of which he took in good spirit, he was the most popular man in the crew.

Purser R. C. Smith, a somewhat dour individual in appearance but in reality a congenial and jolly fellow, was, as befitted his tedious and meticulous calling, "a good man with figures." A veteran of lake shipping, he gave up a job on the car ferry *Ashtabula*, to take over the position of purser when Frank Stone moved up to second mate. His favorite joke, always before an audience at mealtime, was to confront little Manuel Souars with a fistful of supplier's bills and, in a loud voice, accuse the little porter of being responsible for an outrageous shortage of potatoes or meat. The crestfallen look on Manuel's expressive face instantly inspired a chorus of laughs, Smith's being the heartiest. They were really good friends.

Captain McLeod was a bit of a stickler on the matter of wheelsmen, permitting no wavering or lallygagging from the course. William Wilson and John Clancy must have met his approval, for they had been his regular helmsmen for several seasons. Wilson, from Lindsay, Ontario, a man of great humor, had recently become the proud owner of a fine watch, probably his most valued possession. It was a seventeen-jewel Waltham, made for the Canadian Railway Time Service. He had felt quite important when jeweler George W. Beall, of Lindsay, had carefully recorded the serial number of the works as 11,047,297. The guessing in the pilothouse was that it had cost him at least a month's pay. Second Mate Stone, an ex-jeweler himself, agreed.

Beyond those mentioned there were another twenty-four in the car-ferry's normal crew—able seamen, coal passers, oilers, and watchmen. Other than the fact that they were able to be home frequently, the men of the *No. 2* were probably typical of any crew to be found on a Great Lakes vessel in 1909.

There were some exceptions, of course. One of them was William Ray, a coal passer. It was his first trip on a boat and he was nervous. He had been employed on one of the dock's ore unloaders during the summer, but the season was ending, and the opening on the car-ferry black gang roster was his for the asking.

For another, fireman Tom Steele, only three years away

from Edinburgh, Scotland, the coming trip was to be his last. He had spent two years heaving coal into the *No. 2's* furnaces and had found a shore job more to his taste.

Another fireman, Joe Shank, was just returning to the job after a long vacation trip. He, too, was a former dock worker who found the long winter layoff a considerable hardship. It was his second season on the car ferry.

The best storyteller aboard was oiler John "Paddy" Hart, a typical sailor whose home was any place his ship happened to be. Paddy had left Ireland at an early age and landed in Chicago. He joined the Colonel Arthur Lynch Brigade, which left Chicago at the time of the Second Boer War, to help the Boers battle the British in South Africa. His blood-curdling yarns made him a fo'c'sle favorite during his years on the car ferry.

A barber is always welcome on a ship's crew, and Charles Allen, at eighteen a remarkably young one, was no exception. He had operated a shop near the harbor in Conneaut for a time but had quit to become a coal passer, claiming that indoor work was injurious to his health. Why his health would be improved by the hard work and constant breathing of coal dust escaped the reasoning of all but Allen. Nevertheless, he was apparently happy in his new job and was able to pick up a little extra money shearing the locks of his shipmates.

And then there was the ship. She had been built only four years earlier, in 1905. Her owners, the Marquette & Bessemer Dock and Navigation Company, had wanted a sturdy vessel. Nothing fancy, just a good steamboat for efficiently loading and transporting railroad cars across Lake Erie. In all, the fifteen pages of specifications agreed upon with the American Ship Building Company of Cleveland, would indicate a twin-screw vessel of quality. As Hull No. 428, she was to be 350 feet, overall, with a molded beam of fifty-four feet. Power was to be a pair of triple-expansion engines that the builders must guarantee to give her a working speed of twelve miles per hour, loaded. Her cargo deck was to have four tracks capable of holding thirty railroad cars, each of thirty tons capacity. Plates and rivets were to be of open-hearth mild steel, with a phosphorus or sulphur content of not more than .06 percent and with a tensile strength of not less than 54,000 nor more than 62,000 pounds per square inch. Samples of plates, channels, and angles, as stated, must be able to stand being bent double without fracturing. Despite the heavy construction, a load of thirty loaded cars, and two hundred tons of coal in her bunkers, the ship was not to draw more than fourteen feet of water. In due course, having passed her sea trials, she went into service without fanfare, and with Captain McLeod in command.

This, then, was the vessel and the people we find at the car-ferry's dock on the blustery morning of Tuesday, December 7, 1909. It was the usual scene. A puffing locomotive was easing gondola and hopper cars into the cavernous hold, one at a time and on opposite tracks, skillfully balancing the load to keep the ship from listing.

Captain McLeod and Second Mate Frank Stone had gone to their nearby homes to attend to some personal business. Chief Engineer Wood, having said his goodbyes to his children, had stopped off at a grocery store to order some flour for Mrs. Wood. Second cook Harry Thomas and porter Manuel Souars were helping a tradesman carry supplies from his dray to the galley.

On the dock, purser Smith was tallying the cars being loaded, noting the tonnage, commodity, car numbers, and final destinations. When the last car had been shunted aboard, while the safety "key," blocks, clamps, and restraining gear were being noisily hammered into place, he had totaled the lot on his official manifest—twenty-six cars of coal, three cars of structural steel, and one car of iron castings. A rather prosaic cargo but a typical one. The purser had heard

there would also be a passenger this trip—a gentleman from
Erie, Pennsylvania, who was anxious to get to Port Stanley
in a hurry. Noting that he had still not arrived, that the crew
was aboard, and the vessel ready to sail, he commented to a
dock worker that "there's going to be a man left at the dock
if he doesn't get here pretty soon."

There were two car ferries in the service of the Marquette
& Bessemer Dock and Navigation Company, *No. 1*. and *No. 2*.
No. 1's course took her to Rondeau, forty-odd miles west of
Port Stanley, Ontario, the *No. 2*'s daily port of call. Con-
neaut people distinguished between the two by calling the
No. 1, since her cargo was always coal, the "collier." *No. 2*
Ihčhämë, simply, the "car ferry."

No. 1, in the face of rising southwest winds, left the harbor
at six A.M. *No. 2* was ready to go at eight o'clock, but an ore
vessel, being tied up for the winter, had snapped her hawsers
in the high wind, her stern swinging out into the channel.
Captain McLeod waited two hours, until tugs had pushed the
ship back against the dock and secured her, before ordering
his own lines singled-up, and then cast off. The car ferry was
just steaming away from the loading apron at "slow ahead"
when a nattily dressed man, carrying a brown briefcase, came
running along the dock, calling for someone to stop the ship.
Others, on the dock and aboard ship, took up the cry. Somewhat annoyed, Captain McLeod reversed his engines and
permitted the stern of his vessel to swing along the piling of
the loading slip, where the man leaped nimbly aboard.

In purser Smith's office he identified himself as the expected passenger, Albert J. Weiss, treasurer of the Keystone
Fish Company, Erie, but a former resident of Ashtabula. His
business in Canada was apparently of considerable importance. The purser, if he followed his normal routine—and
there is no reason to think he would do otherwise—assigned
him to a cabin and handed him its key. Mr. Weiss, astute as are
most men who become treasurers of companies, undoubtedly

requested Mr. Smith to lock his briefcase in a safe place. Later investigation revealed that it held about $50,000 in bills, to be used, so it was said, to buy out a Canadian fishing company. Whatever the nature of the deal, it was for cash.

Storm signals were snapping taut on the tower overlooking the harbor when, at 10:43 A.M., Captain McLeod straightened his vessel out in the main river channel and headed toward the lake. The wind velocity was mounting, with occasional gusts of fifty miles per hour. At the west breakwall a cluster of tugs and scows, working on a new fog-signal apparatus, were beginning to toss uncomfortably. As the car ferry steamed by the site and began to punch her bow into the making seas, Captain McLeod, standing on the flying-bridge wing, his oilskins and sou'wester flapping in the wind, yelled over to the crew working on the new fog signal.

"Get that thing fixed," he shouted. "I may need it on my trip back."

Edward Pfister, veteran Conneaut lightkeeper, and a good friend of the captain, waved a greeting and playfully struck the new fog bell a crisp blow with a hammer.

McLeod, swinging his arms in acknowledgment, then descended to the lower-level pilothouse and disappeared inside.

A few minutes later, the seas beginning to buffet the floating gear dangerously, Pfister and his crew abandoned their project for the day.

At noon, Mrs. Frank Snyder, wife of a Conneaut commercial fisherman, was seriously concerned about her husband, lifting his nets far out on the lake. Instead of permitting her son, Hugh, to return to school after lunch, she sent him running to the storm-signal hill to look for his father's tug.

"Stay there until you see it and then call me from John Dibbs' store," she ordered.

A couple of hours passed and it had begun to snow before young Hugh could see the inbound tug, wallowing in the big seas. He called his mother, as directed, before dashing down to the dock to help unload the fish. The temperature was forty-two degrees when the *No. 1* departed at six o'clock, but thereafter the mercury plunged steadily until it reached a low of ten degrees above zero. The *Alberta T.* had accumulated considerable ice, and Snyder's crew of Adam Brabender, George Blake, John Keeler, and George Smith hacked some of it away before leaving for home.

For a time the tug crew claimed the rather dubious distinction of having been the last to see the big car ferry. Or were they?

"We passed her a few miles out," reported Frank Snyder. "Captain McLeod came out of the pilothouse with his megaphone and yelled something to us, but the wind was making so much noise we couldn't tell what he was saying. We think he was asking us if we needed any help. We didn't."

An indication of the marked change in temperature was Snyder's observation that, while Captain McLeod was still wearing his sou'wester, he had discarded his oilskins in favor of a fur coat.

If the weather was bad in the morning, it was terrible by mid-afternoon, and sheer hell by nightfall. The official record of the wind, kept at the East Light, on Long Point, revealed a full-blown southwest gale raging at five o'clock. All along the south shore, towns and cities were rocked with seventy-mile winds. Wires came tumbling down, and severe snow squalls all but halted highway traffic. Passenger trains on both the Lake Shore and Nickel Plate Railroads were late and came through Conneaut plastered with several inches of snow, indicating violent weather both east and west of the city.

Out on Lake Erie the most disastrous gale in years was hammering and mauling some of the staunchest ships afloat. The great graybeards, mounting with each passing hour, stalked the shipping lanes like endless regiments of warriors, bent on the final destruction of the enemy. The Anchor Line steamer *Clarion*, was driven up on Southeast Shoal and caught fire. Her captain, E. J. Bell, and the forward crew launched a boat in an attempt to reach the lightship *Kewaunee*, marking the shoal. All were lost. Despite the fire raging below him, the *Clarion*'s chief engineer clung to the smokestack ladder, operating the ship's whistle by hand, sounding a continuous distress signal. Guided by the frantic whistle sounds, the grain-laden steamer *Leonard C. Hanna*, in a magnificent feat of seamanship on the part of her master, plucked the after-end crew from the wreck.

At the other end of the lake, near Buffalo, the *W. C. Richardson* hit Waverly Shoal and was lodged there as the seas marched right over her. Five seamen and a woman cook were swept overboard. More than thirty battered freighters took shelter behind Long Point, many with heavy burdens of ice.

But what of the car ferry?

At 1:30 A.M. on Wednesday, William Rice, a Hulett ore-unloader operator at Conneaut harbor, was outside the cab of his machine when he heard a vessel blowing distress signals.

"She kept sounding these four quick blasts," he explained, "and then she blew five times, which I thought was the at-anchor signal. Pretty soon, as if the anchor chains had parted, she started the distress signal again. I recognized it as the car-ferry's whistle, but in about fifteen minutes all the blowing stopped."

A fellow worker confirmed Rice's story, as did A. H. Brebner, a local man who knew the car-ferry's whistle well.

Both the master and chief engineer of the steamer, *Black*, at anchor outside the Conneaut breakwall because the harbor entrance was too narrow to chance entering in a gale, claimed to have seen the unmistakable profile of the car ferry pass their ship during the night, heading east.

By Thursday afternoon these stories had all been well circulated through the city, inspiring great anxiety among the families of the crew and many tearful inquiries at the office of the Marquette & Bessemer Navigation Company. The Conneaut *News-Herald* and papers in Erie reported that, in some quarters, grave concern was felt for the ship's safety, although the owners still believed her to be safely in shelter somewhere.

In Erie, the horrifying certainty that a dream was coming true, prostrated Sarah Clancy, a sister of one of the *No. 2's* wheelsmen, John Clancy. Three nights before the car ferry sailed on what was to be her last voyage, Sarah experienced a vivid dream of a terrible storm and a ship sinking. Throughout the dream she had heard the voice of brother John, calling out. In the morning her sisters had laughed at her fears. Now the dream was a reality.

General agent and superintendent of the dock operations was Charles J. Magill, a gruff, plain-spoken man who knew his business thoroughly. Mr. Magill was tired of being badgered by reporters and persistent relatives.

"Sure, I think she is safe," he explained again, quite impatiently. "This is all part of the business. If you'll bother to think back, you'll recall that she has been as much as four days late on several occasions when the weather was exceedingly bad. And do you remember the time she had to lay behind Long Point for ten full days, waiting for weather?"

Off the record he wasn't so sure. Early that evening, after learning that the *No. 2* had still not arrived at Port Stanley and was unreported at Rondeau or Port Burwell, he stopped in to see Frank Snyder, the commercial fisherman. A Finnish woman, who lived east of Conneaut, claimed to have heard the car ferry whistling on Tuesday night and to have seen her lights. Since she was known personally by Snyder, Magill wanted him present when he talked to her.

The woman was adamant and would not be shaken in her story.

"I heard the car-ferry's whistle and knew it well," she insisted. "I saw her lights—white in the middle and red and green to each side, like she was headed for the shore. I quickly put a light in the window and watched as the ship's lights dipped out of sight. The next time only the green light was visible [indicating a sharp turn to port], and then I could see only the tall, white stern light as the ship turned safely back to sea."

Mr. Magill went home a very worried man.

On Friday, with the car ferry now seventy-two hours overdue, the steamer, *William B. Davoc*, westbound off Long Point, sent a wireless message to Cleveland, reporting that she had passed through quantities of wreckage, including a green lifeboat, just west of the point. There was nothing to distinguish what vessel it was from, but the portions of woodwork observed were painted green. Green was the predominant color of the *No. 2's* superstructure!

On the Canadian side, where tugs had been searching vainly for a full day and night, there came more stories of the car ferry being sighted or heard. At Port Stanley, Mr. Wheeler, a Canadian customs officer, stated firmly that he had seen her laboring in mountainous seas and trying to make the harbor late Tuesday afternoon, about seven hours after leaving Conneaut. But Captain McLeod, according to Wheeler, was apparently unwilling to chance the narrow entrance with the wind and sea from a dangerous angle, and had then turned to the west, obviously hoping to find shelter at Rondeau. At three o'clock on Wednesday morning Wheeler heard the car-ferry's whistle off the harbor entrance. Two other men, one a schoolteacher, corroborated his story.

Still another north shore resident, a man living at Bruce, seven miles east of Port Stanley, was awakened about five o'clock Wednesday morning by a steamer whistle so close to shore that he thought one had gone aground. He jumped out of bed, lighted a lantern, and went out to investigate.

"She was out there," he insisted. "I could hear her plain as day but couldn't see her because of the snow. Finally, the sound kept getting dimmer, and after a bit I couldn't hear anything but the waves and wind."

Magill, meanwhile, although confiding to associates that it was a rather hopeless quest, ordered the *No. 1* to suspend her usual schedule to concentrate on a search for the missing *No. 2*. The *No. 1* was commanded by Captain Murdock Rowan, first cousin to the McLeod brothers and a seaman of vast experience. He, too, took his ship up the north shore to Rondeau, came back as far as Erie on the south shore, and then steamed over to the Canadian side again and eastward as far as Long Point. At no time did he sight the *No. 2* or any part of her.

The Conneaut *News-Herald*, besieged with requests for information by the families of the crew, did its best to hold out rays of hope, during the search.

> Local people who know Capt. Rowan will suspend discouragement until he reports that there is no hope. He is searching for them and he will go over the coast with a fine tooth comb. If he gives it up, then their fate will be sealed. If they are alive and in serious trouble, he will find them.

Comments from shipmasters who touched at many Lake Erie ports while the car-ferry's fate was still in doubt, inspired the newspaper to ask: "Why did Captain Ben Fox, of the steamer *William B. Davoc*, pass the wreckage and the lifeboat, obviously from the ill-fated *No. 2*, without stopping?"

Captain Rowan tried, but it was of no use. The *No. 2* had vanished somewhere on Lake Erie, probably near dawn on Wednesday, if Mr. Wheeler had correctly identified the desperate bleating of her whistle off Port Stanley at three o'clock that morning. This, too, was undoubtedly the whistle that had awakened the gentleman at Bruce, about two hours later. Those on the Canadian side of the lake had no doubts but that she foundered shortly thereafter as Captain McLeod steamed eastward, trying to get around Long Point to sheltered waters.

At Port Stanley, Alfred Leslie, the company's auditor, had absolutely no doubt but that the car ferry had foundered and what had put her down.

"It is my opinion," said Leslie, "that the heavy seas broke the 'key' that held the cars in place and, weighted as they were, they raced to the stern of the boat, overcoming her keel. She probably turned turtle without a minute's warning."

Superintendent Magill, exhausted from sleepless nights and his long vigil at the telephone, now reluctantly concluded that the ship was lost.

The search for the *No. 2*'s people, however, went on from ports on both sides of the lake. On Sunday, fifteen miles off Erie, the Pennsylvania State fish commissioner's tug, *Commodore Perry*, Captain Jermiah A. Driscoll in command, found the car-ferry's No. 4 lifeboat. Captain Driscoll spotted it first, a dark blotch against the gray of the tossing seas. He summoned fireman Lawrence Scully and engineer James Dally to the pilothouse as the *Commodore Perry* neared the derelict. Its grim cargo removed at once any doubt as to the fate of the ship. There were nine men in the lifeboat, all resembling ice sculptures, hewn by a skillful hand for a festive occasion. Harry Thomas and steward George Smith were sitting upright, as though still scanning the horizon for help that never came. Little Manuel Souars had crawled partly beneath a seat, and four others were sprawled over him as if they had lent the last warmth of their bodies to help keep him alive. Obviously, the boat had at one time held a tenth occupant, one who had apparently gone mad with the horror and hopelessness of their situation and had taken off his clothes and leaped into the sea. His clothes were

found where he left them, wet through and frozen fast to one end of the boat.

With her own flag at half-mast, her grisly consort following astern at the end of a towline, the *Commodore Perry* headed back to Erie. The lifeboat, which had probably been battered against the side of the car ferry during launching and was partially filled with water, was in bad shape. Captain Driscoll wondered what had kept it afloat. Only one oar remained, still grasped by frozen fingers. The men themselves were lightly clad, mute testimony that the end had come quickly, and that they had departed their ship in an atmosphere of utter panic. Strangely, though, despite all evidence that there had been insufficient time to grab warm coats or jackets, steward Smith had taken care to bring along two long galley knives and a meat cleaver!

Once the certainty of the loss was established, many questions arose as to why such a staunch vessel as the car ferry, practically new and designed specifically for the seas she might encounter in her runs across Lake Erie, had gone down when many others had survived the gale. Remarks Captain McLeod had made in confidence to friends and his brother, Hugh, now came to light. They were substantiated by others who had heard similar statements from crew members. In the saloons and ship supply stores along the Conneaut waterfront, there was no mystery as to why the *No. 2* had gone down. It was because she had no stern gate! Although the fifteen pages of specifications dealing with her construction were most detailed and complete, they had not provided for a stern gate that, when raised, gave access to the car or cargo deck but, when lowered after loading, afforded high and adequate protection from overtaking seas. The owners had doubtless concluded that this potentially unpleasant situation could be avoided, should weather conditions dictate, by putting the ship head to in the seas, letting the high bow assume the brunt of the sea assault. But, as is too often the case, these decisions were rarely made by the men who sailed the ships, only by those who stayed ashore, waiting for them to come home.

It was not common knowledge until after she had disappeared, but the folly of not including a stern gate in the *No. 2*'s plans had been adequately dramatized only a month prior to her last trip, when Captain McLeod had come close to losing his ship in a bad November storm. The theory that running head to in high seas eliminated the danger of shipping water over the stern did not work in practice. In the November blow, Captain McLeod confided to brother Hugh, he had kept his vessel headed directly into the seas; when the stern sank down into the troughs between them, the water rushed in, filling her so rapidly that on one occasion the *No. 2* had listed so badly that her upper rails were under water. He had serious doubts that she would ever right herself.

"I damn near lost her," he told Hugh.

Captain McLeod complained quite bitterly, and the Marquette & Bessemer people had promised to install a stern gate when the vessel had finished her season's chores. The December gale had now spared them this expenditure.

Study of the car-ferry's plans revealed that she had four hatches opening directly off the car deck. Two were for the coal bunkers and were always open and exposed; the other two led to the engineroom and were protected by only a thin board covering. Seamen could envision what would happen on the occasion when she must, of necessity, expose her stern to seas running six to eight feet higher than her car deck; they would flood right over her fantail to thunder under and around her lashed-down railroad cars, filling her through her engineroom and bunker hatches. Then, her fires out, she would be helpless and easy prey for succeeding seas.

Compare the two vessels that left Conneaut harbor on that

fateful Tuesday morning. *No. 1*, smaller of the two, had a much lower profile exposed to the wind and seas; what's more, she had a strong and reliable stern gate. When unable to make Rondeau harbor, Captain Rowan had no qualms, therefore, in turning her around and running before the following seas to Port Stanley, which he did.

No. 2 was a bulkier and larger vessel, with high sides and considerable superstructure—a combination of features that would have been a serious handicap in gale winds and high, breaking seas. She would be difficult to turn or maneuver, thus depriving her master of the sailing characteristics most desirable and necessary to make the narrow harbor entrances at either Conneaut or Port Stanley.

In Conneaut groups of sailors huddled around charts on the walls of the waterfront saloons and plotted the probable course of Captain Robert McLeod's last voyage. He had fought his way across the lake all right, as Mr. Wheeler, the Canadian customs man, had testified. Then, again according to Wheeler, he had turned to port, heading west toward Rondeau, meeting the seas head to. This was the only possible course he could have taken to keep the seas from filling his ship over the unprotected stern. It would take many hours, butting into the head seas, for the *No. 2* to cover the forty miles to Rondeau. They assumed that Captain McLeod would be praying for the passing hours to bring about a shift in the wind, a bit of sailor's strategy, or delaying action, that sometimes is successful. But, instead, the gale continued to blow from the southwest with increasing fury. About the time he would arrive off Point aux Pins, which he would have to round to make Rondeau harbor, the seas were more malevolent than at any time during the voyage. They agreed that the captain must have been faced with a terrifying dilemma.

If Mr. Rice and others who claimed to have heard her desperate distress signals at 1:30 A.M. on Wednesday, were correct in their positive identification of her whistle, it would mean that Captain McLeod, in a time of heartbreaking frustration, had then headed for the south shore and Conneaut. Here, the already narrow entrance approach was made even more dangerous by the presence of the steamer, *Black*, anchored just outside the breakwall. The master and chief engineer of the *Black* had recalled seeing the car-ferry's unmistakable silhouette, steaming eastward. Then there was the account of the Finnish woman who was very positive in her statement that she, too, had seen the ship and had prevented it from running aground by placing a light in her window. Later, Mrs. James Holland, who lived near Fairview, west of Erie, revealed that she and her son had heard distress signals out on the lake on Tuesday night, only earlier.

"It was about seven o'clock," she recalled. "My son, Harold, who was out in the barn doing his chores, came running into the house saying that there was a boat in distress almost directly out from us. I went outside and could hear the distress whistle very plainly. The sound then stopped, but later, about midnight, Harold woke me up to say that some boat was surely in sore distress, because it was again sending out a signal for help."

Some hard-pressed ship was out there that night in the wind and snow; that was certain.

If these accounts of the *No. 2* being off Fairview at seven o'clock and again at midnight, and off Conneaut at 1:30 A.M. were to be believed, however, how could Mr. Wheeler have heard her outside Port Stanley, a good five- or six-hour run in good weather, at three A.M.? Or, again, what about the man at Bruce, who had heard her at five o'clock? Either way, Captain McLeod's only course, after being denied safety at Conneaut or Port Stanley, perhaps both, would have been to run to the east to round Long Point and to get in the lee of this long, sandy point that juts southeast from the Ontario mainland. This would have meant exposing the open stern to boarding seas the entire way. But now, of course, he would have had no choice. It was the considered opinion of those performing the saloon autopsies on the *No. 2*, that she had foundered in deep water long before reaching Long Point.

Conneaut, meanwhile, with the majority of the lost vessel's crew numbered among its citizens, was plunged into gloom. The flag over the post office flew at half-mast. All parties and social functions were canceled. The regular meeting of the city council, of which Captain McLeod was a former member, was postponed. Last rites and services were held for the men from lifeboat No. 4—little Manuel Souars, fireman Joe Shank, steward George Smith, coalpasser William Ray, and fireman Thomas Steele. Second Cook Harry Thomas and coalpasser Ray Hines were sent home to Canada, and coalpasser Charles Allen, a sailor for only a month, was returned to his home in Renova, Pennsylvania. Since no relatives could be located, oiler John "Paddy" Hart was buried in Erie, where lifeboat No. 4 made its final port of call.

Nine hundred Conneaut citizens crowded into the new high school building's 750-seat auditorium for memorial services for the vanished ship and her lost people, nineteen of them friends and neighbors. They sang "Rock of Ages" and "Jesus, Lover of My Soul." The Reverend Smith pointed out that: "Our minds are possessed by an element of uncertainty, and will continue to be unless the lake is kind enough to give us added information . . . where they went, what they did, may forever remain a secret . . . the wind swept by and left no written record of its violence . . . the lake is mute; it tells no secrets. . . ."

Most families had lost their breadwinners. Several were almost destitute. One widow was left with eight children, another lacked twenty-five cents to buy coal. Others were hard-pressed to put food on the table.

The Conneaut *News-Herald* commented:

The Elks will attend to these cases as long as their fund holds out and although it is a large and complimentary one, it will not last long if a number of the families need assistance and if the winter continues hard and long.

The newspaper itself organized a relief fund, announcing several points in the community at which contributions could be made. While the idea was most commendable, the first day's yield was only twelve dollars.

The proprietors of the Gem Theater sponsored a benefit matinee for the relief of the widows. When it was over, manager Clyde Torrey turned the receipts over to the newspaper's fund. The total was twenty-eight dollars. Day by day the figure climbed. When the drive was closed the day before Christmas, the total was only a modest $1018.

Such was the fate of sailors and their families in 1909.

The Marquette & Bessemer people, meanwhile, had already authorized the construction of another vessel to replace the lost *No. 2*. Almost an exact duplicate, she was given the same name, *Marquette & Bessemer No. 2*. She had, however, one significant addition—a stern gate. The company also announced that henceforth all of its vessels would be equipped with wireless.

The fate and efficiency of the car-ferry's remaining three lifeboats inspired much speculation among Great Lakes sailors, since there was always the very real possibility that they themselves might one day be in a similar situation. If the crew had left the sinking ship in an orderly manner, custom and tradition would dictate that Second Mate Frank Stone would command one of the lifeboats, First Mate John McLeod, another, and Captain McLeod, the last boat to leave the ship. None of them was aboard the only lifeboat found, the battered No. 4. All indications were that it had left the doomed *No. 2* under conditions of extreme panic.

During the weeks that followed the sinking, a close watch

on the beaches along the Ontario shoreline yielded wreckage, quite a bit of it near Port Burwell. One of the lifeboats was found almost intact, and in the flotsam around it, twelve oars. The paint on the oarlocks being unmarked, it was concluded that the boat had not been launched from the ship, but had broken free because of the air pressure in its flotation chambers. The air tanks of another lifeboat were found not far away, thus accounting for the third boat. Four months later, outside Buffalo harbor, Captain Jackie Farrel, of the tug *Mason*, found the fourth lifeboat, broken in two and impaled on the rocks of the breakwall.

The people of the vanished *No. 2* took their time coming ashore—oiler Patrick Keith and Chief Engineer Eugene Wood among them. Counting the nine from lifeboat No. 4, only fourteen were found.

First Mate John McLeod's journey had been a long one. On April sixth, as a work gang with pike poles was fending off ice from the penstocks of the intake slip of the Niagara Falls Power Company, just above the falls, one of them spotted what appeared to be a body, frozen in an ice floe. He fished it in, saw that it bore a lifebelt marked *"Marquette & Bessemer No. 2,"* and called his superiors. It was Mate McLeod. Among his effects they found $125, two postal money orders, an identification card, and a receipt from the Lambton County, Ontario, tax assessor.

First Mate John McLeod had paid his taxes.

It took wheelsman William Wilson and Captain Robert McLeod ten months to reach Long Point, that haven of refuge they had sought so desperately in the darkness of early morning on December eighth. It was October sixth when they found the captain. Curiously enough, it was the fifth anniversary of the day he had taken his vessel out on her maiden voyage. It was also the day her replacement, the second *Marquette & Bessemer No. 2*, left Conneaut for Port Stanley on her first trip.

There was really no question as to identity. His right arm had long borne a significant bit of tattooing—his name, a Masonic emblem, and clasped hands surmounting the words, "Faith, Hope, Charity." He lay not far from where, months earlier, searchers had found steward Smith's meat block.

Strangely though, Captain McLeod's body bore what were apparently a couple of severe slash wounds. To many, this brought back memories of that terrible night on Lake Erie and the dreadful conditions under which the car ferry must have taken her plunge. Two lifeboats, the one found on the Ontario shore, and the one whose only identifying features were her air tanks, had obviously never been launched, but had broken loose as the vessel foundered. The other two were accounted for by the battered boat in which were found the nine frozen crewmen, and the one discovered broken on the Buffalo breakwall. Captain McLeod had spoken of the terrifying list his ship had taken in the November storm, when she took water over her stern. A severe list to one side or the other would have rendered the two lifeboats on the high side useless. Were these the two that were found on the beach east of Port Burwell?

That being the case, had the entire crew, officers included, rushed to the remaining two boats? Had steward Smith, blaming the officers for the calamity and anticipating just such a contingency, brought along his knives to ward them off? What else would account for the knives and cleaver when the occupants lacked even the clothes to keep them warm? What else could have caused the great gashes on Captain McLeod?

Those who knew him well insisted that Captain McLeod was from the "old school" of shipmasters and would have been the last to leave his ship under any circumstances. They insisted that his presence in a tragic scramble as the lifeboat was being launched would be in the role of the faithful shipmaster trying to bring discipline and order out of chaos.

Photo courtesy Mrs. J. B. Rodebaugh

The *Marquette & Bessemer No. 2,* lost with all hands on Lake Erie, was a frequent victim of late-season ice jams. Here, in a photo taken off Conneaut, Ohio, dynamite charges are being exploded near her starboard side to loosen the packed ice. Inset, Capain Robert McLeod who went down with his ship. BELOW: Grim scene in Erie, Pennsylvania, morgue as the nine frozen men found in Lifeboat No. 4 were identified.

Photo courtesy John A. Tyler, Conneaut, Ohio

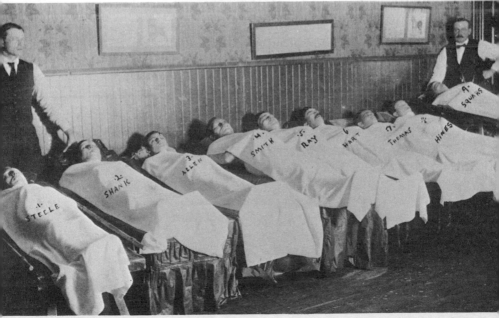

Photo courtesy John A. Tyler, Conneaut, Ohio

Battered No. 4 lifeboat from the lost car ferry *Marquette & Bessemer No. 2* was found with nine ice-encased bodies in it. It was apparently the only boat successfuly lowered from the foundering ship. BELOW: Recorded graph from Captain Sam Moore's depth finder clearly indicates a large wreck jutting up from the bottom of Lake Erie. Many think it is the long lost *Marquette & Bessemer No. 2,* sought since it vanished in December of 1909.

Graph courtesy Mrs. J. B. Rodebaugh

Bow of the *Marquette* after ramming and sinking the automobile-laden steamer *Senator*. It was through one of the big holes in the *Marquette*'s bow that Ralph Ellis, the *Senator*'s wireless operator, climbed to safety after being in the water a short time.

MARQUETTE

THE CLEVELAND-CLIFFS STEAMSHIP CO.

Photo from the author's collection

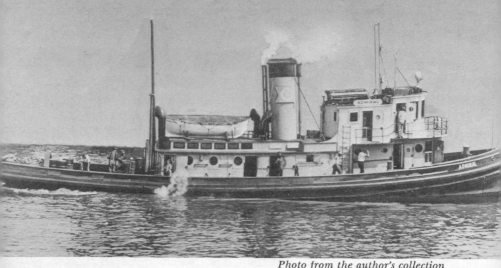

Photo from the author's collection

Photo of the ill-fated tug *Admiral* was taken shortly before she was lost with all hands on Lake Erie, December 2, 1942. BELOW: The passenger and package freight steamer *Chicora,* only three years old and the pride of the Graham & Morton fleet, vanished on Lake Michigan on January 21, 1895, while carrying a cargo of flour from Milwaukee to St. Joseph, Michigan.

Photo from Richard J. Wright collection

Photo courtesy Richard J. Wright

Only two out of a crew of thirty-five lived to tell how the big self-unloading steamer *Carl D. Bradley* broke in half in a Lake Michigan storm in November of 1956. BELOW: A ghost ship that lived to sail again, the tug *Sachem* is shown back in service after lying on the bottom of Lake Erie for ten months. She took her entire crew with her and the reason for her foundering is still a mystery.

Photo by the author

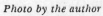

Photo courtesy Elsie Mohr King

The historic old schooner *Our Son,* fifty-five years old when she succumbed to a Lake Michigan gale on September 26, 1930. BE-LOW: Last moments of the schooner *Our Son.* This photo, taken from the deck of the rescue steamer *William Nelson,* was snapped minutes after the schooner's crew had been snatched from certain death.

Photo courtesy Elsie Mohr King

Photo courtesy J. W. Bald, Midland, Ontario

This rare picture, taken from the car ferry *Pere Parquette No. 22*, shows the steamer *William Nelson* nearing the sinking schooner, *Our Son*. Note the schooner's flag, flying upside-down, the international distress signal. Inset, Captain Charles H. Mohr, who was awarded a Congressional Medal for the daring rescue of the schooner's crew. BELOW: Rescued crew of the schooner *Our Son*. Left to right: Walter Schalbert, Charles Schroeder, Peter Olsen, Thomas Larsen, Alfred Peterson, John Olsen and Captain Fred Nelson.

Photo courtesy John A. Chisholm, Muskegon Chronicle

Photo courtesy Parry Sound Historical Society

Brought up from the depths of Georgian Bay, the *Waubuno's* anchor is now "moored" in the town square at Parry Sound, Ontario. Left to right, as appropriate ceremonies marked the event: Ernst Born, the diver who recovered the anchor; W. J. Beatty, whose antecedents owned the *Waubuno;* F. H. McKean, Parry Sound historian; and Ray A. Smith of the Parry Sound Public Library. BELOW: Bottoms up! The hulk of the oil barge *Cleveco,* lost with all hands in December, 1942, rises from her grave off Cleveland. The *Cleveco,* considered a menace to navigation, was towed to deep water and permitted to sink again.

Photo by Dudley Brumbach, Cleveland Plain Dealer

Under such conditions then, did the captain, attempting to halt the precipitous launching of the lifeboat with less than half of its registered capacity of crewmen aboard, meet the senseless wrath of his fear-crazed men?

Wheelsman Wilson came ashore near his commander. They identified him by his pride and joy, the seventeen-jewel Waltham watch, serial number 11,047,297. It had stopped at 10:06. Lighthouse keeper S. B. Cook made a rough coffin, and the *No. 2*'s wheelman was buried there on the point, a plain wooden marker signifying the place where he still sleeps away his personal eternity.

Shortly after he had finally conceded the car ferry to be lost, Mr. Magill had quickly made known the intent of the Marquette & Bessemer Dock and Navigation Company to pay a month's salary to the surviving relatives and to assume the funeral expenses of those whose bodies were recovered. This was really quite a magnanimous gesture, considering the times, but one wonders if the total did not approximate or exceed the cost of a stern gate, had one been included in the vessel's original specifications?

Two men did not require the company's proffered burial money. Nor did their families qualify for a month's pay or relief funds. Instead, hearty congratulations were the order of the day. One was George L. Lawrence, a porter, of Port Stanley. He explained that while the ship was unloading in that port, Chief Engineer Wood had asked him to get off the ship and scout around for men to work in the black gang.

"I had only gone a short distance when I ran into my girl on the street," said Lawrence, "and, of course, forgot everything else for the time being. All of a sudden I heard the 'cast off' signal from the boat, and I made a hike as fast as I could go for the dock. I got there just a minute too late—the boat had cleared the dock and—I missed the trip."

As trips go, he couldn't have picked a better one.

The other man was Max Sparuh, a fireman. On the previous trip the rolling of the ship had resulted in a nasty fall. While the car ferry and her crew were fighting for their lives on that hellish night of December seventh, Sparuh was comfortably bedded down in St. Thomas Hospital.

Fate was kind, too, to young William Dorland of Mount Clemens, Michigan. He had quit his job on the ship only a couple of weeks earlier, making his last trip on Thanksgiving Day.

Of a similar frame of mind, but slower of action, was deckhand John Wirtz. On the morning of December seventh, before the *No. 2* left port, he had mailed a letter to his family in Saginaw, Michigan, saying that, in his opinion, the vessel was a dangerous craft, unstable in rough weather, and that he had a constant fear for his life. "I am going to leave the ferry boat and seek other employment;" he wrote, "the next trip will be my last."

He was right.

The missing *No. 2* has never been positively located. Two schools of thought have held contrasting opinions as to where she went down. Some insist, despite the several reports of her whistle being heard off Conneaut and Port Stanley, that she actually foundered the afternoon of Tuesday, December seventh, the day she left port, somewhere between Port Stanley and Rondeau. A couple of years after she "went missing," as the second *Marquette & Bessemer No. 2* was beating her way to Rondeau, she "touched" a large, uncharted, underwater obstruction. What could it be but the first car ferry, they asked?

Those who hold that the wreck is much farther to the east, have the records of physical evidence to back them up. Had the vessel gone down between Port Stanley and Rondeau, her wreckage, in the southwest gale winds that had persisted for several days, would have come ashore between Point aux Pins and Port Stanley, not far to the east where most of it was found, between Port Burwell and the tip of Long Point.

They, too, point to an underwater obstruction, well offshore, between Conneaut and Erie. In the summer of 1932 the package freighter *Jack*, Buffalo to Duluth, struck wreckage some thirty-five miles southwest of Long Point, breaking her propeller and twisting her rudder. Could this be the *No. 2*, gone now for twenty-three years?

Generations of treasure hunters, and now, growing legions of scuba divers, have spent countless hours searching for her. Over the years there have been many reports of the hulk being found, but, in each instance, they have proved to be other wrecks. The sought-after prize, of course, is the *No. 2*'s purser's locked desk which, hopefully, still holds Albert J. Weiss's brown briefcase, stuffed with currency. It is still there, inside the elusive wreck, guarded by the ghosts of the eighteen men who went down with the ship.

For many years the tragic story of the *No. 2* and her people has been the compelling interest of Mrs. Joseph Rodebaugh, of Ashtabula, Ohio, another major Lake Erie port a few miles west of Conneaut. A daughter of Captain Hugh McLeod and niece of the missing car-ferry's captain and first mate, she has patiently tracked down every published and oral clue, compiling a mass of evidence that would indicate that the wreck is indeed somewhere off Long Point. This is where Captain Hugh McLeod has always maintained the ship went down. While visiting in Port Dover aboard their cabin cruiser in 1964, Joseph and Donna Rodebaugh learned that a commercial fisherman had recently lost some equipment on an underwater obstruction near Long Point. Tracking down the lead, they found him to be Captain Sam Moore of the fishing tug *Trimac II*. Trawling in 145 feet of water in August of 1963, he had lost a $600 trawl on some sort of wreck. The chart on his recording depth finder indicated a rather massive object that jutted up about forty-five feet from the bottom. With the graph that Captain Moore turned over to them, and armed with shoreline reference points he pro-

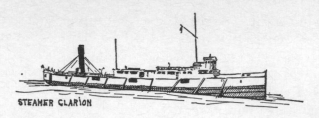

STEAMER CLARION

vided, they hope some day to organize an expedition to establish at long last, the grave of the ill-fated *No. 2*.

The car-ferry days on Lake Erie are gone forever. The change to oil for heat in homes and the power plants of industry, took away most of the coal traffic. High-speed freight trains or trucks now carry other commodities around the lake. It was a glorious era in lake shipping, despite the occasional dangers and losses. Today, wherever Great Lakes buffs gather to yarn about the past and the treasure still within the hulks of long-vanished ships, a frequent topic is the old *No. 2* and the tangled circumstances surrounding her disappearance. Several mysteries, as yet unsolved and likely never to be, still plague the amateur historians. Finding the wreck and a subsequent examination by divers would clear up three questions. If Mr. Weiss turned his money-laden briefcase over to purser Smith for safekeeping in the purser's desk, it will still be there. If the thirty cars that made up the cargo, or most of them, are still in the ship, Mr. Alfred Leslie's assumption that they had broken free and foundered the ship as they rolled off her stern, is proved wrong. More likely, then, if the railroad cars are still within the ship, she was sunk by hundreds of tons of wild water piling over her open stern, seeking out her four hatches as Captain McLeod frantically sought shelter.

And, of course, there are the puzzles that will never be solved. Did Captain McLeod receive his wounds while trying to halt a hasty launching of the No. 4 lifeboat? Why, the ship buffs ask, did steward George Smith, abandoning ship in a December gale of wind and snow, bring along his knives and cleaver while neglecting to pick up a coat or jacket to keep himself warm? The incongruities are many. The theories just as plentiful. Only one thing is certain: on the night of Tuesday, December seventh, or the morning of December eighth, 1909, the *Marquette & Bessemer No. 2* joined the lost and silent fleet whose last voyages were for. eternity.

The Prophetic Passing of
Captain Napier

Under the circumstances it would have been completely understandable if young Nelson Napier had chosen to live inland, seeking his future in farming, railroading, or clerking in a store—anything but steamboating. One brush with death on Lake Michigan would have been enough for most people, but Napier, greatly to his mother's distress, loathed farming, found no lure in the expanding railroad industry, and was most adamant in his dislike of store work. The alternative, if one was growing up along the eastern shore of Lake Michigan in post-Civil War days, was decidedly more promising and romantic—a career on one of the new big steamboats. The growing fleets of steam passenger and freight vessels were fast becoming the economic lifeblood of towns and cities on both sides of the lake. At sunset, with the smoke plumes of distant steamers silhouetted against a red sky, the distinctive smell of fresh water in the air and the mellow blasts of departing night-boat chime whistles echoing along the St. Joseph waterfront, a fellow is likely to forget the horrors of shipwreck, especially when he is only four at the time.

It happened right out there on the outer bar at St. Joseph,

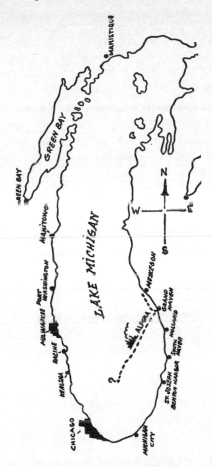

Michigan. Some, his mother in particular, claimed it was a miracle. Personally, he couldn't remember any of the details, but she had recounted the story so often that he could repeat it, almost word for word; he knew, too, at what points she would sigh and shake her head. Always at the end, she would raise her eyes heavenward, as if thanking the Almighty again for their deliverance. Maybe it was a miracle.

The little schooner, *Experiment*, Chicago to St. Joseph, had almost completed her journey. She was only a couple of miles from her destination when overtaken at dusk by a sudden and fierce gale that came booming down the lake. Despite some hectic and skillful maneuvering, she broached to and capsized a half mile out from the harbor. All the crew was apparently lost in the pounding surf. After ascertaining that there were no lives to save, the thrifty residents of St. Joseph spent the night salvaging for themselves what items of cargo the seas brought swiftly to their shore. The *Experiment*, meanwhile, was upside down on the offshore sand bar, anchored there by what remained of her masts. All night long the seas climbed aboard, rolling, pounding, twisting, and wracking her hull. But she was still there the next morning when, with the seas again quiet, a dozen men put out to her in small boats, hoping to salvage her anchors and ironwork. They were stamping around and wondering at the skill of men who could build a ship that would stand such punishment when, from inside the hull, they heard a muted hammering and faint cries. Quickly axes were produced and several men began hacking through the four-inch oak planking and heavy ribs. It took the better part of half an hour to chop a hole big enough to accommodate a person. After the job was done, tender hands lifted out Mrs. Napier, a baby daughter, and four-year-old Nelson.

When the ship had capsized so suddenly, Mrs. Napier and her three children were huddled in a lower cabin. So quickly had the *Experiment* gone over that a pocket of air remained trapped in the cabin. There, through that long and terrible night, as the ship was assaulted by Lake Michigan's mighty seas, she and two of her children had managed to stay alive. Sometime, as the ship was rocked and battered, one son had been torn from his mother's arms and was drowned.

This was Nelson Napier's introduction to Lake Michigan. But the memories of that dreadful night in the *Experiment*'s lower cabin were soon lost in a flood tide of happy boyhood adventures. Little wonder, however, that Mrs. Napier sought recourse in tearful efforts to dissuade her son from following a career as a fresh-water sailor. But at fifteen young Nelson Napier had "steamboat fever," wanted to go sailing—and did.

"He's a good, steady lad," Mrs. Napier told a neighbor. "But he's a bit headstrong, too, once he sets his mind to something. I fear that dreadful lake will be the end of him."

Things were booming in the lake-boat business, and a clean-cut, alert young chap like Napier had little trouble getting a job. New ships were coming out nearly every year, and experience was the sole prerequisite for advancement. One might begin as a deckhand or ship's clerk and bide his time until there was an opening for a wheelsman. From this rather exalted position the next step was third mate and from there the course to the top was clearly charted. With the blessings of good health, a desire to learn his trade, and a normal rate of attrition among the senior skippers, recognition of faithful service by his owners would eventually elevate him to command. On the other hand, if one judged that his progress in one vessel line was unduly slow, there were always others to whom a few seasons of experience in a pilothouse was the most desired recommendation.

The early years in Nelson Napier's steamboating career had included several job changes. Each one put him one step closer to his goal. He had finally settled on the Goodrich Transportation Company as the line for which he wanted to work. It was managed by Captain Albert E. Goodrich, a man still in his thirties, who was fast becoming the shipping tycoon of Lake Michigan. In addition to operating a night-boat shuttle service between Grand Haven and Muskegon to Milwaukee and Chicago, he had other vessels on steady daylight and night runs that included stops at many cities and towns on the west shore. His ships were smartly run by experienced skippers. Each vessel, in its own way, became part of the growing legends of the communities that depended upon them. Early histories are replete with many accounts of the famous old *Huron, Ogontz, Wabash Valley, Comet,* and *Sunbeam.* Then came the *Planet, May Queen, Orion, Northwest, Truesdell, Ottawa,* and *Manitowoc.* These were followed by the *Seabird, Alpena, Muskegon, Sheboygan, Corona,* and, through the years, many more.

Nelson Napier chose his employer wisely and his advancement through the ranks was steady if not spectacular. There came finally that happy spring day when he strode aboard the *Alpena* as her commander. The *Alpena's* regular route was the long-established cross-lake night-boat service between Muskegon and Grand Haven to Chicago. It was an old, familiar passage. He had made it hundreds of times as wheelsman, third mate, second mate, and as chief officer. During that time he had become a well-known figure to a host of passengers, shippers, sailors, and the leading citizens of his ship's ports of call. It was a good life, and on dark nights in the pilothouse, when the mood was on him, he was fond of telling his mates, as if to remind them that the road to the captain's cabin was a long one, of his early affliction of steamboat fever and his subsequent experiences. Often, too, he would relate the story of that morning when his mother lifted him up through the hole on the bottom of the old *Experiment* and his unorthodox arrival at the village of St. Joseph.

Captain Goodrich usually preferred to have his vessels built for him, constructed to plans he and his builder devised to best serve the combined passenger and freight business in which they were to be employed. But there were instances when the volume of business would not permit time for building a ship to order. Occasionally, too, the loss of a vessel through some unfortunate mishap necessitated finding a replacement in short order. The *Alpena* was such a ship.

On her first trip of the season down the west shore to Chicago, in April of 1868, the Goodrich steamer *Seabird* caught fire off Waukegan and foundered with the loss of nearly all her crew and passengers, seventy-two in number. It was a dreadful disaster, commemorated several times in prose and poetry.

For Captain Goodrich the loss of the *Seabird* meant finding a replacement immediately. He transferred another vessel to the *Seabird*'s busy route and went looking for a steamer suited for the night-boat trade. He found the 653-gross-ton side-wheeler, *Alpena*, at Detroit. Built in 1867 at Marine City, Michigan, she was practically new, and her physical dimensions and passenger and freight capabilities were about as well proportioned as he could hope to find in an existing vessel. Her big walking-beam engine was the type that usually outlasted a couple of steamers. She had passenger accommodations practically the full length of the upper deck, with her lower deck big and roomy for the variety of package freight that would likely come her way. Wide gangways would permit freight wagons to back right up to them. There were several changes he would have liked to make but time was of the essence, so he bought her on the spot for $80,000.

The *Alpena* was still essentially a new boat when Captain Nelson Napier moved into her captain's quarters. He knew she had her own personality and peculiarities as every ship had. He set about learning them with the dedicated thoroughness he had displayed throughout his career. In a few weeks he knew her intimately, studying her handling characteristics both on the open lake and in the confined waters of the harbors as she departed or made up to a dock. He knew that no two boats, even though built from the same plans, responded to the seas in exactly the same way. One might require a little more of the freight tonnage to be stowed forward to make maximum speed with minimum hull stress. The other vessel, seemingly identical, assumed her ideal "squat" or steaming-while-loaded stature with more weight aft. The *Alpena*, he discovered, handled best and burrowed her way into cross seas with the least commotion and pounding when she had some weight forward, giving her forefoot a little more "bite." Personally, he would have preferred a propeller-driven ship, being convinced that side-wheelers were not the best craft in any kind of seaway.

"They're great on the rivers," he once confided to a friend, "but out there on the open lake with a bit of sea running, it's another matter. If you follow your course, you sometimes have to meet the seas at an angle. Then you find that most of the time one wheel is completely buried in the water while the other one is clawin' air. Bound to put a big strain on the shafts and machinery."

Despite this disadvantage the side-wheelers of the Goodrich line continued to make steamboat history on Lake Michigan. Good freight tonnages were always offered and passenger traffic revenue was high. Considerable emphasis was placed on comfort and convenience in the passenger quarters, and the well-advertised deluxe accommodations usually resulted in a "sold out" cabin deck.

The *Alpena's* normal schedule called for her to load both passengers and freight at Muskegon in late afternoon and early evening, steaming twelve miles south, then, for Grand Haven, where the freight cargo would be "topped off," and more passengers would be assigned quarters, if any remained. One advantage of the two-port coverage was that those seeking passage at Muskegon, if they were tardy and missed the boat, could always charter a rig at the livery stable and still catch the ship at Grand Haven, usually with time to spare. At about ten o'clock the *Alpena* would back from her dock, blow one long, melodious blast from her chime whistle and depart for Chicago. Sometime during the night, visibility permitting, she would meet and pass another Goodrich night boat, usually the *Muskegon*, outbound from Chicago, headed for Grand Haven and Muskegon. The *Alpena* would arrive at her Chicago dock early in the morning and begin discharging passengers and freight. That night, burdened again with both, she would depart once more for the neighboring ports on the east coast of Lake Michigan. Again, weather conditions being favorable, she would meet the *Muskegon* and exchange whistle signals. Passengers making the trip for the first time were often vexed at this unexpected and sometime alarming interruption of their sleep, but it was a tradition of steamboatin' and, after all, Captain Napier was, and always had been, a steamboat man.

The weather on October 15, 1880, was delightful. Temperatures throughout the day had held between sixty-five and seventy degrees, typical of Indian summer in Michigan. In Grand Haven that evening, it was still warm as the noisy dock crews trundled crates, boxes, and barrels through the *Alpena*'s gangways. Teamsters bawled orders to their horses and backed their wagons as close to the ship as they could get. Mosquitoes, gnats, and the full spectrum of summer insects were still out in force, swirling around the oil lights and bedeviling the sweating stevedores.

"Blimey," grumbled one, obviously a recent arrival from distant shores, "them bloody bugs bites like ruddy fox-'ounds."

At ten o'clock, loading completed, the ship's hawsers were cast off, and the *Alpena*, her great side-wheels turning slowly astern, backed into the Grand River channel, turned, and steamed slowly toward the mouth of the river and Lake Michigan. Once more, and it never varied more than a few minutes, the big chime whistle reverberated over the waterfront. On the upper deck, enjoying the warm weather, most of the seventy-five passengers waved to anybody they could see. On the freight deck the big wooden gangway doors boomed shut, and shortly thereafter the sturdy oak "strong-backs" were dropped across them and driven tight with wedges. The *Alpena* was ready for sea, and her crew of twenty-two automatically fell into their accustomed routine.

Light northerly winds had prevailed over Lake Superior and Lake Michigan throughout the day, rippling up a gentle swell that the *Alpena* accepted with a slow and modest roll. It was typical of midsummer sailing and remained so for some time. At about one o'clock on the morning of the sixteenth, again entirely routine, the *Muskegon*, all lights burning, hove into sight and passed nearby on the port side. Again the *Alpena*'s whistle sounded, its echo blending with a similar salute from the *Muskegon*. The *Alpena*, all well aboard, gradually faded from sight.

It was the last anybody saw of her. Not long after that friendly salute, traditional of the two ships passing in the night, the *Alpena* simply vanished!

Shortly after the two ships passed, Indian summer of 1880 became a matter of history. The northerly breezes died out and, within minutes, conditions on Lake Michigan changed violently from the sublime to the atrocious. The transformation, originating over land, burst out with winds that some observers interpreted as tornadoes. Massive and conflicting weather fronts spawned meteorological excesses that brought about the most drastic reversal of temperatures veteran shipmasters could recall. In little over an hour the thermometer dropped thirty-three degrees, from a high of sixty-five degrees to thirty-two degrees Fahrenheit, the freezing point. The wind, with demoniac fury, swept up the lake on a southwest to northeast track, moving with such speed that skippers were unable to get their sails down before they were blown to shreds. Sometimes the masts went first, breaking with terrifying reports and sweeping overboard in a grinding, tangled avalanche of shrouds, stays, braces, shattered cabins, ironwork, cordage, and men. Worst of all, the winds brought with them snow—great driving, choking blizzards that limited a helmsman's vision, when indeed he could open his eyes, to a bare five feet beyond his assigned post.

The season was a busy one, and the storm caught all manner of craft at sea, hauling one commodity or another. In the two-day blow nearly one hundred vessels, sail and steam, were driven ashore, twenty of them between Kewaunee and Death's Door, a distance of fifty miles. More "went on" in the vicinity of Plum Island, including the schooner, *Colonel Cook*, loaded with coal. The schooner, *Guido Pfister*, went ashore at North Bay with a cargo of corn. While her crew was jettisoning the corn to keep it from swelling and bursting the decks, the wheat-laden schooner, *Two Friends*, came pounding ashore beside her, broadside to the beach, with the seas cleaning off her bulwarks. Wrecked nearby were the schooners, *Lem Ellsworth*, Buffalo to Chicago with coal, the *Cascade*, *James Platt*, *Letty May*, *Josephine Lawrence*, and *Pauline*, the latter spewing out her cargo of shingles. Here, too, Captain J. G. Hurlbut brought his ship, the *George Murray*, into what he thought was safe anchorage. Loaded with coal, the *Murray*'s anchors were holding well when the schooner *Montauk*, carrying pig iron, came charging in, minus her foreboom and sail, and before Captain Gunderson could get her under control the *Montauk* crashed into the *Murray* and went hard aground, the seas, even in the semi-protected harbor, sweeping everything from her decks. Moments later another anchored ship, the *Fiorette*, was rammed by the *Louise McDonald*, fleeing into the harbor for shelter.

At Baileys Harbor the lumber-laden *Peoria*, went hard on the lighthouse reef just after dark on the night of the sixteenth. The wracking seas broke her open almost immediately, and Captain Peter A. Hogan and his crew were forced to climb the masts and rigging to keep from being swept away. Although their plight was discovered almost at once, no rescue craft dared make an attempt to reach the stricken schooner. Seas climbed over her, littering the shore and lacing the surf with big timbers from her lumber cargo. All night and most of the next day they clung to their perilous roosts while on shore several unsuccessful rescue expeditions were mounted. Finally Captain Lewis Lawson of the schooner *Conway* launched a small boat and with a picked crew managed to pluck the half-frozen sailors from the wreck.

At Sturgeon Bay the latest word on the wrecks and the names of overdue vessels and local skippers made news bulletins that were placed in the window of the local newspaper, the Door County *Advocate*. They revealed that the schooner, *Ebeneezer*, had foundered with a load of stone—the schooners *Hungarian*, *City of Woodstock*, and the scow, *Dunham*, were ashore at Whitefish Bay while the dismasted *David Van Valkenburg* was at anchor, but in a sinking condition—at Mud Bay the schooner, *Contest*, loaded with railroad ties, posts, and poles, was on a reef; an unknown steamer with only its masts above water was reported sunk off Two Rivers, and the schooner *Nabob* was sighted, aground and badly broken up. No word as to the fate of her crew, at Jacksonport the *Perry Hannah* was a total loss; the schooners *George B. Sloan* and *Shandon* were also ashore and wrecked at Jacksonport; the lighthouse-supply steamer, *Dahlia*, reported that at little Cana Island the seas were so high during the storm that water surged into the window of the lighthouse, ten feet above its base and fifty feet back from the shore. The keeper had to flee with his family into the boathouse. The seas also tore up the walks around his house, drowned his chickens, and smashed things up generally. The schooner *Anna Maria* was capsized off Two Rivers; the *America*, Captain Lovedale in command, reported seas so high that when the *America* went down into the trough between them she hit bottom several times although the normal water depth at that particular point, near the harbor entrance, was thirty feet. The schooner *Glad Tidings*, reported missing, finally turned up at Chicago; the steamer *Alpena*, however, had not been sighted since the morning of the sixteenth when she was met and acknowledged by her sister ship, the *Muskegon*!

Considering the severity of the storm and the widespread

disruption of all marine traffic on Lake Michigan, no immediate alarm was expressed when the *Alpena* failed to dock at Chicago on the morning of the sixteenth. It was assumed that in order to show his passengers every consideration as to their safety, Captain Napier had probably made for a nearer port—Racine, Kenosha, or, perhaps, even Waukegan. But as reports of staggering losses and groundings came in, Goodrich officials concluded that he had been forced to turn before the storm and run with the seas at his stern. Before that monumental wind and the great seas they built up, he might have had to steam far up the lake before he could find a lee behind the Manitous, there to anchor in safety until the gale had spent itself. There was no cause for alarm, they assured anxious relatives, the *Alpena* was the staunchest of ships and could come to no harm. The heavy losses, they pointed out, were to sailing vessels, and that was to be expected because they were literally helpless in a real gale. The *Alpena*, however, was a powerful steamboat and was not likely to become a victim of the elements since she had the power to take herself anywhere. No doubt, they advised, she had even then left her shelter and would reach Chicago in the normal running time from wherever she was at anchor.

Behind the scenes those in charge were not quite so confident as their public statements might indicate. The *Muskegon* and *Menominee* had resumed their shuttle runs from Grand Haven to Chicago and Milwaukee, but they were quietly instructed to put extra lookouts on duty and to investigate any sign of wreckage. Chartered tugs also steamed up the eastern shoreline and cruised around the Manitous, the Fox Islands, and the Beavers. There were plenty of wrecked schooners to be found wherever they went but not a sign of the *Alpena*.

From Sturgeon Bay came belated word from the captain of a steamer that had been in the same general location as the

Alpena on the night the gale broke. He had not seen her, he explained, but he had heard her whistle.

"I'd know that whistle anywhere," he told Captain Goodrich, "but it was blowing a gale and snowing so hard I couldn't see my own bow. And, sir, she was blowing distress signals. They were terrible to hear, but I couldn't do a thing, even if I could have found her. We were having a bad time of it ourselves. Yes, sir, them was distress signals I heard from the *Alpena*."

Faint hope was held in some quarters that the *Alpena* had been forced to run the full length of the lake before the gale and, there, blinded by snow and completely lost, had gone hard aground. The northern shore of Lake Michigan was sparsely inhabited, and a ship might thus be stranded a week before her master could notify his owners. Then, too, the optimists opined, had she been at last able to find shelter behind some lonely island, she would in all probability have long since exhausted her fuel supply. This, too, could explain her failure to return home. But the theories did not explain why, out there in the dark of night, while the furious seas marched over the decks of a hundred ships and the snow came in smothering blasts, the *Alpena* was heard sounding desperate signals of distress. Or was it the *Alpena* that the Sturgeon Bay skipper heard? No other steamer known to be in the area went missing that night.

Where was the *Alpena*? She was gone, most certainly, but where and why? Goodrich officials were as puzzled as those who kept demanding news of the ship and those aboard her. Then, in a few days, the dread news began to come to the company offices from scattered points. Residents along a seventy-mile stretch of the eastern shoreline were reporting wreckage on the beaches. Six of the Goodrich marine staff chartered rigs and drove to several distant areas to view the mass of debris. Back in Muskegon they closeted themselves in an office, compared notes, and finally admitted publicly and quite regretfully, that in their opinion, the flotsam and jetsam had, indeed, once been part of the *Alpena*.

It was unanimously agreed in a hundred waterfront taprooms and in the dock offices where knowledgeable marine men were wont to gather, that the *Alpena* had gotten herself down in the troughs of the mountainous seas and had been overwhelmed. Some could remember Captain Napier's expressed reservations about the sea characteristics of a sidewheeler, and his remark that they were not the handiest type of ship to be maneuvered in any kind of a seaway.

Those who still preferred sail, and there were many of them, pointed out that steamboats should be required to carry at least one sail, preferably on her foremast. Then, even though she might fall off into the troughs by reason of insufficient power or a mechanical breakdown, they argued, the sail, properly handled, would lift her out of the troughs. It was a well-known fact, they insisted, that a single sail, even on salt-water steamers, was carried for just such an eventuality.

Most steamboat people, including Goodrich officials, were unimpressed.

Captain Goodrich, aware that this philosophy was getting a lot of attention in the newspapers of the lake cities, countered quickly.

"Every sailing ship on the southern end of Lake Michigan had her sails blown out that night . . . stripped to bare poles in a minute. The same thing would have happened to a sail on the *Alpena*, if she had been equipped with one."

As usual, a number of unpleasant rumors began to circulate in the port cities along Lake Michigan. There were unfounded stories of hull and engine deficiencies, of needed repairs going uncorrected, and of outrageous overloading, most of them traced to disgruntled former employees or people who knew absolutely nothing about steamships. Why, it was asked, did a large and supposedly powerful steamer fail to survive a storm that had failed to sink the sailing ships near her? Although the schooners and brigs had been shorn of sails and some dismasted, most had lived to sail another day. Could it be that side-wheelers, by the very nature of their design and motive power, had insufficient power and maneuverability in really severe weather? The ship driven by a single propeller at its stern and in the proximity of its rudder certainly seemed to have an advantage when heavy seas were running.

The rumors and damaging stories finally reached such proportions that the Manitowoc *Tribune* denounced as "malicious falsehoods" the stories circulated representing the lost steamer, *Alpena*, to have been been unseaworthy.

The newspaper also printed a statement by G. S. Rand of the Manitowoc shipyard.

The steamer *Alpena*, during the winter of 1876-77 was thoroughly rebuilt. She was docked, refastened, and recalked, received new arches, new deck frames and deck, new gallous frame, ceiling and planking wherever required, an entire new stern, new breast yokes forward and aft, and had her cabin improved and strengthened and was considered by everyone as better and stronger than ever. The work was done at a cost of $20,000.

Considering that the Goodrich line wintered its boats in Manitowoc, maintained extensive headquarters and repair shops, and accounted for a fair share of the winter employment in that city, the newspaper could scarcely have done less. Nor could Mr. Rand whose company had traditionally built and rebuilt most of the Goodrich vessels. Nevertheless, it was the considered opinion of all responsible shipping men that the *Alpena* was, and always had been, a staunch and dependable ship. It was simply a case, they declared again and again, of a vessel being completely overwhelmed by an unprecedented storm, the most severe within memory.

The *Alpena* was a favorite subject of conversation through-out the winter. A hundred theories attempted to account for her last moments and the succession of events that must have led to her foundering. Experienced seamen held to the now oft-expressed view that side-wheelers were really not sea boats at all and that the big wheels themselves were subject to damage by high seas. Others were of the opinion that she had caught fire, that the engineroom and black gang had been forced to abandon their posts, and the resulting loss of steam had left the steamer helpless. Another favorite theory was that she had been in collision during the blizzard with a scow that had later been reported missing. One viewpoint was as good as another since none could be proved.

The *Alpena* was gone but not forgotten. The Goodrich people wrote her off and did their best, once the grim details associated with the tragedy were disposed of, to let the past slip quietly into the dusty drawers of history. It was the sailors who wouldn't forget her. They, particularly the old sailing-ship men, were a superstitious lot, given to proverbs, adages, omens, and, occasionally, apparitions and super-natural manifestations. More than one, on watch as his ship slipped silently through the wraithlike evening fogs, claimed to have seen the missing *Alpena* steaming by—lights burning, her big walking-beam engine clanking, and wisps of steam curling up from her boiler room skylight. For years, or as long as old sailors spun their yarns, the *Alpena* was known as the "ghost ship" of Lake Michigan . . . a specter ship upon an endless voyage, haunting the steamer lanes of her past, but with never a friendly passing signal from her stirring old chime whistle.

Actually, what most likely happened came to light the next summer, but even then some considered it to be a grisly hoax.

On July 19, 1881, the St. Joseph and Benton Harbor *Daily Evening Herald* reported:

The keeper of the Point Betsie Life Saving Station yesterday found a bottle with the following note, kindly handed to your correspondent by the Frankfort *Express*;

> October 16, 3 o'clock, on board the *Alpena* . . . she has broke her port wheel; is at mercy of seas; is half full of water; God help us, Capt. Napier washed overboard.
>
> —GEORGE A. N. MOORE
> 856 South Halsted Street
> Chicago, Ill.

The other side of the note read:

> The finder of this note will please communicate with my wife and let her know of my death.

Superstitions, omens, ominous premonitions, or notes in bottles notwithstanding, it was just as Nelson Napier's mother had feared . . . that dreadful lake had been the end of him.

12

Don't Change Her Name ... !

There is an old adage, popular among superstitious sailors
of past generations, that to change a vessel's name is to in-
vite all manner of ill luck. A ship is endowed with a soul
when she is launched, they claimed, born with her own individual and highly personal traits and habits . . . , little characteristics her people must learn to know and accept. Being
a woman—since all ships are "she" even though they bear
masculine names—she will need a good bit of understanding.
Her skippers and crews, for she may have many during her
lifetime, will soon discover whether she is "tender" or "stiff,"
how she responds under given conditions of wind and water,
how she behaves in a seaway, and will learn to recognize her
own peculiar way of expressing her displeasures and com-
plaints. A wise master will heed them. The old-timers say
she will be a good ship if those responsible for her care and
management give her the understanding treatment they
would tender a temperamental mistress . . . sensing when to
coax her and correctly judging the moment when firmness is
the best policy. But to strip her of the name she has always
known is to ask for an end to all the blessings and good-luck
wishes bestowed upon her as she rumbled down the ways—
champagne still dripping from her stem.

Shipping people of today pay little heed to shipyard superstitions, old wives' tales, adages, or the doleful laments and
predictions of old sailors. Ships' names are changed quite
frequently, particularly when they are purchased by new
owners. Some vessels have had half a dozen names without
becoming addicted to groundings, mechanical breakdowns,
fouled lines, fires, or collisions with docks or other vessels.
Business expediencies of the times often result in a ship being
shorn of her old name and rechristened in honor of a high
official of a company or corporation for whom she hauls
prodigious tonnages of iron ore, coal, or grain. There is no
gloomy talk of bad luck, preordained disaster, or a future of
doom. All is gaiety. Happy speeches are made, blessings are
asked, congratulations are in order, and champagne from
another era drips on their bows.

Yet, there are instances—enough to make prophets out of
many old seamen—when the changing of a name has eventually foretold tragedy, giving a sense of authenticity to the
sinister and foreboding aphorisms so often recalled and
changed to fit the occasion by the grizzled old fo'c'sle sooth-
sayers or prophesiers of doom. They might, indeed, find a
grisly sense of self-satisfaction in the fate of three sturdy tugs
that vanished in the murky depth of Lake Erie—ghost ships
that took their entire crews, thirty-four men, down with
them. Their disappearances are still regarded as great mysteries but, curiously, one of them is still in service today, the
only "ghost ship" to sail again! Strangely, too, the reason for
her sinking is as much a puzzle as it was the day she was lost.
The three tugs were the *Cornell*, *Admiral*, and *Sachem*.
These were not their original names. That, cackle the tooth-
less old prognosticators, was their problem, their cross to
bear, the reason for their certain, predestined, rendezvous
with disaster. The inevitable date with destiny that was supposedly inherited by a ship whose name had been changed,
according to the seers, might be far in the future, but it was,

beyond a doubt, preordained. It took twenty-two years for the name-changing jinx to catch up with the *Cornell,* twenty-six years for the *Sachem,* but less than three months for the *Admiral.*

The durable wooden harbor tug, *Grace Danforth,* was built and so christened in 1888 when she became a part of the fleet of the Hand & Johnson Tug Line in Buffalo. For the better part of twelve years she was active in the daily routine of the busy harbor. In summer she worked around the clock, aiding schooners and steamers in and out of the many docks and slips along the Buffalo River and the Union Canal. Iron ore and grain were the chief inbound cargoes, but outbound vessels were usually down to their marks with coal. During the winter the *Grace Danforth* was occupied shifting grain vessels. At the close of the season many ships traditionally came down from the upper lakes ports with grain cargoes. The capacity of the elevators at Buffalo, although it was the largest milling center in the world, was limited. The grain-laden ships were moored wherever space was available. During the winter, as space developed, they would be shifted from their moorings to the long suction spouts of the elevators. This shifting was the job of the *Grace Danforth* and her sister tugs. The bitter winters of the Buffalo area often resulted in major ice-breaking operations before the "dead" storage vessels could be moved.

Just before the turn of the century the newly organized Great Lakes Towing Company was acquiring the fleets and facilities of many independent towing companies in all the major lake ports. The lake vessels were growing in size while the harbor-towing situation was becoming more confused and less efficient. Rates were uncertain and competition between rival independent tug operators so bitter that agreements between them became necessary if they were to survive. Thus, if they agreed to take turns towing vessels in particular ports, the incoming ship might be forced to wait a full day until the company whose turn it was had tugs available. And often as not, the tug assigned was too small or underpowered for the job.

The objective of the Great Lakes Towing Company was to construct a fleet of large, modern tugs to meet the changing needs of the Great Lakes ports. Meanwhile, they set about buying out many existing independent operators, redistributing the equipment according to the needs of the various ports, and forging ahead with their program of building tugs adequately powered to meet the challenges of the burgeoning fleets of big steel bulk carriers.

By 1900 the Hand and Johnson Tug Line, its fleet, and facilities became part of the Great Lakes Towing Company, active by now, from Buffalo to Duluth, although sometimes operating under the names of predecessor companies.

The *Grace Danforth*, after due consideration, was renamed the *Cornell*. As such she continued to earn her keep for a number of years, laboring in the various harbors she was assigned to and performing her tasks as well as could be expected, considering her size, power, and wooden construction. Still, she could not approach the efficiency of the new and more powerful tugs that were joining the ranks every year. She was eventually reduced to the "reserve fleet" status in Cleveland, where she lay idle for several years.

In late 1922 the Syracuse Sand Company was looking for just such a vessel as the *Cornell* for their modest armada of tugs, scows, and barges operating on the New York State Barge Canal. The *Cornell*, inadequate for the demands now being made on harbor tugs, was available and, in consideration of a modest sum, was sold to the New York firm. The price included delivery to the new owner at Syracuse, thus necessitating a long trek eastward on Lake Erie, a stop at Buffalo, and then through the Welland Canal and down Lake Ontario to Oswego, New York, the terminus of the Oswego Canal, part of the New York State Barge Canal.

The *Cornell*, after minor repairs and a thorough inspection by the company's marine superintendent, the underwriters, and the United States Steamboat Inspection Service was cleared to leave Cleveland, which she did on the afternoon of Thursday, December twenty-first. Due to the length of the journey she was provided with two full crews, eight men. The weather, as she steamed out between the harbor piers at two-thirty, was clear and cold with only a hint of a breeze. Her modest speed would put her in her old home port of Buffalo late the following afternoon.

On Saturday, when a telephone call from Buffalo revealed that the *Cornell* had not yet arrived, some immediate concern was shown. More calls from Cleveland to the Erie office and the Dunkirk harbor master confirmed that she had not put into either of those ports. Quite obviously she had broken down, possibly from some infirmity resulting from her long layup and undetected by the several inspections. Lake Erie in December is no place for a vessel with the low freeboard of a harbor tug. A search was instituted immediately by other larger company tugs, the *T. C. Lutz* steaming out of Cleveland and the *Tennessee* heading west from Buffalo. The *Oregon* and *Q. A. Gillmore* also left for Erie, where the search was centered. At the request of the company, Government air mail planes were requested to fly over the *Cornell's* course, where, it was supposed, the disabled tug lay helpless and at the mercy of the wind and waves.

The search pattern, with the tugs crossing and recrossing the *Cornell's* projected route and likely course of drift, continued on through Christmas Day. Then, on December twenty-sixth, the *Gillmore* came upon the *Cornell's* single lifeboat. In it, staring out with sightless eyes, was the ice-encased body of one man, a fireman. Whether the boat had earlier been occupied by more of the crew could not be determined. The fireman was lightly clad, indicating that there had been no time to gather up warm clothing. Whatever the reason for the tug's foundering, it had apparently come with little or no warning. A fire aboard the *Cornell*, even though it spread swiftly, would have permitted her crew a moment or two to gather the warm clothing they knew would be needed. A boiler explosion would have demolished her instantly, probably catapulting the lifeboat from its cradle over the engineroom. Those who reached it would have to do so after they found themselves in the water. Several possible reasons for the disappearance of the *Cornell* have been advanced through the years, each one a logical explanation under a certain, prescribed set of circumstances. No one will ever really know. The only clue was the little ice-encrusted lifeboat, wallowing in the tossing seas east of Long Point with a dead man as her skipper.

The very year the *Cornell* vanished on Lake Erie, a larger tug was being completed at Manitowoc, Wisconsin. She was the *W. H. Meyer*, a ninety-foot steel vessel of 130 gross tons, constructed on order from the Milwaukee Towing Company. Her launching was the usual affair, attended by toasts, good-luck wishes, and the traditional breaking of a bottle of champagne on her stem. The blessings and petitions of good will and luck asked in her behalf held for exactly twenty years, or as long as she kept her original name of *W. H. Meyer*. On July 14, 1942, she was purchased by the Cleveland Tankers Incorporated. Her name was changed to *Admiral*, officially, as recorded on an amended certificate issued at Toledo, Ohio, on September third of that year. Still young as age is reckoned in fresh-water vessels, the *Admiral* had only eighty-nine days to live.

The Cleveland Tankers people had purchased the former *W. H. Meyer* to tow their big 250-foot, 30,000-barrel-capacity oil barge *Cleveco*. To engage in open-lake towing, however, some changes had to be made on the tug. She got a new, raised pilothouse, built above the forward cabins, thus providing for the better visibility needed on the long hauls between lake ports. Her normal crew, to man her around the clock, would number fourteen, far more than she had required in harbor work. Accommodations for them, and a larger galley and mess room involved some rebuilding of her interior spaces. In the end she was an efficient vessel, adequately powered and manned to do the job expected of her.

Changes in a vessel's superstructure usually result in altering or modifying her center of gravity. Following the reconstruction work, the United States Coast Guard had subjected the *Admiral* to a stability or inclination test, as a result of which it issued a certificate of inspection expressly stating that the tug "has satisfactory stability for all reasonable operations, subject to the following restrictions." The restrictions involved normal operating draft, fore and aft, the frequent pumping of her bilges and, most importantly, that "the towline shall be maintained in as nearly a fore and aft line as practical." The officer who conducted the stability test, however, prepared a memorandum for his Washington office that had the effect of contradicting the certificate, stating that "the *Admiral* was slightly deficient in stability." This memorandum, strangely, was not furnished to the owners or their marine superintendent. In seaman's vernacular, the *Admiral* was apparently a bit tender.

The *Admiral* went into service with Captain John Swanson as her master. Prior to his assignment to the tug, his first experience with such a vessel, he had been commander of the *Cleveco*. Upon his transfer to the tug, Captain Swanson's first mate, William H. Smith, assumed command of the barge. Edwin Smith, second mate on the *Cleveco*, and a brother of Captain William H. Smith, was elevated to the post of first mate.

On the morning of December first, the two vessels lay at the Sun Oil Company dock in Toledo as the *Cleveco* took aboard her oil cargo. Fireman Joseph Callahan and watchman Leo Frost, both of the *Cleveco*, were Toledoans and had left to visit their homes as soon as the tug and her consort docked. Pay checks had arrived and a helpful dispatcher at the Great Lakes Towing Company office volunteered to take several crewmen "downtown" to cash them. Earlier in the day William Rocks, the tug's chief engineer, had been quite determined about quitting his job. Others had persuaded him to finish out the season, thus qualifying for the usual bonus. Despite the cold and a biting wind that promised a "nasty bit of slop" running out on the lake, the crews were in good spirits. The pay checks obviously had something to do with it.

Late in the morning the tug had shifted the barge to the Gulf Refining Company's Maumee River marine terminal to finish loading. Now, at approximately two o'clock in the afternoon, the *Admiral* sidled up to the *Cleveco*'s bow and took aboard her towing hawser. As she pulled the barge from the oil dock Captain Swanson was already sounding three long blasts on the tug's whistle, signaling for the opening of the Wheeling and Lake Erie bridge. A few minutes later, when he had drawn the *Cleveco* to midstream and was pulling ahead on the shortened line used in harbors and rivers, he noted that the drawbridge had been opened promptly.

At three o'clock the tug and her loaded consort were seen as they passed the Chesapeake & Ohio Railroad's coal docks, steaming out into Maumee Bay and the open lake, the towline now lengthened out. A strong northwest wind had been blowing most of the day, although up to the time of departure, no storm warnings had been issued for the Lake Erie area between Toledo and Cleveland. It was nearly dusk when the tug and barge, far beyond Toledo Light, turned to the east on the Pelee Passage course, thereby taking the brunt of the thundering graybeards marching before a steadily increasing northwest wind.

All night long, through the dangerous Pelee Passage and on the Southeast Shoals course, the tug and her tow plugged ahead. Her decks constantly awash, the *Admiral* was properly "buttoned up," with all her watertight doors dogged down. Darkness had brought plunging temperatures. Both vessels were now beginning to accumulate a modest burden of ice. Heavy snow flurries prevented the two vessels from seeing each other. At four o'clock on the morning of December second, Captain Smith became aware that the rolling and pitching motion of his ship had changed abruptly. Whereas she had been swept by overtaking seas all through the night, the *Cleveco* was now meeting them head to! The wind had not changed direction, but obviously the *Cleveco* had. In company with a deck watchman the captain fought his way through the snow and boarding seas to the bow. The towline, still bar tight and obviously still secured to the tug's towing winch, angled directly down into the water. The *Admiral*, apparently without warning, had plunged to the bottom with all hands! Thus anchored to the sunken tug, the *Cleveco* had swung around, facing directly into the wind and seas.

Captain Smith was a practical man, whatever the emergency. His first duty was to contact his owners to apprise them of the *Admiral*'s fate and permit them to make shoreside arrangements to save his own vessel. Awakened by radiotelephone call from Captain Smith, Captain L. M. Jonassen, manager of the Cleveland Tankers fleet, immediately made contact with the Coast Guard. Within minutes motor lifeboats from Lorain and Cleveland were on their way to the scene of the foundering. The Cleveland boat was skippered by Chief Boatswain's mate, John Needham, who had a special reason for urgency that morning. One of the *Admiral*'s wheelsmen was John Tierney, Needham's cousin. The Coast Guard Cutter, *Ossipee*, was also dispatched to the location given by Captain Smith, and the Civil Air Patrol prepared to put planes up at daylight. Captain Jonassen also arranged with the Great Lakes Towing Company for tugs to bring in the *Cleveco*, the tug *Pennsylvania* departing Lorain, the *California* from Cleveland.

The Cleveland-bound steamer, *Marquette*, passed four miles to the leeward of the *Cleveco* at about the time the Coast Guard vessels were departing their stations, but Captain Douglas Jackson had heard the ship-to-shore radio-telephone conversations, knew the *Cleveco* was then not in immediate danger, and was aware that rescue craft were on the way.

The position given by Captain Smith proved to be substantially incorrect. The *Cleveco* was actually a number of miles east of the position he had indicated, as so discovered by the Civil Air Patrol pilot Clara W. Livingston. She found the barge ten miles due north of Cleveland harbor. Given the right location, the cutter *Ossipee* changed its course and closed on the drifting barge.

Many have wondered if the hawser between the *Admiral* and *Cleveco* had parted or whether Captain Smith had ordered it severed. Certainly the rescue craft would have had little difficulty locating him had his position, "anchored" to the sunken tug, remained constant. In any event, the *Cleveco* was loose and drifting. Powerless, she would be down in the trough of the seas every mile of her fearful journey.

The *Ossipee* established radio and, later, visual contact with the *Cleveco*. His crew, Captain Smith reported, wanted to be removed. The barge was taking water through her hawse pipes, and it was only a question of time, he indicated, when it would rise high enough to put out the fire in the donkey boiler, thus shutting down the generator and eliminating further use of the radio-telephone. But although the *Ossipee* was at one time within 150 yards of the *Cleveco*, she could not maintain visual contact. She carried two six-pound line-throwing guns, a shoulder line-throwing gun, and a sturdy manila-towing hawser. She was never, after one brief sighting, able to see the barge again. Driving snow flurries in winds of between fifty and seventy miles per hour, high seas, and a condition known as "Arctic mist," which hovered over the water constantly, prevented any of the rescue vessels from again sighting the doomed *Cleveco*. In spite of severe icing conditions, the *Ossipee* continued to search for the balance of the afternoon and night. The motor lifeboats, so heavily encased in ice that their self-bailing facilities were inoperable, had to return to their stations. Sometime during that wild night the barge went to the bottom with all hands. It is significant to note, too, that her name had recently been changed, from *Gotham 85* to *Cleveco*!

Why did the *Admiral* perish so quickly? It was obvious to sailors that she had simply flipped over without a second's warning. This is readily understandable when one reviews the condition of the sea that night, and the known fact that she was tender. The inspector had certified her stability "under reasonable operating conditions," further indicating that her stability would be doubtful if the towline were not maintained in as nearly a fore and aft line as practical. His memorandum in Washington stated flatly that "the *Admiral* was slightly deficient in stability."

Imagine then, in violent seas, the wind or a faulty steering gear, possibly both, sending the *Cleveco* in a sheer to starboard. Both vessels rising on the crests of different seas, the *Cleveco* rolling to starboard, the tug falling off to her port. The sudden strain on the taut towing hawser would have flipped the tender tug over like a pancake. There would be no time to escape, no time to open the dogged-down doors, no time, even, to think. It would be all over in a minute for the *Admiral* and her crew of fourteen. And it was.

There is little doubt but that the strong, steel, steam tug built by Benjamin L. Cowles was a good one. Mr. Cowles took great pride in the vessels his Buffalo yard turned out, and the one in question was not an exception. The seventy-one-foot, eighty-five-gross-ton tug, after the usual ceremonies and a blow from a champagne bottle, came sliding and smoking down the ways in 1907, bearing the name of the man for whom she was built—*John Kelderhouse*. In the service of her owner she did all that was asked of her for many years and continued, with the same name, to perform efficiently for the Empire Engineering Company, the firm that later acquired her. In 1924 she appeared to be just what the Dunbar & Sullivan Dredging Company of Detroit was looking for in the way of another craft to tow and service their rather considerable fleet of dipper, hydraulic, and clamshell dredges along with a complementary armada of scows, drill boats, and associated gear. They bought her and immediately changed her name to *Sachem*, a title signifying the mightiest of Indian chiefs. Someone with a delightful sense of humor, probably an Irishman, is responsible for naming the assorted craft belonging to the Dunbar & Sullivan organization. They have some conventional names, too, but imagine tugs named *Sachem*, *Shaughraun*, *Shaun Rhue*, *Spalpeen*, *Paddy Miles*, and *Nanny Goat*. Fancy such names for dredges, big ones, too, as *Omadhoun*, *Old Hickory*, *Tipperary Boy*, *Pocantico*, *Handy Andy*, and a drill boat named *Earthquake*. Glorious!

The *Sachem* fitted in perfectly with the dredging firm. It is not glamorous work hauling mud scows out to the dumping grounds or shifting them under the dredge buckets or hauling a lumbering big dipper dredge hundreds of miles to a new working site. The Dunbar & Sullivan firm had extensive contracts all over the Great Lakes. Its equipment had to be mobile and adaptable to any of many varying working conditions.

The quality Mr. Cowles built into the old tug was still apparent when the dredging firm had her completely reconditioned in 1947 and during the winter of 1949-50 had her aged steam engine and boiler replaced with a big diesel engine. The diesel equipment was smaller than the old steam plant but much more powerful.

In 1950 the Dunbar & Sullivan people had work in the Dunkirk, New York, harbor. The usual array of equipment was on hand, including the sturdy and revitalized old *Sachem*. As was customary on a long job, many dredge and tug crews had found temporary homes in Dunkirk, many of them staying at the Park Avenue Hotel. By mid-December cold weather brought progress on the dredging project to a near halt. It was time to batten down for the season, remove the large dredges and scows to protected winter moorings, and secure all floating gear. This was the *Sachem*'s job. Many of the casual laborers on the project had already been dismissed for the season. There remained a considerable number of men responsible for the floating equipment.

The *Sachem* was scheduled to depart Dunkirk on Saturday morning, December sixteenth, 1950, with the big dipper dredge *Omadhaun* in tow. She would take her east to Buffalo where the ponderous dredge would be moored for the winter. The *Sachem* would then return to Dunkirk to tow the derrick scow, *Ohio*, to Detroit. Presumably, then, her labors would be over for the year.

The holiday spirit was in the air. After being away from home since April, all hands were looking forward to Christmas with their families. Daniel Ryan, the *Sachem*'s substitute cook, was taking the place of Sidney O'Laughlin, the regular cook. O'Laughlin had taken a nasty fall on the tug's deck and was taken to Brooks Hospital, in Dunkirk, for observation. Ryan had already done his Christmas shopping for his wife and five children, back in Port Clinton, Ohio. Employees at the Park Avenue Hotel had helped him wrap the presents. He had placed them in his car, which he had driven to the Central Avenue dock so he could leave for home immediately when the *Sachem* returned from Buffalo.

Russell McKinney would be leaving for Sault Ste. Marie, Michigan, as soon as the tug docked. He parked his car in a service station near the dock.

Ten of the men scheduled to leave with the *Sachem*, on Saturday morning, had been residents of the hotel all summer. Since they would not see many of the other dredge and vessel people until the following spring, they held their annual Christmas party at the hotel on Friday night. The men in the marine construction and dredging field have earned a reputation for being a hardworking lot who play just as hard as they labor. A friendly, outgoing, and often boisterous group when relaxing, they are usually not averse to taking a drop or two of spirits, sometimes many drops. They did nothing that Friday night to tarnish their reputation. They laughed long and loud over humorous incidents of the past season and recalled choice stories from others. The Park Avenue Hotel was a happy place that night. It was a splendid affair.

Early on Saturday morning Captain Hector Church maneuvered the *Sachem* into position, took aboard the big towing hawser, and proceeded to pull the cumbersome *Omadhaun* slowly out the main channel, protected on the west side by a pier nearly 1500 feet long. Holding her steady until he reached deep water, Captain Church then hauled to starboard on a northeasterly course to Buffalo, thirty-seven miles away. The morning was cold and clear, the lake almost "flat," ideal towing weather. It remained so all day and in midafternoon the *Sachem* duly delivered her charge to its assigned winter mooring quarters. Captain Church told all hands that the tug would be leaving for Dunkirk at six o'clock Monday morning. Some stayed aboard the *Sachem*. Others, left to their own devices, scattered to the favorite haunts of sailors and dredgemen. Buffalo provided a wealth of diversions, and they would find them.

The weather on Monday morning, December eighteenth,

was below freezing—twenty-three degrees, to be exact. The wind was from the north, northwest, with intermittent snow squalls. There was nothing to be concerned about, weather-wise. Not all the men were on hand at six o'clock and Captain Church delayed departure for about twenty minutes. One by one the tardy ones arrived, some by taxi. Finally, all were aboard and accounted for but Max Tobin. Captain Church reluctantly ordered the lines cast off. Tobin could still catch a Greyhound bus for Dunkirk, and would probably arrive before the tug.

There were twelve men on the *Sachem* when she cleared Buffalo piers, some of them members of the dredge crew. One man aboard was not a Dunbar & Sullivan employee. He was Hans Von Frankenstein, of Winnetka, Illinois, a diesel expert who was making some minor adjustments on the tug's new diesel engine. It had given Chief Engineer George Burns no serious trouble; the work was routine.

At ten minutes after seven Captain Irwin P. Paulson, master of the steamer, *Venus*, sighted the *Sachem* about one mile west of Waverly Shoal Buoy. As far as is known, he was the last mortal to see her afloat.

When, in due course of time, the *Sachem* failed to make Dunkirk harbor, the Coast Guard began a massive search program. On the chance that there had been a misunder-standing as to the tug's destination, and Captain Church had set a course for Detroit, a radar-equipped Coast Guard cutter stayed "on station" near the Pelee Passage to intercept her. Police at all United States and Canadian ports were requested to check their harbors, in the event the tug had put in with mechanical troubles. The *Sachem* had no transmitter but could receive radio messages. Motor lifeboats from the Erie and Buffalo lifesaving stations put out to retrace the *Sachem*'s course. The Coast Guard cutters *Tupelo* and *Acacia* joined the search, and one of the service's Catalina planes ranged low and far, covering both Canadian and American waters. The few lake steamers still operating on Lake Erie were advised to keep a sharp watch for survivors or debris. The intensive hunt failed to turn up a single life jacket, oar, the tug's lifeboat, or a single scrap of evidence of any kind.

Ten days after the *Sachem* disappeared, wreckage began to come ashore—not much, to be sure, but enough to indicate that she had gone down off Silver Creek, New York, not far from Dunkirk. A couple of life preservers and three oil drums were little enough in the way of clues, but they were enough.

An oil slick out in the lake was investigated by the cutter *Tupelo* on December twenty-third, and her sounding apparatus indicated an unidentified underwater object of some proportions in eighty feet of water. A buoy was dropped to mark the location. The Dunbar & Sullivan people began to bring in other tugs and divers.

On December twenty-ninth the word spread quickly that the *Sachem*'s lifeboat had been found. It was discovered in the shorefast ice at Sunset Bay, overturned, and almost buried by the ice. It was in fairly good condition, except for a deep dent in one side. The name, *Sachem*, was clearly stenciled on its thwarts. Trucked back to Buffalo, the lifeboat was being unloaded when a worker noticed scratches near the keel. From the right angle they spelled out a message: "T. Boice . . . Can't hold." Thomas Boice was an oiler on the *Sachem*!

Working against deteriorating weather, ice floes, and winter winds, the divers finally reached the object in early January, confirmed that it was, indeed, the ill-fated *Sachem*, and made a search for bodies. They found none. Curiously, the life-belt chest had been emptied and the cover replaced! During their thorough examinations, the only ones they were able to make before ice and high seas brought a halt to all salvage work, they found no evidence of an explosion or fire, no ruptured plating, no reason at all, actually, for the tug to be on the bottom of Lake Erie.

The *Sachem*'s people, as if penitent for missing Christmas at home with their loved ones and reluctant to foregather with friends as they had that Friday night at the Park Avenue Hotel, came wandering ashore at various places, from the fifth of January until late September.

During the winter there were indications that long and bitter litigation would follow, with legal action instigated by the surviving kin of the lost crew. Much would depend, though, on what was found when the *Sachem* was raised, which the Dunbar & Sullivan people had indicated would be done.

In June of 1951 the salvage flotilla hovered once more over the grave of the *Sachem*. Divers searched the hull again without finding any reason for the foundering. There was no dislocation of equipment to indicate an explosion of any kind. Glass in the engineer's gauges was intact. The tug, however, had settled in mud almost up to her gunwales. Luggage and personal effects were sent up as they were found. One bag, belonging to the diesel expert, Hans Von Frankenstein, contained gaily wrapped neckties he had apparently intended as Christmas gifts for crewmen.

It took all summer to prepare the *Sachem* for lifting, placing slings under the hull and attaching them to a steel framework that would prevent them from slipping. The lift was to be made not by the Dunbar & Sullivan equipment but by the big derrick scow *Cherokee* of the Merritt-Chapman & Scott Corporation, another major dredging and marine contracting firm. The *Cherokee*, anchored almost directly over the wreck, broke the tug loose from her blanket of mud and brought her to the surface on Monday, October twenty-second. Lashed to the stern of the monster scow, the *Sachem* made a slow and solem trip to Dunkirk harbor, the scene of her happy departure ten months earlier. Scarcely had the equipment been tied up to the Central Avenue dock when pumps were put to work dewatering the tug. It didn't take long. When the pumps were shut off the *Sachem* floated dry and free. Alternate lifts of the bow and stern ends revealed no damage of any kind to the hull . . . no evidence of an explosion or collision with an underwater object. Captain George P. Kennedy, chairman of the Coast Guard investigating board, and Commander Willis Bruso made a close-up inspection from a rowboat. The hull was, apparently, as sound as a dollar.

Inside a layer of silt and mud lay over everything. Down in the engineroom the investigating board found nothing in the way of a clue to the sinking. The engine was connected with the pilothouse control. It was in the "stop" position. Sediment, silt, and rust clearly indicated that it had not been moved during the salvage operations. The engine itself was securely mounted to its "bed," with no signs of excessive vibration. The framing and plating on the engineroom shipsides were found in good condition, with no cracked paint or loose rivets or other signs of severe vibration. The seacocks and all piping were found to be in a sound condition, without breaks or fractures.

In the pilothouse the helm and rudder were found to be in the "hard right" position. In the presence of board members the helm was moved and the rudder brought back to amidships. Nothing was wrong with the steering mechanism. Significantly, too, the emergency alarm switch was in the open position, indicating that the alarm bells had not been sounded.

Over a fire extinguisher in the galley—and this is important only to those who lean to superstitions—a horseshoe hung, placed there, no doubt, by a crewman who sought good luck for his ship. But, possibly due to misinformation on his part, it hung with the open end down, supposedly an omen of bad luck.

The *Sachem*, afloat and dry, yielded no more clues as to

what had happened than she had while still under eighty feet of water, off Silver Creek.

Coincidentally, as the enigma of the *Sachem* was being studied, President Herbert L. Daggett of the National Marine Engineers Beneficial Association was in Washington, pointing up some distressing facts to a House subcommittee.

Mr. Daggett was referring to technicalities that rendered operators of most diesel-powered craft exempt from the annual Coast Guard inspections of their vessels. His particular concern was not necessarily the motive power involved, but the lifesaving gear that normally came under Coast Guard scrutiny—life vests, flares, rafts, lifeboats, davits, and, of course, the hull itself. He did not refer directly to the *Sachem*, but cited the loss of the diesel tug, *Lorraine*, and her crew in Chesapeake Bay only two months earlier. The tug's lifeboat had proved practically useless, he claimed, because of neglect and deterioration—a condition that would not have been permitted to exist had the fact she was diesel-driven not exempted her from an annual inspection by the Coast Guard.

The Coast Guard board investigating the loss of the *Sachem* did its best to solve the riddle of why an apparently sound vessel should suddenly go missing. Usually in a case of this kind they had little to work with. But now, even with "exhibit A"—the tug itself—they could point to no definite or even probable cause. The *Sachem* was last inspected as a steam tug on September 2, 1949. Upon her conversion to diesel power she commenced operation as an uninspected motor vessel in late September of 1950.

The board interviewed thirteen persons and took depositions from two more. They included Edward A. Koonman and Erbin D. Wattles, vice president and superintendent, respectively, of the Dunbar & Sullivan Dredging Company; William Booth, a former master of the *Sachem*; Captain

Irwin P. Paulson, master of the steamer, *Venus*, and the last person to see the tug before it was lost; three tugmen who had worked on the *Sachem*; George Boice, brother of the tug's oiler, Thomas Boice; Donald MacGregor, superintendent of the Merritt-Chapman & Scott salvage team; five professional divers who had worked on the project; and John F. Finnegan, Jr., a salvage worker. None could shed any light on the strange disappearance of the *Sachem*.

The ship's log and the personal diaries and records kept by Assistant Engineer Frank Reynolds and diesel expert Hans Von Frankenstein had been salvaged on one of the early dives, shortly after the sunken tug had been located. Neither the log nor individual accounts had noted any mechanical difficulties, either with the new diesel engine or any of the ancillary equipment. The board did indicate, however, that the change from steam to diesel probably resulted in a great increase in power.

> It appears [said the board's report] that a possible corresponding marked increase in rudder forces and in the size and proportion of the bow wave may have been a contributing factor to the *Sachem*'s foundering. To conclude this report, the evidence indicates that the vessel was swamped and sank, rather than capsized and sank. The vessel has been salvaged and towed to Detroit, Michigan, for possible reconditioning and employment again as a towing tug.

Life aboard tugs has changed greatly since the end of World War II and the great swing to diesel power. Gone are the days of steaming out to sea to "dump ashes," and the frequent trips upriver to get coal bunkers. Gone are the rusty and dirty boiler casings, coal on the firehold floor, the stifling heat, and the great, oily, clanking engine. Today, the harbor-tug captain could come to work in his Sunday suit and often takes his towing assignment by radio-telephone from a dispatcher a couple of hundred miles away. The engineer works in clean surroundings around his big gray and chrome diesel engine. His fuel supply may last him a month, and the dust, ashes, and clinkers of the steam-tug days are but a memory.

Something has been lost, however, that can never be replaced. Today's harbor tugs, operating around the clock, will have three different crews in a twenty-four-hour period, and may frequently switch from one tug to another. There is no bond of feeling such as once existed between men and the vessels they sailed. Around the turn of the century, amidst the brawling and competitive years of tugboating on the Great Lakes, a sailor developed a great affection for his tug. His tug, since few sailors had an abode ashore or a family to return to when the day was done, was his home. Here, he worked, ate, and slept. He shared its adventures and accidents. The crew and tug passed through lean years and fat. In spring freshet or winter storm they worked as one, each aware of the other's imperfections and each, in his way, forgiving and repentant. Long ago, probably about the time the *Sachem* first felt the touch of fresh water, an eloquent sailor, long since gone to his reward, best expressed the feeling of an old tugboat man for his ship:

> *In the heart of ev'ry human is a feelin' kinder soft.*
> *Fer the bidin' place he's used to, even if it's a loft,*
> *An' a-settin' on the towpost when we're docked here,*
>   *all alone,*
> *I feel sorry fer the man that has no place to call*
>   *his own.*
>
> *With my pipe lit an' a-puffin', with the bridge lamps*
>   *shinin' red,*
> *An' the black smoke hangin' heavy in the air just*
>   *overhead,*
> *An' the garbage in the river bobbin' up an' down,*
>   *you see*
> *There's a heap o' satisfaction to a homebody like me.*

Other men may have their millions an' their houses,
    big and grand,
But I ain't got any envy fer them people of this land;
Twenty years I've bunked down forrard in the old
    Rebecca Nye—
She has been my home an' will be, if I'm lucky,
    till I die.

Home—yes, home is where the heart is, an' the old
    Rebecca's mine;
I blowed up with in in '80, sunk with her in '89.
Ev'ry plank an' rope an' rivet, ev'ry bolthead is
    a friend,
True an' firm an' tried an' trusted, on the which I
    can depend.

Twenty years I've slept down forrard in the same
    familiar bunk
With exception of occasions when it happened I
    was drunk.
With exception of occasions of a sorry kind when I
Let the wicked city tempt me from the old
    Rebecca Nye.

This is home—the greasy water an' the sulphur an'
    the smoke,
An' the smell that comes a-floatin' up the river till
    you choke,
An' the tootin' o' the whistle, an' the crashin', splashin'
    sound
As the whizzin' old propeller swings some passin'
    boat around.

This is home—the steward callin' like a voice out
    of the tomb,
Tellin' us to come to supper down there aft the
    engineroom.
This is home—with us a-groanin' up the river, pullin'
    slow,

An' as we go chasin' outside nosin' round to find
  a tow.

Let them kings who live in castles be as proudish as
  they please;
Let them wade around in carpets that reach up to
  their knees,
That an' such things may be their idy of a home,
  but I'd
Ruther have my bunk down forrard on the old
  Rebecca Nye.

The old *Sachem*, née *John Kelderhouse*, still goes about her workaday tasks for the Dunbar & Sullivan Dredging Company, towing muddy scows out to the dumping ground, hauling the big dredges from port to port, and nudging a fleet of scows and barges into position. She is often seen, thus employed, and, of those who view her, only the real sailors will recall that her name was changed and remember her as the ghost ship that took her entire crew down with her, but lived to sail another day.

One would hope that the horseshoe hanging in the galley, if it is still there, has been reversed.

13

That Damnable Nuisance, Mrs. Doupe

GEORGIAN BAY—AN INTRODUCTION

This is the story of Georgian Bay, three ships, the prophetic dream of a young bride, five sailors' caps, and of a young couple named Duncan Tinkiss and Christine Morrison. The latter two, meeting for the first time in a lifeboat, should, in the time-honored, storyland world of the romanticist, have lived happily together ever after. But while they may indeed have lived happily it was not together. All the elements of drama were there, but it just didn't work out that way.

First, there is Georgian Bay, sort of an eastern extension of Lake Huron, and a body of water so large that it rivals Lake Ontario in size. The Bruce Peninsula, jutting up from the level farmland of lower Ontario, curves gradually westward in a crescent-shaped arm that extends and ends far up on Lake Huron. Then, like offshore jewels, Flowerpot and Cove islands, both south of the main channel between Georgian Bay and Lake Huron, seem to beckon the venturesome onward. Beyond the main channel—as though the Supreme Architect had missed a step or two while blazing a watery trail of stepping-stones to the setting sun—come Yoe Island, Fitzwilliam Island, and, then, still following a westward curve,

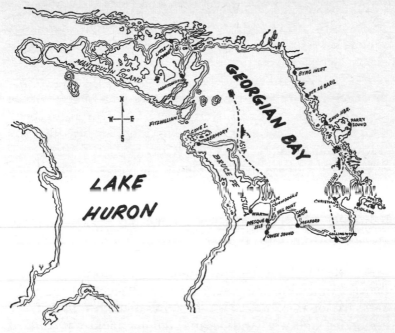

is big, sprawling Manitoulin Island. Beyond Manitoulin lie Cockburn and Drummond islands, only the latter is in United States waters. To the east of the Bruce Peninsula and the lower end of the chain of oddly assorted islands stretches Georgian Bay, to the west the vastness of upper Lake Huron.

Lake Attigouaton, as the Ojibways called Georgian Bay, was the first of the great sweet-water seas to be discovered by a white man, explorer Samuel de Champlain, who was really searching for the legendary Northwest Passage to China. Strangely, too, it is still the least known of the great chain of fresh-water lakes. With the exception of the cottages and lodges of summer vacationers, pleasant towns, and charming little villages, the area has, most fortunately, been bypassed by the great despoilers—big cities and heavy industry. The water is clear, cool, and deep, the air unsullied by the smoke, dust, and fumes that typify the the great cities to the south.

Thirty-thousand islands, most of them along its eastern shore, and a truly amazing number of reefs, banks, and barely submerged rocks have helped Georgian Bay acquire its reputation among navigators as the "Graveyard of the Lakes." Nor do the Bruce Peninsula or the islands of the western approaches deter the great northwest gales that come romping down Lake Superior and over upper Lake Huron, to spend their full fury on Georgian Bay, building up seas that are truly monumental.

"You have to see 'em to believe 'em," philosophized one old skipper.

In 1879, when our saga begins, the hand of man had but lightly touched the shores of Georgian Bay. At the southern end the towns of note, simply because they were the jumping-off point for whatever and whoever went north, were Collingwood, Meaford, and Owen Sound. To the north and along the eastern area of the bay, the few settlements of the maps or charts of the inletted shore were there because of the lumbering industry. And because the mainland was studded with a thousand lakes, laced with ridges of pre-Cambrian rock, and overgrown with dense pine forests, roads were few and those existing impassable much of the year. The ships that plied Georgian Bay then were the only really dependable tie to the civilization to the south, an indispensable lifeline without which significant economic progress would have been almost impossible.

In addition to the people who were dependent upon them for transportation, the creaking but sturdy old package freighters hauled in every commodity used or needed—from cook stoves, livestock, and hay to canned foods, dry goods, flour, sawmill machinery, and patent medicines. The village-store or lumber-camp commissary could not have long existed without them. During the last few stormy weeks of fall, before ice ended all navigation, they brought in truly staggering cargoes of winter supplies—their holds, even their decks and spare cabins piled high with bags, bales, boxes, and crates. Some made Parry Sound, Byng Inlet, and Little Current their major stops. Others ranged through the main channel, touched at docks along rocky and lonely Manitoulin Island and the wooded shores of the North Channel, before wandering up the historic St. Marys River to the fabled Soo country. Their hauntingly mellow old chime whistles were the harbinger of spring in a quiet land where timber was king. The "Gallant Old Ladies of Georgian Bay" the land-lubbers often called them and one wonders, considering the uncounted hazards of navigating those specific waters in gales and blizzards, if, indeed, the old saying, "the days of wooden ships and iron men," did not originate here, or at least the fresh-water version. Of the many vessels that plied the almost unknown waters over the years and left their bones in the dark and cold waters, three are pertinent to our tale of Georgian Bay . . . the *Waubuno, Jane Miller*, and the *Asia*.

*   *   *   *   *

At noon on November 21, 1879, the side-wheel steamer *Waubuno* lay moored to her dock at Collingwood with a very unhappy skipper pacing the pilothouse. Capt. George Burkett was, under normal conditions, a patient, kindly man. But conditions had not been normal for some time and every hour seemed to add to his burdens, little problems, big problems, all vexing. The *Waubuno* should have been halfway to Parry Sound at the moment, but a heavy fall gale had been pounding Georgian Bay since late the previous evening. Even in the harbor the fourteen-year-old ship had grown restless under the booming winds, creaking and groaning while her hawsers whined protestingly at the extra duty demanded of them. Captain Burkett had been forced to postpone sailing until the weather moderated. The usual heavy November freight had always been an exceedingly heterogeneous mixture that, already aboard the ship, included a team of horses, several cows, a quantity of boxed apples, hundreds of boxes of miscellaneous goods, a donkey engine, bagged oats, sugar, and a number of cartons of tea. The cargo had long since been safely stowed, the animals led to close-confinement stalls. The captain was ready to go and so was the *Waubuno*, if only the persistent gale would moderate. And then there were the passengers, the usual lot—some uncomplaining, others querulous and annoying—insisting upon knowing when the winds would abate and just when the *Waubuno* would sail, as if Captain Burkett had the power to still the storm and quiet the waters. Even the animals seemed to be nervous and unhappy, whinnying and mooing at inconvenient hours.

One of the passengers the captain knew well, a Mr. B. Noel Fisher, publisher of the Parry Sound newspaper, the *North Star*. Mr. Fisher had every confidence in Captain Burkett, knew he would sail when it became possible to do so without undue risk to the ship and her passengers. Others were people he knew on sight, the Sylvesters, Mr. Griffith, and a half-dozen men he recognized as connected with the lumber business.

Quite another matter were young Dr. and Mrs. W. D. Doupe, the newlyweds. Dr. Doupe was undoubtedly a noble fellow. He had recently completed his medical training, and, instead of hanging out his shingle in a populous community where success would certainly have come sooner, he chose to begin a pioneering practice in remote and lonely McKeller Village, far beyond Parry Sound, where the Doupes would debark with his modest medical paraphernalia, their furniture, and luggage. But while Dr. Doupe obviously viewed his profession with idealistic dedication, Mrs. Doupe, although young and pretty, was a damnable nuisance.

During the previous night, while the wind howled around the *Waubuno*'s rigging, Mrs. Doupe had been visited by a particularly horrifying and realistic dream, during which

she saw the *Waubuno* wrecked and her husband and fellow
passengers in the cold water fighting for their lives. In the
morning she told the doctor about the dream and tearfully
begged him not to depart on the *Waubuno* but to wait for
another ship, better weather, or, best of all, another means
of getting to McKeller Village. But the doctor made light of
the entire matter, attributing his wife's fear to a bad case of
nerves.

Born with a great dread of water and a vivid imagination,
Mrs. Doupe was also highly articulate, and compulsively related her dream to all the other passengers and the crew.
Before noon everybody scheduled to sail on the *Waubuno*
and many in the town of Collingwood had heard the grim
details, either from Mrs. Doupe or those in whom she had
confided.

Meeting the doctor and his wife in a companionway, Captain Burkett had sought to allay her fears. This had led to
some rather firm words between the young couple, perhaps
their first lovers' quarrel. The good doctor had, in no uncertain terms, told his wife that their furniture and effects
were already on board, their tickets paid for, and that, in any
event, they could not afford the long trip by land—by way of
Gravenhurst. In the end, still tearful, Mrs. Doupe retired to
her cabin, promising to say no more about the matter.

As the evening of November twenty-first wore on, Captain
Burkett sat in the pilothouse. Intermittent snow squalls
lashed the windows, the snow melted as it touched the glass,
turning to rivulets that dripped steadily off the outside sills.
Many of the passengers, certain that the *Waubuno* would not
sail until the following morning, had taken rooms at the
local hotel or were staying the night with friends. Tongues
were wagging all over town, he concluded, but there was little
he could do about that now. His primary responsibility was
his ship, her cargo, and future cargoes.

The *Waubuno* was built in 1865, a strong side-wheeler

about a hundred and fifty feet long and forty feet of beam. *Waubuno* was in itself an odd name for a ship since in the member tribes of the Algonquin Indian family, Waubuno was the highest form of "black art," or magic. Practitioners of the art, or Waubunos, and they were few, were said to be able to cast an evil spell upon their enemies—a spell from which there was no escape.

In her early years the *Waubuno* had combed the entire north shore, picking up and dropping off freight and passengers wherever such trade offered, sometimes at ports where the only sign of civilization was a Hudson's Bay Company post. She had worked hard and well, her earnings helping to pay for larger and faster vessels. But, more recently, somewhat weakened by age and her machinery no longer able to cope with the gales encountered in Lake Superior and upper Lake Huron, she had been relegated to the shorter Parry Sound-to-Collingwood route, where the trade, while growing enormously, did not commit the vessel to extended periods of wracking seas. During the years, because of her pioneering prowling in the uncharted waters along the north shore, her skippers had become more or less legendary figures. First, there was Captain Symes, a magnificent seaman who could "smell a rock" a mile before its menacing bulk appeared. Then came Captain Peter ("Black Pete") Campbell, the man who feared no seas and put his ship head to in the worst of them. And, finally, there was Captain Burkett who sometimes wondered if Captain Campbell's insistence on bucking the gales rather than anchoring behind a sheltering island had not contributed to the *Waubuno*'s infirmities.

The *Waubuno* and several other vessels were owned, in part, by William Beatty, of Parry Sound, who also had extensive lumber interests. Mr. Beatty had once hoped to carve a model temperance community out of the forest. But the lumbering industry required many lumberjacks, a roistering breed of men, he discovered, who were the least likely candididates for the temperance philosophy. So, thereafter, Mr. Beatty had concentrated on owning ships and selling lumber, both highly profitable.

Compounding Captain Burkett's problems was a situation over which he had no control, although his owners were loathe to face the facts. A rival company, the Georgian Bay Lumber Company, had entered the trade, putting on the Parry Sound-to-Collingwood run a much newer and faster steamer, the *Magnettawan*, skippered by Captain John O'Donnell.

The *Magnettawan*, due to her superior speed and ability to dodge in and out of ports with a minimum of time lost, was picking up freight and passengers ahead of the *Waubuno* with embarrassing and exasperating frequency. It was no secret, either, that Captain Burkett had been chided more than once by his owners for permitting this to happen, although the *Waubuno* was in no position to outsail or out-weather her adversary. As a matter of fact, the *Magnettawan* was even then tethered to a nearby dock, taking on freight and passengers, her scheduled sailing time ten o'clock on the morning of the twenty-second. And Captain Burkett did not take kindly to the idea of being outsailed. He knew, too, from long experience that the dock at Parry Sound would undoubtedly hold a heavy freight consignment, and that shippers, not being particular, usually gave it to the first vessel on the scene.

These considerations, perhaps subconsciously, may have weighed heavily in the decision Captain Burkett made when he noted that, at three o'clock on the morning of the twenty-second, the force of the wind had abated considerably. At three o'clock he was notified that George Playter, a young man who had been scheduled to join the crew as a wheels-man, had decided not to make the trip. Mrs. Doupe's dream had had nothing to do with the decision, Playter told the mate; he had just concluded to "call it a season." The matter was a minor one since Captain Burkett, if necessary, could take a turn at the wheel. At three-thirty the Captain, after stealing a glance at the dock where the *Magnettawan* lay dark and quiet, with only her red and green running lights aglow, notified his chief engineer that the ship would sail in half an hour, promptly at four o'clock!

No attempt was made to notify those who had scattered to various private homes to spend the night, but John Rowland, the *Waubuno*'s purser, was sent running to the Globe Hotel, operated by his father, John, Sr., to rouse as many passengers as he could. The response was not great, and Captain Burkett was in no mood to spend another hour, perhaps two, rounding them up, listening to their protests, and counting noses once they were aboard. He was going to beat the *Magnettawan* to Parry Sound. Slowly, one by one, a few of those quartered at the hotel found their way to the dock, fighting the cold wind every inch of the way and in a bit of a temper when they arrived. Counting the sleeping doctor and his wife, the passengers aboard the *Waubuno* at four o'clock numbered ten. The crew roster was fourteen.

Captain Burkett was probably hoping that Mrs. Doupe would not have another dream, but, if so, he knew that she would very likely be too seasick to tell anybody about it.

Despite the almost secret departure of the *Waubuno*, word of the intended sailing did reach a few of her intended passengers, staying either at the hotel or with friends, but when they arrived at the dock the ship was already a hundred yards away and fast disappearing in the darkness of a cold and windy November morn. However loud their cries of anger and disappointment, the deed was done. They would not sail on the *Waubuno* that trip.

Steaming almost directly north from Collingwood, the *Waubuno* came abreast of Christian Island a short time later. On shore, lighthouse keeper John Hoar, recognizing her lights, duly logged her passing, reporting: "A stiff wind from the nor'west but ship seemed to be riding well with full cargo."

On the normal route of the *Waubuno* the twenty-eight miles between Hope Island and Lone Rock was really the only exposed area where she would be subject to the full force of the winds sweeping in from the northwest, a considerable part of which could be avoided by steering for Moose Point and running into the sound by way of the South Channel. The decision to do this, however, was usually predicated upon the visibility at the time, since the entire area is a maze of reefs and rocks. A shipmaster had to know exactly where he was at any given moment.

It is supposed that Captain Burkett, for a time, had enjoyed good visibility, since he had obviously chosen the protected passage. But the wiles of Mother Nature are unpredictable. Eight hours after the *Waubuno*'s departure from Collingwood, while the snow came in impenetrable, wind-driven sheets, lumbermen working near Moose Point heard her whistle, somewhere off the point, coming in sharp, repeated, desperate blasts. A mariner would have instantly recognized the sound of a ship in distress, but mariners weren't chopping wood on Moose Point that day. The lumbermen concluded that the ship was signaling to someone on an island, a rather common practice.

Six hours after the *Waubuno* had taken French leave of some of her passengers, the *Magnettawan*, true to her announced schedule, also left her Collingwood dock. The weather, however, once his ship got out in the bay, did not meet with the approval of Captain O'Donnell. His ship, rolling badly in high seas, was causing considerable discomfort to his passengers and knocking the freight cargo about. Captain O'Donnell, quickly concluding that this was not a day to be testing the seaworthiness of his vessel, wisely hauled to starboard and the shelter offered behind Christian Island.

What's more, he lay there at anchor for nearly forty hours while the gale built up monstrous seas on Georgian Bay and the snow was so heavy he rarely caught a glimpse of the island that protected him.

At noon on Monday, the twenty-fourth, Captain O'Donnell, bringing the *Magnettawan* to her dock at Parry Sound, was agreeably surprised to see a large pile of freight on hand, but was somewhat mystified by the absence of the *Waubuno*. He had fully expected to meet her, outbound, with the freight that still lay there, waiting. Obviously, the *Waubuno* had never arrived!

The search started immediately with the tug, *Mittie Grew*, of the Parry Sound Lumber Company, and other craft, exploring the South Channel and the thousands of coves and inlets where the *Waubuno* might have been driven ashore, her people still safe. Of the *Waubuno* they found nothing, but lacing the rocks and shore was much of her cargo—apples by the thousands and scores of boxes and crates—flotsam from which the Indians and half-breeds salvaged enough calico and ready-made clothing to keep them living in high style for years.

Strangely, too, every one of the *Waubuno*'s life jackets were recovered, none of them showing any sign of having been used. Whatever happened, the end came quickly.

Experienced seamen later reconstructed what must have been the terrible dilemma faced by Captain Burkett. Visibility at Christian Island, when the *Waubuno* passed, had been good, but when she came to the end of the northern leg of the course, at Lone Rock, she encountered a blinding snowstorm. No captain, without being able to see the rock, would risk turning into the narrow western entrance to the sound. Captain Burkett, then, apparently turned back and headed for the gap between Moose Deer Point and Copperhead. His navigation was excellent, but he was not aware of an uncharted shoal known now as the Haystacks. In despera-

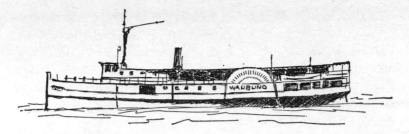

tion he must have dropped his anchors. They did not hold, and it is thought that it was there, trapped in the wild breakers, he began sounding the distress signals heard by the lumberjacks on Moose Point.

Four months after she vanished, the hull of the *Waubuno* was found floating upside down in a serene bay behind Moose Point and east of the Haystacks. All her machinery and cabins were gone, again the theory being that she was rolled over, her machinery and cargo carrying her cabins and people to the bottom.

In 1962 the *Waubuno's* big anchor, discovered and recovered by scuba divers, was placed in the town square at Parry Sound, with appropriate services. It was eighty-three years late in making port.

Curiously, none of the *Waubuno's* company of ten passengers was ever found, although the search continued until the winter freeze-up and was resumed the following spring. More wreckage was discovered but no bodies.

Still, one cannot say that the *Waubuno* went her tragic way without leaving her mark on the charts of today—charts that, had they existed in 1879, would have undoubtedly guided Captain Burkett safely into Parry Sound. The narrow, western rock-studded entrance to the sound, where Captain Burkett apparently turned back, is now on the charts as Waubuno Channel. The island behind which the overturned hull was found the following March, is, significantly, marked Wreck Island. And directly downwind from where the *Wau-*

buno was struggling for her life in the breakers, a stone out-cropping, barely breaking the surface, is called Burkett Rock. Farther to the south and slightly west is Rowland Rock, named, no doubt, for John Rowland, the *Waubuno*'s purser. Even John Hoar, the Christian Island lighthouse keeper, the last mortal to see the vanished ship, is remembered by Hoar Point, off Hope Island.

There is, however, nothing in the way of a reef, rock, or landmark named for Mrs. Doupe, the young bride whose dream revealed the terrible and last voyage of the *Waubuno*, well in advance of her sailing.

Mrs. Doupe, from her spot in Heaven, would undoubtedly have given her approval to such a project. It would have been her way of saying, throughout eternity: "I told you so!"

14

. . . And Then There Were Two

By their late arrival at the Owen Sound dock of the Northwestern Transportation Company's steamer *Asia*, Duncan Tinkiss and his uncle, J. H. Tinkiss, missed much of the last-minute confusion that is inherent in the loading of a passenger and freight ship—the bawling of the teamsters, the grumbling of the purser, the shouting stevedores, and the thumping and bumping as heavy crates, boxes, bags, and bales are manhandled through the gangways. It was the organized bedlam that always preceded the departure of the combination vessels carrying people and supplies to the northern Georgian Bay ports. The present cargo was the *Asia*'s largest of the season, much of it winter stocks for north shore merchants. It was eleven o'clock on a cold and windy night in September of 1882, the thirteenth, to be specific. Fortunately, the Tinkiss cabin was snug and warm. Duncan, stepping around crates and bales lashed to the passenger deck to take another look at the scene before retiring, saw the last of the *Asia*'s cargo coming aboard: four teams of heavy workhorses, destined for a winter of labor in the lumber camps, and five cows consigned to a proud and hopeful farmer somewhere on Manitoulin Island. The impatient animals had been tethered at the dock most of the day, snort ing and mooing their discontent. But they clumped aboard to their close-confinement stalls without protest, thankful, perhaps, for the shelter.

Not far down the passenger deck from the Tinkiss cabin was that of Miss Christine Morrison, who was also aboard by reason of being late—not for the *Asia* but the *Northern Belle*, which had departed that morning. Miss Morrison, bound for Grand Marais, Michigan, to visit an aunt, had arrived too late to board the *Northern Belle*, but had immediately booked passage to the Soo on the *Asia*, then just beginning to load. She had discovered, in the process of arranging for her ticket, that a cousin, John McDonald, was the *Asia*'s first mate. She had gone aboard in midafternoon, heard the usual commotion as the ship took on cargo, but had emerged from her cabin only to partake of the evening meal in the dining room. She was fast asleep when Duncan Tinkiss arrived. Both were eighteen, exactly twice the age of the vessel.

The propeller, *Asia*, was typical of the several ships then calling regularly at Georgian Bay and other northern lake ports in the 1800s. Built of wood, but considered very sturdy, she was one hundred thirty-eight feet long and nearly twenty-five feet of beam. With a little crowding, such as on that night of September thirteenth, and by making the couches and chairs in the lounge available for sleeping, she could accommodate about a hundred passengers. The crew numbered twenty-five. In the Collingwood and Owen Sound to Sault Ste. Marie (Soo) run to which she was presently assigned, the *Asia* was taking the place of the regular vessel on the route, the *Manitoulin*, damaged by fire the previous May. Prior to that time the *Asia* had operated almost exclusively between Sarnia and Fort William. In 1881 she sank, but in shallow water, and so she had been raised and refitted, apparently without ill effects.

It was not more than five minutes after midnight when,

being assured that the freight gangways had been closed and secured, Captain John Savage, shouting to make himself heard above the wind that strummed and sang in the rigging, ordered the *Asia*'s lines cast off. It is a matter of record that storm warnings were supposedly in effect and that the company had considered holding the vessel in port. However, possibly after consulting Captain Savage, she was permitted to depart, although the ominous weather information was not communicated to the passengers.

Leaving Owen Sound harbor, the *Asia*, for the first eight miles of her voyage, was able to stay in the immediate lee of the Bruce Peninsula as far as Presque Isle, near Gravelly Bay, where she took on a full load of cordwood fuel. Captain Savage presumably was hoping that the heavy wood, stowed low in the ship, would tend to lessen the rather miserable roll the vessel had exhibited between Owen Sound and Presque Isle, in what he still considered to be sheltered waters. Some of it was undoubtedly the result of much of the freight being piled on the passenger deck, altering considerably the *Asia*'s normal stability characteristics.

The refueling operation took less than an hour, the ship's deckhands forming a line to relay the cordwood to the bunker pile on the firehold deck.

From Pyette Point the *Asia*'s course took her well out from land to clear Griffith Island and, later, Wingfield Point. Here, crawling northward at reduced speed because of the heavy weather, and leaving the shelter of the Bruce Peninsula, she encountered the full force of the gale on open water. The wind and seas, sweeping the full breadth of northern Lake Huron and humping noisily over Georgian Bay, were undeterred by the islands in their path. The night was pitch black, and the air filled with the spray from seas that ran as high as the *Asia*'s steering pole.

The tremendous seas were, apparently, more than Captain Savage had bargained for. The overburdened ship showed a marked tendency to fall off into the trough of the rearing graybeards, and this the captain made every effort to avoid. Duncan Tinkiss slept blissfully on. Christine Morrison, a few cabins away, was awake, on her feet, and wretchedly seasick. Once, during the terrible night, as the wind seemingly wanted to tear the ship apart and while the seas rose like black mountains, she heard a great commotion on the passenger deck. Opening her door, she inquired of the only person she knew, her cousin, First Mate John McDonald, what was going on.

"We're just untying the horses and cattle in our cargo and driving them overboard," he said in an effort to calm her fears. "Just you go back to your cabin and don't worry."

The animals, however, were quartered below, on the main freight deck, the only egress for the creatures being the freight gangways, which could not possibly be opened under the prevailing sea conditions. In any event it would not account for the deck crew being topsides. She did not question him further but noted that the men under him were cutting the lashings that held the freight to the upper-deck rails. Some they threw overboard; the rest was swept away as the rolling *Asia* occasionally put her rails into the crests of the boiling seas.

At seven-thirty the next morning Duncan Tinkiss and his uncle arose and found their way to the dining room for breakfast. Only the hardiest ate that morning and, having unwisely done so, immediately began to feel seasick and found their way back to their bunks. Tinkiss recalled that the ship's lounge was well tenanted, many people reclining on the sofas and even on the floor. The wind was still blowing a gale, the clouds were low and threatening, and the seas were still tremendous. But, perhaps, because the scene was less awesome in daylight than at night, there seemed to be not the slightest fear for the safety of the ship, among the passengers, at least. If the crew had any reservations they, of course, did not voice them. Duncan and his uncle climbed back into their bunks, where both fell asleep again, almost at once.

At nine o'clock the intensity of the gale increased, the wind literally tore the tops off the seas, sending scud and spume flying over the ship. High at daybreak, the seas now rose in the form of dark, roaring monsters, battering the wooden hull until it seemed that no work of man could continue to endure the pounding. At eleven o'clock the *Asia* fell into the troughs between the seas, and no amount of steam could get her out. Now she rolled fearfully over on her beam ends with every sea. She was done.

At the second such breathtaking roll, J. H. Tinkiss leaped from his bunk and tugged at his nephew. "Dunc," he shouted. "Jump up, the boat is doomed."

Rushing out on deck they found all confusion, the rails and stanchions crowded with people, most of them on their knees, praying. Others rushed frantically about, calling out to friends, grabbing life preservers, and adding to the madness of the moment. Duncan Tinkiss did not see the captain or any of the crew, but heard a single order to throw more cargo overboard. No effort was made, at the moment, to launch the ship's three boats, it being instantly apparent that they would have been dashed to bits against the wallowing and helpless *Asia*. Each great sea that swept over the doomed vessel rolled her almost over, and she was agonizingly slow in making even a partial recovery. With each such roll, those clinging to her expected the ship to keep on going over until she was upside down. Finally there came a sea destined to finish her. She went over, slowly enough for many to clamber up on the huricane deck. When the *Asia* went over and sank, stern first, this final outpost of salvation broke free from the superstructure and floated almost intact for a few moments before malevolent seas systematically plucked it apart.

At the moment the ship capsized, Duncan Tinkiss saw one of the lifeboats floating by, and calling for his uncle to follow, he dived into the water after it. Duncan never saw his uncle again; the boat, badly overloaded, quickly overturned and sank. The *Asia*'s people, alternately lifted to the crests and then dropped into the dark valleys, probably behaved as any large group would have under similar circumstances. Some thrashed around senselessly, shouting and clawing at bits of wreckage that could not possibly support them and tried to wrest larger pieces from those who had already claimed them for their own. Others, dazed and discouraged, just drifted away in their life preservers. One of them was William Henry, father of a boy who was later to become premier of Canada. Tinkiss, an excellent swimmer, struck out away from the wreckage and the crazed passengers who clutched at him, threatening to pull him down after them.

Christine Morrison, coming on deck when the *Asia* began to go to pieces, had a different impression. To her it seemed that only part of the ship's complement of passengers responded to the crew's efforts to get them on deck. She concluded that most of them were too seasick to care what happened. She remembered Captain Savage ordering the boats lowered when it was certain the ship was doomed. Minutes later she jumped or was swept from the disintegrating hurricane deck into the cold and punishing seas.

By a strange coincidence she was picked up by the only one of the *Asia*'s lifeboats adequate for the task it was designed to perform. Of the ship's three boats, two were ordinary double-enders, without buoyancy chambers. Both, after turning over and dumping their cargo of frightened souls into the water, floated upside down, later sinking. Captain Savage, First Mate McDonald, Second Mate Robert McNabb, purser John McDougall, a couple of passengers, a few of the crew, and three lumberjacks, bound for Little Current, had, again by some coincidence, chosen the only

self-righting lifeboat, equipped with air chambers so it would
not sink. When it drifted by him, Tinkiss swam over and
requested the help of purser John McDougall to get aboard.

Mr. McDougall, thoroughly disheartened, complied but
grumbled, "Oh, I don't think it of any use."

There were eighteen in the lifeboat when the winds
carried it beyond the spreading circle of wreckage and
screaming survivors. Tinkiss was relieved to have the scene
of misery and suffering behind him.

Under the direction of Captain Savage, the ship's crew
settled down to the oars and pulled for land, twenty miles to
the east, according to the Captain's reckoning. But the first
really big sea overturned the boat. When it righted itself,
all but one oar was gone. So were four of the occupants.

Then there were fourteen.

Soon the boat went over again. This time, instead of climbing back into the craft, Christine Morrison and Duncan
Tinkiss stayed in the water, hanging on to the looped life
ropes fastened to the boat's gunnels, he at the bow, she at the
stern. Thus, the ropes acting as swivels, they remained wet
but safe as the boat, overturning four more times, inflicted
severe injuries to those thrown out. Each time fewer climbed
back into the boat. Those who were lost made no outcry;
they just weren't there when the boat righted itself. After the
second capsizing there were twelve left, after the third, only
ten. And then, once more, the boat rolled over and slowly . . .
ever so slowly, recovered, almost full of water.

And then there were seven—Christine Morrison, Duncan
Tinkiss, Captain Savage, First Mate McDonald, two lumberjacks, and a gentleman named Mr. Little who had almost
missed the *Asia* at Owen Sound, and who now wished most
fervently that he had.

The seas moderated as the hours passed. No longer concerned with more capsizings, both Tinkiss and Christine
Morrison climbed back into the boat. With no means of

propelling the lifeboat and the wind being very cold, the second battle to stay alive began. Some were shivering uncontrollably.

Night began to fall. With darkness came a blink of hope off to the east—a glimmering which Captain Savage identified as the lighthouse at Byng Inlet. The sighting had a miraculous effect on the spirits of the seven survivors, all of whom had helped to bail the boat almost dry, using caps, cupped hands, and even their shoes.

Mate McDonald, who had evinced little hope for their ever reaching shore alive, now joined in the rejoicing and led the group in several croaking renditions of "Pull for the Shore, Sailor," and "In the Sweet Bye and Bye."

But since they had nothing to "pull" with, it became a matter of waiting, endless hours, it seemed, as the beacon drew nearer with agonizing slowness. Quite suddenly, the wind, now light but shifting, began to blow the boat away from the still-distant shore. It was almost more than human emotion could endure. Those who moments before had been brave and confident, although near collapse from exposure and their earlier efforts to right and bail the boat, now seemed to give up.

The first to succumb was one of the two lumberjacks. Two hours later the other one leaned back against the side of the lifeboat and died. He was put in the bottom of the boat with his comrade. Tinkiss and Christine Morrison attempted to raise the spirits of their remaining shipmates by again singing, "In the Sweet Bye and Bye." Shortly after the last notes died away, Mr. Little, who was on his way home to Sault Ste. Marie, lay down and breathed his last.

Then there were four.

Mate McDonald was the next to go, dying while his weary head was supported by his cousin, Christine Morrison.

Then there were three.

Captain Savage had been alert early in the morning, but,

shortly after his first officer expired, seemed to fall into a deep sleep. Tinkiss shook him vigorously, telling him to wake up. But the captain was far gone and in a world of complete physical exhaustion. Responding as he had so many times when the ship's porter had shaken him to announce a change of watch or the nearing of a port, he nodded his head and muttered, "Yes, yes, I'll be up in a minute." A wave hit the boat at that moment, knocking Tinkiss off balance and tumbing him to the bottom of the boat, on top of the corpses. When he returned to the captain it was too late.

Then there were two . . . Christine Morrison and Duncan Tinkiss.

The morning dawned sunny and beautiful. The warmth of the rising sun was received on the *Asia*'s lifeboat, despite its grisly cargo, with great appreciation and a lightening of spirits. The water was calm. With the help of an onshore breeze, the boat was driftly slowly but steadily toward an island. Which one it was, neither Duncan Tinkiss nor Christine Morrison knew nor cared. It was land. That was all that mattered. It was later discovered to be an offshore island near Pointe au Baril.

It was still early when the boat ground ashore on a rocky beach. Almost unable to believe that they were still alive, the couple moored the craft and struck off toward what they had earlier sighted and thought to be houses. But after an hour of pushing through the underbrush they found the objects to be but stone cliffs. Weak with hunger, they stumbled back to the beach. Earlier they had spotted, around a precipitous headland, what appeared to be a lighthouse. Assuming that there would be life there, at least the keeper, they decided to take the boat around the point. Tinkiss then removed the five bodies and with boughs cut from nearby trees serving as oars, they set out for the lighthouse. They made only a half mile before dark, spending the night on the beach. The next morning, still famished but somewhat refreshed, they managed to propel the boat around the headland, only to find that the "lighthouse" was an abandoned derrick. Back at their original landing point once more, Tinkiss harvested some berries in the nearby underbrush, and after sharing them with his companion, loaded the five bodies back into the boat.

Christine Morrison, too weak and exhausted to help, was resting on the beach when she heard a noise. Thinking it was a prowling bear, she called to Tinkiss to come quickly. The noise turned out to be an Indian and his squaw, in a small sailboat. This, in itself, Miss Morrison always considered to be somewhat of an unexplained miracle.

The couple had been picking berries on the island and had already left for the mainland when the squaw was seized with an unaccountable desire to return. In what is probably one of the few instances of an Indian giving in to the whim of his spouse, the taciturn Ojibway, probably grumbling all the while, put about and ran his craft ashore within a few feet of the shipwrecked couple.

Having lost all his money, Tinkiss offered the Indian his sole remaining possession, a gold watch, to take them to Parry Sound. The Indian somewhat grudgingly agreed. Late in the afternoon, after the squaw had prepared a simple meal and brewed tea, they set out. But at dusk the wind failed, and the sail drooped. Claiming they were too tired to row, even though Tinkiss offered to do his share, the adamant Indians lay down in the boat to rest. Their passengers could do little but follow suit.

At noon on Sunday, just about three days after the *Asia* dove to her final port of call, the little sailboat tacked up to the town dock at Parry Sound. The news of the *Asia*'s sinking was already known and reports of bodies coming ashore at many points had led to the logical belief that all had perished. Helping hands now reached down to welcome and assist the only two survivors. Miss Morrison was so weak that she could scarcely stand or talk.

This is where, in the movies, the emotional, heart-throbbing climax should come. In the age-old Hollywood-script formula, the couple, strangers before their perilous adventure, should melt into each other's arms before the delighted onlookers, vowing eternal love and devotion. But it didn't happen that way. Christine Morrison was borne off to the home of a town official, where she was bedfast for two weeks. The hardy Duncan Tinkiss, after a meal that would have shamed an iron puddler, joined a tug crew to return to the island for the lifeboat and its silent crew of five.

Duncan Tinkiss and Christine Morrison met twice in later years. It is common knowledge that neither mentioned those terrible hours and days they shared together. Tinkiss and his father later operated the Mansion House, at Little Current, before the younger man moved to Manitowaning, where he died in 1910 at the age of thirty-eight. Christine Morrison married Albert Fleming, brother of the distinguished Great Lakes historian, Roy Fleming, and died in 1937, at the age of seventy-four.

All the ingredients for a good, they lived happily ever after, true-love drama were there on the Parry Sound dock on that September morning in 1882, but it just didn't come off.

Real-life situations often vary from the Hollywood versions.

15

A Family Affair

It is axiomatic that a cargo vessel, when designed, should provide for enough weight below the waterline, loaded or light, to keep the ship from becoming top-heavy or unstable in a seaway, and have sufficient weight to enable her to right herself no matter how severe the roll, and to do so at an even, measured pace. She must not tend to "stick" or be overly slow in recovering from a roll. But neither should she right herself so quickly as to cause discomfort or danger of injury to her people. The properly designed and ballasted ship recovers from her roll in an orderly, businesslike, no-nonsense manner, but in time to meet the next sea on even terms.

In a steam vessel the power plant itself—engine, boilers, shaft, and all the myriad auxiliary gear whose workings are the province of the engineer—provides some measure of ballast in themselves. Fuel, if it be coal or oil, is another weight factor. In modern ships with double bottoms, the tanks between them are filled with water ballast, sometimes fuel oil if the voyage is to be a long one, the oil being replaced by water as successive tanks are consumed. Heavy cargo is quite logically placed on the floor of the hold, a procedure to get the maximum weight as low in the ship as possible. This is no problem when the ship is a bulk carrier,

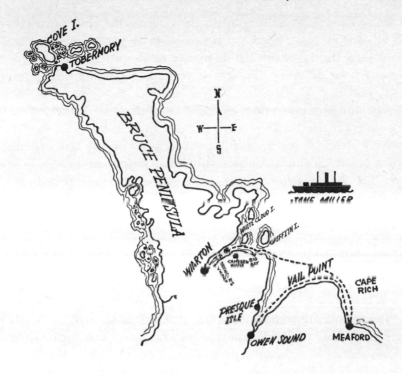

hauling iron ore, coal, or stone. In the general cargo or
package freighter, however, proper loading, in respect to the
stability of the vessel, is an exact science. In the old days,
particularly in tugs, pig iron was favored as permanent ballast, the "pigs" being covered with hot tar that, when it
hardened, kept the iron from shifting. Shipbuilders of today
utilize side and bottom ballast tanks to give the ship whatever
stability she needs when running light. On the other hand,
the tanks can be pumped dry as the cargo comes aboard,
permitting a minimum of draft when loaded. Many factors
are, or should be, considered in depth when designing and
building stability into a ship.

But the shipbuilder can only provide the finished vessel,
built to the best of his ability and from plans approved by

the owners. The responsibility for keeping the ship properly ballasted and in a good condition of stability throughout her working life is in the hands of her master. It is his burden every hour of every day, for he is blamed if something goes amiss.

In the disappearance of the steamer *Jane Miller*, one wonders if the builders were at fault in delivering an excessively "tender" vessel, or if her commander on her last voyage was guilty of almost unbelievably bad judgment.

The *Jane Miller* was a wooden freight and passenger propeller ship built in 1879, on order for James Miller & Son, at Crop's shipyard at Little Current, on Manitoulin Island. She was modest in size, seventy-eight feet long and eighteen feet of beam, with a gross tonnage of 210. By any of the aesthetic standards of a seafarer she was not a beautiful vessel. The primary consideration in her design and building was her ability to pay her way, not pleasing lines that would cause a true ship fancier to nod his head in approval.

"The *Jane Miller*," reported an observer, "was built high above the water, with a pair of large freight ports on both starboard and port sides, a large cabin superstructure with lifeboats near the stern. A small wheelhouse was attached to the cabins near the bow."

It is important to note that the builders, perhaps on orders from the owners, made no provision for permanent ballast. Consequently, despite her considerable freeboard and bulky superstructure, she drew only seven-and-a-half feet of water. Supposedly, the owner-operator would furnish whatever ballast he deemed advisable for the varying weather and sea conditions the vessel might encounter, according to the season.

She was sold in 1880 to Andrew Port. Perhaps the deciding statistic in the transaction was the *Jane Miller*'s shallow draft. She was, in every respect, ideally suited for the freight and passenger trade Mr. Port intended her for—running between

Collingwood, Owen Sound, and Meaford, at the southern end of Georgian Bay, to points along the Bruce Peninsula and the south shore of Manitoulin Island. Her home port was Wiarton. She was what salt-water sailors would call a "coaster," a small freighter, often family operated, working in and out of ports too small to justify the services of a larger vessel, or where the available depth of water would not accommodate a deep-draft ship. And the rocky shores of Georgian Bay, along the *Jane Miller's* projected steaming course, boasted many such ports, often just a cluster of buildings near the end of a makeshift dock.

Like his salt-water counterparts, Andrew Port kept the *Jane Miller's* operation just as much a family affair as he could. His brother, R. D. Port, a shipmaster of long experience, was named captain. A son, Frank Port, took over the duties of purser. Her normal crew, in addition to the Ports, was eight, and one can assume that they would have been replaced with more Ports, had the clan so provided.

One of the *Jane Miller's* disadvantages, and it was one shared by her many competitors, was that she burned wood in her boiler furnace. Again, like the others, she burned cords of it. In fact, the Georgian Bay coast was dotted with the docks of woodcutters—Indians and whites—who made their living supplying cordwood for the steamboats. Most skippers patronized regular sources of supply, but when head winds or high seas resulted in excessive consumption, there was always a supply not too far distant. Obviously, too, the cordwood, stowed below where it was needed, served as ballast, when there was enough of it.

The *Jane Miller*, as far as is known, had never shown any inclination to misbehave in a seaway or exhibit the characteristics of a "tender" ship. Had she done so, word of it would have been common knowledge at every dock and port. Shipping a crew, although jobs were scarce, would have presented a problem on every voyage. Sailors well knew the tragic shipwreck history of Georgian Bay, and memories of the *Waubuno* were still vivid.

On November 25, 1881, the *Jane Miller*, having taken on a heavy load of freight assigned to her, departed the town of Owen Sound. However, before she could head up the bay on her normal course to Wiarton, she was under orders from owner Andrew Port, who was aboard, to "backtrack" to Meaford, where a late-arriving consignment of thirty tons of freight awaited her. This meant steaming nearly thirty miles around Vail Point and Cape Rich to Meaford, on the west shore of Nottawasaga Bay. Here, although there was room below and large gangways through which to load it, most of the thirty tons of boxes, crates, and machinery parts, was stowed on deck, along with some of the cargo from Owen Sound. The reason given at the time was that the vessel was getting low on fuel and that Captain Port apparently wanted room for a good load of it below. Thus, when she left Meaford, the ship was already top-heavy, although this fact seemed to escape both Andrew Port and his brother, the Captain. Worse yet, the condition would obviously grow more serious as the little remaining cordwood in the firehold was steadily devoured by the boiler furnace. She was literally burning up her only ballast.

Captain Port had the dubious reputation of being very daring, although "foolhardy" was a term often applied to his exploits. Many were the tales of his recklessness and contempt for the elements. Yet, luck always seemed to be with him. Many, sailors and landlubbers alike, recalled his fantastic voyage in the ice during the winter of 1880. With his tug, *Prince Albert*, and a company of dignitaries aboard that included R. A. Lyon, M.P., Captain Port had attempted to reach Michael Bay, on Manitoulin Island. It was a wild day. Seas marched up over the tug's bow, battering the cabins. Spray washed down her funnel, almost extinguishing the fires. Still, Captain Port drove her on until at last even he had to admit defeat. The tug was finally driven back to Tobermory, on the northernmost tip of the Bruce Peninsula, where the shaken and ashen-faced passengers thankfully clambered ashore. At Tobermory the tug was frozen-in for nearly a month. During a brief December thaw the captain broke his tug free and tried to make his home port of Wiarton. Vast fields of pack ice were roaming Georgian Bay, and in one of them the *Prince Albert*, trapped again, lost her rudder. Then, for over two weeks, she drifted thither and yon, all over the bay, a pawn of ice and wind. It was a hungry and tired Captain Port who peered ruefully from his pilot-house window as another vessel towed him home to Wiarton.

Including owner Andrew Port, Captain R. D. Port and purser Frank Port, there were twenty-eight people aboard the *Jane Miller* when she cast off her lines at Meaford late on the afternoon of November twenty-fifth, to plod out into Georgian Bay in the face of a southwest gale. Wheelsman Alex Scales was at his post, August Keppel and Gilbert Colbert were down below, heaving the dwindling supply of cordwood into the boiler furnace, Engineer James Christie tended the throttle. The passengers included twelve area businessmen, one of whom, Leon Butchart, had his wife with him. The rest were laborers under contract to work at Watt's Mill at Lion Head, and for Mr. McLaunderer's lumbering enterprise at Tobermory.

Considering the direction and velocity of the wind, the lack of ballast, and the *Jane Miller*'s rather high profile, there is little doubt but that she immediately assumed a bit of a list to starboard. The wind alone would have taken care of that. On most of her coasting voyages the vessel would rarely be required to stay more than half a mile from shore. But the backtracking to Meaford for the thirty tons of freight changed all that. Now, after leaving the sheltered waters behind Cape Rich, she would have to steam northwest across fifteen miles of exposed waters on Owen Sound before she again found surcease from the winds at Cape Commodore and Colpoy Bay, at the extreme western end of which was the town of Wiarton, her destination.

The snow began shortly after the ship left Meaford, blowing a blizzard that must have left her rolling and pitching in a perilous world of her own, with all landmarks and lights obliterated by the driving, relentless storm. Elsewhere in the same general vicinity, the propeller, *City of Owen Sound*, was fighting her way home from Collingwood. She was heading into the seas, barely making steerageway, her anchors ready for instant release. Her master later reported that it was the worst blow he or his ship had ever encountered. And not far away the *Jane Miller*, top-heavy, low on fuel, and with only the foolhardy luck of Captain Port on her side, wallowed on toward Cape Commodore.

The captain had already announced his intention of stopping at Spencer's Wharf, on Colpoy Bay, for a full load of cordwood. It was a regular stop and one where he enjoyed favorable rates. And, somehow, the miraculous luck of Captain Port brought the battered *Jane Miller* through the furious gale and blizzard in Owen Sound, although the battle apparently exhausted his fuel supply completely. This is deduced by the fact that, after rounding Cape Commodore and reaching the somewhat sheltered waters between the mainland of the Bruce Peninsula and the offshore Griffith and White Cloud Islands, he put into Big Bay for wood, probably just enough to carry him to Spencer's Wharf. The ship was sighted leaving Big Bay between eight and nine o'clock that night.

A few miles west of Big Bay, along the southern shores of Colpoy Bay, Mr. Roderick Cameron and his son were anxiously peering from their windows, hoping to see the lights of the *Wiarton Belle*, bringing another son home from Owen Sound. But the snow came again in driven sheets. Only occasionally could they see the waters of the bay. Shortly after nine o'clock, however, they did see the lights of a steamer passing a half mile offshore, apparently headed for Spencer's Wharf, two miles to the west. Strangely, though, when abreast of the dock, she appeared to be stationary. Then the snow came again and the Camerons saw no more of her. Nor did anybody else. She never arrived at Wiarton nor did she reach Spencer's Wharf, for no wood was taken that night. After surviving the terrible seas and blizzard crossing Owen Sound, the *Jane Miller* simply vanished in the comparatively quiet waters of Colpoy Bay!

The Camerons, although it was undoubtedly the *Jane Miller* they had briefly sighted, could not tell whether the ship was listing or in any difficulty. Had the rolling and pitching, severe as it must have been, shifted the cargo she had on deck instead of in the hold where it properly belonged? And if she was in danger because of shifting cargo, why was the matter not put to rights when the vessel was taking on wood at Big Bay? Could it be that the daring Captain Port, concluding that the cargo would shift no more in the milder seas of Colpoy Bay, had fatally misjudged the stability of his ship? Or had he decided that the task of restowing cargo would be simplified after the wood ballast at Spencer's Wharf had eliminated much of the list? And then, when abreast of the wharf and while turning to port, had a single, malevolent sea, encountered seconds after the Camerons sighted her, proved to be the straw that, so to speak, broke the camel's back?

Although there were several and varied opinions expressed as to why, and exactly where the *Jane Miller* disappeared, the editor of the Wiarton *Echo*, although his words were bound to reflect unpleasantly on the manner in which the ship was managed, minced no words in printing the most popular consensus:

It is surmised, and we think correct, that after taking on the extra freight at Meaford, the steamer was top-heavy, and the fact that nearly all, if not all, of her load was on the deck . . . and there being no ballast, she has simply rolled over without giving a moment's warning. That not one of the victims of the disaster has been found need not be wondered at, when it is considered that the strong gale and snow storm which was raging at the time, no doubt compelled every gangway and other avenue of escape to be closely closed against the elements without.

Thus, completely penned in, and before the slightest effort could be made to save themselves, twenty-eight souls were hurled into eternity without time to utter a prayer.

A few days after the storm, when regular patrols of the rocky shores of Colpoy Bay had revealed no trace of the *Jane Miller* or her people, a Wiarton man named McGregor, and two other men started out from near Spencer's Wharf to see if any wreckage had come ashore on White Cloud Island. A half mile off the wharf, at about the point the Camerons had reported the bobbing lights of the *Jane Miller*, the trio noted large bubbles coming up from the depths and a distinct discoloration in the water. McGregor took rough bearings on mainland objects before the boat continued to the island. There, in a little bay on the island, they found all that was ever recovered from the missing ship. It was not much . . . a broken flagstaff, her fire-bucket rack, the cradles on which her lifeboats once rested, a couple of oars with the name *Jane Miller* painted on them, and five uniform caps identitied immediately as belonging to crew members.

Armed with Mr. McGregor's bearings and equipped with sounding leads, ropes, and grappling hooks, another party of Wiartonians, in the tug *Tommy Wright*, went out to locate the wreck. In addition to the tug's owners, James Inksetter and Hugh Boyd, the group included D. B. Miller, Samuel Parke, and William Bull. Starting at Spencer's Wharf, with grapnels out, they dragged for one hour without making contact with anything resembling a sunken ship. This is quite understandable since the bottom of Colpoy Bay is as rough and broken as the mainland itself, and a vessel the size of the *Jane Miller* could easily lie undetected in a crevasse or fissure. Soundings, however, were consistent, thirty-three fathoms, or almost two hundred feet.

On White Cloud Island the tug, by prearrangement, met Mr. McGregor who again, consulting his bearings, pointed out the spot where the water had been discolored and he and his companions had witnessed the air bubbles. It was almost exactly a half mile, slightly northeast, from Spencer's Wharf. While they failed to locate the hull, all members of the party were convinced, without a doubt, that it lay on the bottom in two hundred feet of water within a radius of a quarter of a mile from the place indicated by McGregor. It was directly in line with the home of Roderick Cameron, from where she was last sighted, between flurries of snow.

The pitiful debris from the lost ship was brought to Spencer's Wharf; the five caps were hung in a row on the dock spilings to dry out. They were still there the next morning, frozen stiff as boards and somehow resembling the helmets of fallen soldiers, hanging on makeshift battlefield crosses. They hung there in the cold morning breeze, nodding slowly up and down in the direction of White Cloud Island, as if pointing out the eternal grave of the *Jane Miller*, her twenty-eight victims, and the point where the foolhardy Captain Port's luck had at last run out.

16

~~~~~~~~~

⚓

"Telegram for Captain Stines"

The name of Graham, as one biographer put it, "is inseparably woven into the historic fabric of St. Joseph and Benton Harbor." The "Twin Cities," as they are called today, are located on the eastern shore of Lake Michigan, not far north of the Indiana-Michigan border. St. Joseph is at the mouth of the St. Joseph River, Benton Harbor less than two miles inland, beyond where the Paw Paw River joins the larger stream. Both communities flank the widening St. Joseph as it meanders south and east through some of America's richest agricultural land. Now, as in the waning years of the last century, although old rivalries are sometimes apparent, the cities are almost as one, with common interests, problems and aspirations.

The Grahams referred to by the biographer of the 1890s were John H. and Edmon A. Graham, Illinois-born brothers who came to Berrien County in 1864 to engage in the lumber business with their father. John later formed a partnership with Andrew Crawford in the sawmill and hardwood lumber field, at considerable profit. Early in the 1870s, he, with J. Stanley Morton and several associates, began a steamboat service between Benton Harbor, St. Joseph, and Chicago.

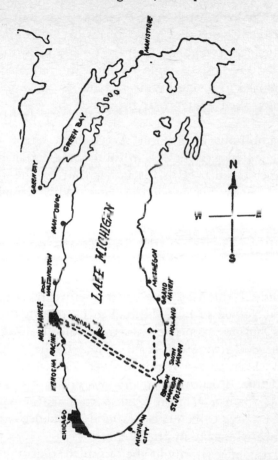

The name of the firm was Graham, Morton & Company. In 1880 this merged into a stock company known as Graham & Morton Transportation Company, with John Graham as president. Business was excellent, and in due time John Graham, by practicing the cardinal principles of success—great energy, hard work, honesty, and the ability to make the right decisions, had achieved a position of civic eminence in both communities. By 1895, the year with which our story is intimately associated, he was also president of the Alden

Canning Company of Benton Harbor, President of the St. Joseph Hotel Company, and a director of the Union Banking Company in St. Joseph. In Chicago he and his shipping firm constituted the largest single business interest on the docks and employed over one hundred men. By the usual criteria with which such affluence is measured, he was a self-made man.

The ambitions of Edmon A. Graham, eight years his brother's senior, were no less inhibited. He, too, had been in the lumber business with his father, but by the 1870s had branched out in his own enterprises. With Captain James Brooks he purchased the sternwheel steamboat, *Union*, and ran her in the excursion and freight business up the St. Joseph River. Later, at the lumberyard of Preston and Shaw, he built the first *May Graham*, a side-wheeler named for his daughter, May Belle. With a passenger capacity of four hundred, the *May Graham*, Captain James S. Fikes in command, served so long she had to be rebuilt three times. Another business venture was the acquisition of the old Morrison docks at St. Joseph. These Graham rebuilt extensively, lengthening them to over 750 feet. They were renamed the Graham Docks and obviously became "home" for the Graham & Morton Transportation Company's fleet. By some strange coincidence, Edmon A. chanced to become the Company's agent in St. Joseph.

At first glance it might be assumed that the Graham brothers had gone their separate ways. But, as in the case of the docks, their commercial ventures were tightly dovetailed. Berrien County and the entire countryside drained by the St. Joseph River, comprised the most extensive fruit-growing area in the Midwest. Beginning in June with sweet cherries and throughout the growing season, the orchards and vineyards yielded fabulous harvests of peaches, pears, plums, grapes, and apples. In 1872 Berrien County alone was shipping out 140,000 bushels of peaches. And beyond its great fruit yields, the lovely St. Joseph River area was a favorite summer resort and vacation home for sweltering Chicagoans. There was John Graham's St. Joseph Hotel, a great, sprawling structure, and hundreds of smaller hotels and cottages, scattered for miles along the verdant banks. The Graham & Morton Transportation Company's steamers brought the vacationers from Chicago to the Graham Docks and the *May Graham* delivered them to their upriver destinations. Coming back down the river the side-wheeler stopped at scores of small docks, picked up thousands of crates of fruit, most of which found its way to the Graham Docks and aboard a Chicago-bound Graham & Morton Transportation Company steamer. Much of the harvest not shipped out to Chicago or Milwaukee went directly to the Benton Harbor dock of brother John's Alden Canning Company. Long after the summer visitors had gone, their cottages boarded up for the winter, until the orchards and vinyards were white with frost on late October mornings, the old *May Graham* thrashed her way up and down the St. Joseph, her deck stacked high, her superstructure almost hidden by crates of peaches and apples, and her passage sweetened by the fragrance of ripe grapes. It was, by the standards of the day, a highly efficient and presumably profitable operation. As in the case of brother John, the biographer of Edmon A. Graham summed up the net results of his business acumen by stating simply, "He has accumulated a fair share of this world's goods."

The vessels of the Graham & Morton fleet had the dual purpose of carrying substantial tonnages of general freight in addition to the seasonal fruit harvest, and of providing handsome passenger quarters, not only for the heat-weary Chicagoans, but for other discriminating travelers whose comings and goings had nothing to do with the vacation season.

Competition among the lines offering passenger service was keen. Great emphasis was placed on the luxury accommodations and conveniences of the individual vessels. The rival Goodrich Transportation Company had always ballyhooed the superlative appointments of its vessels. The Graham & Morton people, if they wanted their share of the business, could but do likewise. Speed, too, was essential in advertising. It was the considered opinion in steamboat offices that passengers wanted to get to their destinations just as fast as was humanly possible. Thus, the prevailing speeds of the competing vessels were featured in posters and newspaper advertisements, although rare was the occasion when they made the exact passage time.

As business was excellent, Mr. John H. Graham was compelled, in the winter of 1881, to make another momentous decision. The firm, in the light of projected commitments to Chicago wholesalers, increasing tonnages from the fruit growers, and improving passenger quarters demands, was reaching a point where additional vessel capacity would soon be required. John Graham was accustomed to making decisions. His whole career had shaped up most favorably because of his ability to make the right decisions at the right time. Consequently, after discussing the matter with the board of directors and revealing statistics of anticipated growth, he contracted with the Detroit Ship Dry Dock Company for a new vessel, the building to start almost at once, acceptance to take place the following year when she was completed. A wooden propeller-driven ship, 217 feet long and thirty-five feet wide, she was hull No. 111 launched on June 25, 1882. The *Chicora*, as she was to be named, gave every indication of being Graham & Morton's final answer to the matter of superb passenger accommodations, in addition to being able to carry six hundred tons of freight. Her cabins were constructed for the utmost comfort of those who would favor her with their custom. Skilled ship's carpenters and joiners paneled them in mahogany and cherry. Expensive draperies covered her passenger-deck windows, and "elegant" paintings lined her companionways and halls. Down below, the shipbuilders installed a veritable giant of an engine, a triple-expansion creation of thirteen hundred horsepower. Little wonder that her owners, when she had passed her sea trials and had been accepted, gleefully announced that the *Chicora* would have a "guaranteed speed of seventeen miles per hour!" Boasting a gross tonnage of 1122, she was impressively commissioned. Captain Edward George Stines, a thirty-year veteran of the lakes, was named her commander.

Early in the planning stages, friends and associates had tried to persuade Mr. Graham to consider building a side-wheeler rather than a propeller ship. They pointed out that present vessels of that design had experienced no problems that could be attributed to the fact that they were side-wheelers. Besides, they were wider, more handily loaded, and should, on the whole, be able to carry more freight. Wasn't this, in essence, what they were in business for?

But Mr. Graham had been somewhat adamant. Had they forgotten, he asked, that only a few years ago the *Alpena*, a side-wheeler belonging to the rival Goodrich Transportation Company, had disappeared with all hands? And following that disaster, did they recall, common dockside gossip had it that the side-wheel design was impractical in bad weather? Unfortunately, too, he pointed out, this theory, right or wrong, had been widely publicized in the newspapers and would undoubtedly have an adverse effect on the passenger trade. So, he held, since the business required that the vessels encounter a good deal of bad weather, let us look to the advantages of a propeller ship. The final decision was that of Mr. Graham.

There is little doubt that memories of the old *Hippocampus*, subconscious or otherwise, were a factor in the thinking of Mr. Graham's associates. She, a propeller ship, loaded with over seven thousand crates of peaches, had foundered quickly with a loss of twenty-six lives some twenty-four years earlier. There was still some unpleasant talk of overloading and poor seamanship.

Mr. Graham was aware of this but placed no stock in the fact that she, too, was a propeller. He sincerely believed the *Hippocampus* to be a badly designed vessel, with more importance placed on her ability to carry a heavy load, rather than upon her stability when under way in a seaway. She had been owned by Curtis Boughton, the pioneer of the local fruit-shipping industry. On the night of September 7, 1868, she departed St. Joseph for Chicago at eleven o'clock, burdened down with 7000 boxes of fresh peaches. The tendency of owners in loading fruit, bearing in mind the numbers of men required to relay the crates deep down into the hold, was to keep as many crates as possible topside, making for greater ease in loading and unloading. Unfortunately, this greatly altered the ship's stability. It worked out well enough in good weather, but made the vessel dangerously top-heavy in any kind of wind or sea.

There was a modest sea running when the *Hippocampus* left port. Captain H. M. Brown was in command, having temporarily succeeded her regular skipper, Captain Morrison, who was ill. When she blew her departure whistle the *Hippocampus* had hundreds of crates of peaches on her promenade deck; some even lined the walkway between the cabins and rails. At two o'clock on the morning of September eighth, she was rolling badly and shipping some water through her after gangway. Greatly alarmed, Captain Brown checked the engines down and, in a loud voice that aroused and alarmed the passengers, ordered crewmen to lighten the ship by throwing peaches overboard. But it was too late. The *Hippocampus* suddenly heeled over on her port side and went down in less than two minutes!

Peaches were in good supply all along the southern shores

of Lake Michigan that fall, but the ugly implications that followed the deaths of many St. Joseph residents were not quickly forgotten or dispelled.

With considerable fanfare and a commendable surge of interest on the part of passengers, the *Chicora* went into service in the fall of 1882, fitting into the Chicago-St. Joseph night run as if the course between those ports were her own private waterway. During the next summer's vacation season, her passenger deck was sold out weeks in advance, and even the off-season commercial travelers were favoring her with their trade. In the matter of freight she more than lived up to expectations. It was noted that it took twenty men all afternoon and the early part of the evening to load her with crated and boxed fruit. And, strangely, there was no more talk of the advantages of a side-wheeler around the docks and offices. Wise heads now nodded approval of Mr. Graham's decision to build a propeller ship.

In the marine columns the *Chicora* was getting her share of space. One item quoted the experience of a Chicagoan who spoke feelingly of "falling gently off to sleep in a most luxurious cabin on that wonderfully mild October night, while my nostrils were tantalized by a most agreeable odor wafting up from the hold . . . the smell of freshly picked apples from the lovely St. Joseph River Valley."

So it went until the late fall of 1894 when, her season's chores completed, the *Chicora* was laid up at St. Joseph. The winter freeze-up was at hand. Trade had reached its seasonal decline. Only the steamer, *Petoskey*, of the Graham & Morton fleet, continued to operate, and then on a limited basis, weather and ice permitting. The *Chicora*'s boilers grew stone cold, and her crew scattered to their respective homes.

The harvest season had been late in the northerly plains states. Milwaukee refiners and millers had experienced a rush of grain long after the normal arrival dates. As a result they had on hand large amounts of bagged and barreled flour, with the stockpile growing day by day. On the other hand, they had customers waiting for it in the east, wholesalers whom they normally serviced by sending it across the lake to St. Joseph where it would be transshipped by rail.

Would the Graham & Morton Transportation Company, they asked, be receptive to the idea of commissioning a ship to relieve them of this overstock of flour?

The *Petoskey* was already in service but had her own commitments and, in any event, was too small to do the job efficiently. For one reason or another, primarily because winter repair work was already underway, the other Graham & Morton vessels were not available. This left only the big and practically new *Chicora*.

Ordinarily Mr. Graham would have dismissed the request as being highly impractical. First of all the cut-off date for marine insurance had long since passed. Reinsurance, even for one voyage, was out of the question. The *Petoskey* was operating without insurance, but she was an older ship, and the shippers who favored her with freight at this late date were also aware that no insurance was in effect, either on the ship or her cargo. The marine insurance people were entirely cognizant, painfully so, of the hazards of winter navigation on Lake Michigan, of the great gales that swoop down most unexpectedly, and of the vast fields of moving ice that can trap and crush the staunchest of vessels. Obviously, they wanted no part of such risks and sought to discourage winter sailing by arbitrarily withdrawing their coverage at a specific date . . . and were adamant about it.

On the other hand, Mr. Graham probably reasoned, most of the vessels in the package-freight business, his own and those of competitors, often operated without insurance since their normal freight commitments could not be met entirely within the alloted period of insurance coverage. Most of them were sailing days, sometimes weeks, after the expiration date. Indeed, if one were timid and refused to permit his vessels

out before or after the insurance was in effect, the year's
revenues would be substantially lighter, to say nothing of a
vessel's profit-or-loss statement. It was something one had to
accept, in order to stay in the lake freight business. Then, too,
after a harsh December and early January that left a modest
ice field anchored to shore and extending out a couple of
hundred yards, the weather had unaccountably turned very
mild. In fact, local fishermen, following the channel cut
through the ice by the *Petoskey*, were going out every day,
setting and lifting their nets. The lake had been flat calm
for days, and there was no indication of any worsening conditions, according to known weather reports. And, of course,
there was the matter of freight money. It would, coming
more or less as an unexpected windfall, be very welcome.
Flour is heavy, dense, and stows well. It makes a compact
cargo that amounts to excellent ballast and requires a
minimum of space, tonnagewise. It is just the kind of cargo
a shipowner would always choose, if he had a choice.

Mr. Graham was again faced with a decision, and it was
not an easy one. He knew that the *Chicora* had been laid up
for a month, her boilers cold, and all her piping cleared of
water. The luxury furnishings had been carried ashore for
storage, along with her compasses and lights. Moreover, she
was frozen in at her dock with her eight mooring hawsers
festooned with ice left from the early January gales. The *Petoskey* could break her free with little trouble. The other details
would merely take time. Captain Stines and Chief Engineer
McClure were home and available, and both St. Joseph and
Benton Harbor housed the makings of a dozen crews—men
who would welcome the opportunity of making a few unexpected dollars. Still, there was the inevitable risk.

In the end, apparently after some soul searching, Mr.
Graham made his decision. He wired the Milwaukee shippers
that he would fit out the *Chicora* as quickly as possible, and
luck and weather holding, she should be at the Graham &

Morton dock on the afternoon of January nineteenth. Furthermore, he would like, again considering the season, to be able to begin loading as soon as she arrived. He confided to his associates that there was a very real possibility, if the balmy temperatures held, the *Chicora* might be able to make a second trip, perhaps three. He had information to indicate that the tonnage of flour on hand in Milwaukee would certainly justify more than one trip, and the expense of fitting out the ship.

Rounding up a crew on short notice had not been as easy as Captain Stines and Chief Engineer McClure had anticipated. Many of the *Chicora*'s regular crew had found winter employment and declined to abandon it for the financial returns of a single trip. Deckhand Archie Bentley, for example, had already been working at a lumber mill at Hersey, Michigan, for a couple of weeks, and could get no assurance that his job would still be open if he went back on the *Chicora*. At the last minute, the ship's second mate reported ill, and, anxious to get his personnel problems solved, Captain Stines signed on his twenty-three-year-old son, Benjamin. Will Hancock, the ship's clerk, had agreed to make the trip, but a misunderstanding about departure time brought him to the dock too late to catch the ship. His place was taken by James R. Clarke.

On the morning of the nineteenth the *Petoskey* steamed from her own moorings to break away the ice that held the *Chicora* fast. It was slow work, but once the imprisoned vessel was able to move her own propeller she made short work of the job of turning, alternately working her screw full astern and full ahead to clear the channel in the slip. Once that was done she plowed her way out to open water, following the "lead" the *Petoskey* had kept open by her arrivals and departures. Counting Captain Stines, the ship's company numbered twenty-three.

Other than the very slight difficulty with the ice at St. Joseph and similar conditions encountered at Milwaukee, Captain Stines found it just like summer sailing, the flat calm prevailing. The *Chicora*, being light and not running at full speed, made the ninety-six mile crossing in six and a half hours, mooring at the Milwaukee dock at four o'clock that afternoon.

Having turned his vessel at the dock so she would be "headed out" when loaded, Captain Stines observed the hawsers being secured and the port-side gangway doors being swung open before he went ashore to consult the Company's agent at the office. There, after confirming the gross weight of the cargo to be loaded and commenting appropriately on the unusually fine weather, he excused himself and went back aboard to dinner and a well-earned rest.

The loading of packaged freight in the 1890s, the barreled flour qualifying as such, was a far cry from today's conveyor or palletized systems. Strong gangplanks were placed between the horse-drawn drays that backed up to the freight shed doors. Others bridged the gap between the shed and ship. The heavy barrels, one hundred and ninety-six pounds of flour in each, were rolled from the drays, through the freight shed, and into the *Chicora* through her gangways. Inside the ship the barrels were placed on end in neat rows. The hour was late. The number of available drays was limited. The result was that despite Mr. Graham's expressed desire for a quick dispatch of the cargo, only a couple of dozen barrels were loaded that day. However, the promise was that early on the morning of the twentieth an efficient shuttle would begin between the milling company warehouses and the Graham & Morton freight shed. The promise was sincere, but the execution deplorable. Extra drays had been hired, but for some reason—Captain Stines suspected the plethora of saloons along the route—the drays seemed to arrive in groups. Then there would be long periods of inactivity when the freight-shed gang and the *Chicora*'s crew would be idle, while the captain stewed and fretted.

"I've a good notion to wire Mr. Graham about this monkey business," he complained bitterly to the dock agent. For some reason, probably because he feared to cause friction between his owners and the milling firms who were ordinarily very good customers, he contented himself with kicking savagely at a flour barrel and stomping off to his cabin.

It was long after dark when the prescribed tonnage of flour had been delivered to the shed and stowed in the *Chicora*'s hold. The gangway doors were banged shut and properly secured at nine o'clock. It had been a long, hard day. Mr. Schmidt, the freight-shed foreman, searched his memory but could not recall a more frustrating one.

Captain Stines had earnestly hoped that the loading would be completed early in the afternoon, in which event he would have departed immediately. But his men were tired, and he had no desire for a night crossing. No point would be gained by arriving at St. Joseph in the small hours of the morning. Besides, who knew what errant ice fields had come wandering down the lake while his ship lay at dock for over a full day? He had spent a good many years fighting his way in and out of harbors through ice, and he much preferred that any additional experience along this line might come his way during daylight hours.

"We'll get a night's sleep and depart early in the morning, about five o'clock," he told Chief Engineer J. D. McClure.

A few hours later, back in St. Joseph, Mr. John Graham, the man who always made the right decisions, was apparently having belated second thoughts about his order to recommission the *Chicora* for a winter crossing. This is deduced by the fact that about four o'clock on the morning of the twenty-first he had occasion to refer to his trusty barometer. What he saw sent panic clutching at his heart. It registered twenty-eight, the lowest reading he had ever seen! By all the tried and true principles of barometric pressures that have guided mariners for centuries, the reading of twenty-eight indicated a massive low pressure system of unprecedented intensity! Mr. Graham was appalled.

Down at her St. Joseph moorings the *Petoskey* was loaded and scheduled to leave at six o'clock. With all the energy he could muster, Mr. Graham sped to the dock, awakened the *Petoskey's* master and in unmistakable terms ordered him not to sail until the anticipated storm had passed. Quickly then, or as quickly as such things can be managed, he sent a ship's watchman uptown to awaken the local telegraph operator. Meeting that unhappy individual at his office door, Mr. Graham dispatched an urgent wire to Captain Stines, ordering him, too, to stay at the dock until the atmospheric disturbance was over.

Undoubtedly the wire made its way to Milwaukee with the customary speed of such dispatches. In due time a sleepy bicycle messenger was peddling his way to the Graham & Morton freight office through a misty, light rain. It was five o'clock when he arrived, only to find the *Chicora*, lights aglow, already underway and fifty yards from the dock.

"Telegram for Captain Stines," he cried at the top of his voice. "Telegram for Captain Stines."

He could see figures moving on her deck but he had no light to attract attention. Nor could he make himself heard. The steamer's boilers were blowing off steam, her propeller was churning up a lather of water, and overhead came the petulant cries of a thousand gulls, piqued at being aroused by the thrashings of a steamboat at such unlikely an hour. It was a moment of extreme frustration.

One wonders at the reactions of Captain Stines and his officers that morning when they observed the ominous dropping of the barometer, if, indeed, they did consult it. It is highly unlikely that they had failed to note such an astounding reading since such details are periodically included in the ship's log, especially at the start of a voyage. No, Captain Stines must certainly have been aware of a reading as low as twenty-eight. But like all sailors he also knew that while a falling barometer most surely presages bad weather, it cannot predict how soon it will arrive. Calculating that it would take the loaded *Chicora* approximately seven and a half hours to make the crossing to St. Joseph, he probably felt that he would be safely moored to his "home" dock before the foul weather descended upon his ship. It could be, too, that this vain hope inspired him to order his lines cast off a little sooner than his announced five o'clock sailing.

For a time the captain's judgment appeared to be sound. The *Chicora* steamed on, but under lowering skies. The rain, light and fitful, back in Milwaukee, became heavier and steady when she was an hour out of port. Then, very suddenly, the rain began to come in lashing sheets as the wind velocity increased violently. By nine o'clock Lake Michigan was being raked by gusts of hurricane force. The rain quickly turned to snow, a smothering wilderness that shut up the *Chicora* and her people in a little world of their own, a world that knew only two colors—the blinding whiteness of the driving snow and the ominous gray of the mounting seas. The temperature had plunged downward almost as spectacularly as the barometer. Each sea that climbed her rails and piled over her forepeak built up a thickening layer of ice.

Under normal sailing conditions the *Chicora* would be "making her dock" at St. Joseph at twelve-thirty that afternoon. When she failed to put in an appearance at three o'clock, Mr. Graham, notified by his Milwaukee office that his telegram had not arrived in time, began to show concern. His first conclusion was that Captain Stines, probably finding the approach to St. Joseph harbor too hazardous in the gale, had turned his vessel and headed north to Grand Haven, perhaps even Muskegon. This was completely understandable, particularly since untold tons of ice, shore-fast before the gale, were now roving free before the wind and accumulating at the southern end of the lake.

Telegrams to Grand Haven and Muskegon brought no news of the ship, although residents along the shore at Grand Haven had earlier reported the lights of a ship bobbing out on the lake. But they disappeared after a short time, hidden perhaps by the gale-driven snow and spume. At South Haven, sixteen-year-old Henry Cross reported that he had heard a ship's whistle, blowing repeatedly, at a point seven miles below that community. William Hare, traveling along the shore from Saugatuck to his South Haven home, saw a ship, obviously headed for shore, during a lull in the blizzard.

"It was the *Chicora*, I'm sure," he reported. "Her stern was down and she appeared to be sinking. There were no spars and I saw no signs of life nor did I hear any disaster signals."

Still later came word from another resident that he had seen a vessel battling the storm, heading toward South Haven. According to him she was rolling heavily and her whistle was blowing almost continuously, obviously signaling that she was in distress. He said he watched her for some time, then a huge wave blotted the ship from sight.

The winter hurricane raged for two days with unrelenting fury. All along the shore the wind-driven ice rafted and piled up in towering windrows, twenty and thirty feet high. Despite the wind and snow, shore watchers continued to look vainly for the *Chicora*. Volunteers from many points along the eastern shoreline of Lake Michigan, as far north as Ludington, mounted regular patrols of the beach. There was still a forlorn hope that the vessel had been driven ashore and that her people might still be safe although marooned somewhere where communication lines were down or nonexistent.

Back in St. Joseph it was becoming very apparent to Mr. Graham and Mr. Morton that the *Chicora*, prize of their fleet, was gone, tragically, perhaps unnecessarily, but quite definitely—gone.

At long last one of Mr. Graham's decisions had been the wrong one. Or, perhaps, the blame should have been laid at the door of Captain Stines. After all, he was the master of the vessel. Since the responsibility for the ship and her crew was ultimately his, the decision of whether to sail or stay at the dock was traditionally and rightly his, and his alone. He could have stayed safely moored and would have been fully justified in doing so. But Captain Stines knew Lake Michigan's winter weather and that in all probability the startling drop in barometric pressure would mean the start of the winter gales that would bring all navigation to a halt until spring. And there he would be in Milwaukee with his ship frozen in and its cargo undelivered. While it would not be his fault, the situation would mean some embarrassment for Mr. Graham, particularly if the anticipated storm did not strike for many hours—hours during which the *Chicora* could have safely made her crossing to the satisfaction and profit of all. And Mr. Graham, the Captain knew, did not relish being embarrassed. It is the sort of situation a shipmaster does not like to dwell upon, and apparently Captain Stines did not.

Mr. Graham would undoubtedly have preferred not to dwell upon it either, but he was busy filling out dreadfully long and complicated forms connected with vessel losses and reminding important customers that neither ship nor cargo was insured.

Strangely, none of the *Chicora*'s people were ever found. They, like their phantom ship, had vanished into that endless dark world under the seas . . . where every voyage is forever.

Mr. Graham, meanwhile, was enmeshed in all manner of unpleasant details and duties, most of them the kind that would not permit him the luxury of forgetting . . . forgetting the decision that had sent his ship on her final passage. Each day brought new reminders. Several times he was advised that families of the *Chicora*'s lost crew were in painful and distressing circumstances. Above and beyond the economic hardships, there was common gossip to the effect that poor Mrs. Stines, unable to bear up under the shock of losing her husband and only son, had retreated from reality and would probably never again resume a sane and normal life. Nor did it help when shoreline residents, seeking to be helpful, brought in pitiful bits of wreckage for identification. A boy named Herman Hirner came in dragging a cabin-window shutter, another had found a piece of a pilothouse door, complete with lock, and others had discovered the vessel's spars.

As always, curious and unfounded rumors got ready circulation. Stories went the rounds that the company knew where the wreck was but refused to divulge the location for fear it would inspire a flood of insurance claims. This was rather ridiculous because no insurance was in effect and the shippers were well aware of the circumstances. To put these stories to rest the company later offered a reward of $10,000 for the discovery of the hull. Other groundless tales hinted that in the haste to fit out the *Chicora* to make a few unexpected dollars her lifesaving equipment had not been made ready. Nor, it was said, had the owners taken the time to round up fully experienced crewmen, the incident of Captain Stines signing on his son, being an example.

The total effect was rather demoralizing. Mr. Graham felt that every time he walked down the street a thousand accusing eyes were staring at him. It was most uncomfortable, and, he felt, undeserved. In all the years they had been in business, Graham & Morton had never before lost a ship. This was a record that could not be matched by any other firm. Being an intelligent man, Mr. Graham knew that only the passage of time would still the rumors and heal the wounds. Yet, the days passed so slowly.

It was early evening of a late March day, two months after the *Chicora* vanished. From his desk president Graham could look out over the docks. Lights were flickering on all over town, dispelling somewhat the cheerless gloom of what had been a depressing day. Earlier, word had come from a point near South Haven that a hundred or more barrels of flour were coming ashore, while others bobbed in the surf. It was another distressing reminder of a decision he had once been called upon to make. And now it was raining outside, a cold, quiet, and misty rain. Mr. Graham reflected that conditions were similar to those in Milwaukee that fateful morning back in January—the morning his message had failed to stay the *Chicora*.

As a matter of fact he wouldn't have been surprised at that very moment to hear a youthful voice, loud and strong, crying, "Telegram for Captain Stines . . . telegram for Captain Stines."

17

Our Son . . . and E.S.P.

Beginning early on the morning of September 26, 1930, a series of singularly curious and inexplicable events occurred on gale-wracked Lake Michigan. Three men, one ashore, two at sea, miles apart, were directly involved. The somewhat eerie chain of events that took place between dawn and mid-afternoon still defies rational and reasonable explanation. Old-time sailors might describe what happened merely as a man "following a hunch." Others would proclaim it an outstanding example of extrasensory perception. One of the three men concerned termed it "three-way mental contact." Whatever the analysis, it saved the lives of seven sailors.

It began with Captain Fred Nelson, seventy-three years old and a man about to lose his vessel, the schooner *Our Son*. The battered three-master was not of great value, dollarwise. She was fifty-five years old and tired. And as if she were transmitting her burden of weariness to her master, a psychological surge of sympathy, Captain Nelson was suddenly beginning to feel his age.

The westerly gale had developed suddenly on the evening of the twenty-fifth as the *Our Son* had been romping along quietly enough and minding her own business. She was carrying pulpwood to the Central Paper Company (now the S. D.

Warren Mill) at Muskegon, Michigan, and would have arrived there the following afternoon had fair winds held. Before the crew of six could muster forces, the westerly winds, accelerating quickly to near hurricane force, had stripped the schooner of her aged canvas. It was all over in a moment or two . . . a great booming like nearby cannon fire. Then there was only the clatter of now useless mast hoops and the strumming of the gale in her shrouds and stays.

A sailing ship without her sails is prey to all the malevolent tricks the sea can play, and, one by one, the *Our Son* fell heir to them. No longer maneuverable, she lay supine in the troughs of the great gray seas which, abuilding the full width of Lake Michigan, now reared twenty and thirty feet above her bulwarks. Many of them broke over her, sweeping the deck and seeking out her most vulnerable defenses, her hatches. They were well-battened down, for Captain Nelson was a cautious and thorough man. But he had expected a routine voyage, nothing like this. The boarding seas, like a clumsy puppy at play, had swept the *Our Son*'s deck gear— cordage, spare lines, boxes, and barrels—into a huge tangled pile, a sliding, smashing avalanche that roved at will from rail to rail as the schooner rolled perilously. The tons of water dropping over her counter put more strain on the old hull than she could be expected to withstand for long. Captain Nelson could sense a growing sluggishness in her movements. He knew that her seams were opening.

"There's water in the hold, lots of it," one of the crew reported.

Captain Nelson was realistic, as well as cautious. He knew the *Our Son* was done for, and what he should properly do as prescribed by regulations and centuries of tradition. He should promptly order the ship abandoned. But the realistic part of Captain Nelson told him that to attempt to launch the schooner's single yawl boat into the maelstrom would be the end for all of them. He knew, too, that his ship had been driven far out of the shipping lanes, that she would be unlikely to encounter another vessel before it was too late. It would not be reasonable to expect rescue from any of the conventional ore, coal, or limestone carriers. They would be on the usual downbound or upbound courses, either to the east, on the Manitou Passage, or, considering the deplorable weather, far to the west, hugging the lee of the Wisconsin shore.

"Anyway," he commented to Peter Olsen, "that's where I'd be tonight . . . if I had me a steamboat."

There was really no choice but to stick with the slowly sinking schooner and to pray that dawn would bring moderating weather that would permit the launching of the yawl. Sometimes, when the wind shifts, there is a brief period of calm. This would be the opportune moment to muster the crew and lower the boat, which hung from davits over the schooner's stern. That would be the proper time to order "abandon ship," Captain Nelson decided. Just in case a distant vessel might see them when morning came, the Captain had the ship's flag hoisted to the top of the aftermast, upside down, the international distress signal. Again, it was proper procedure.

The *Our Son* had no radio or wireless, but Captain Nelson, a firm believer in the Almighty, was sending out some powerful and personal signals of distress, praying that, come daylight, some errant vessel, far from its prescribed course, would happen upon them. What a potential rescuer could do to help was problematical. The seas would still be too high for them to launch a boat. His own yawl would very likely be swept under the schooner's counter and smashed to splinters. Still, Captain Nelson was hoping fervently that help would come from somewhere. When and if such assistance appeared on hand he would know instinctively what to do. Whatever the direction of the winds he would have no choice but to order "abandon ship."

Unbeknownst to Captain Nelson, far to the north and west, the Valley Camp Steamship Company's self-unloading steamer *William Nelson* was bound down Lake Michigan with a cargo of sand for South Chicago. Coming through the Straits of Mackinac and meeting the gale head on at dawn, Captain Charles H. Mohr didn't like the weather a bit. He had observed the seas breaking over St. Helena Shoal and had already concluded that later, after hugging Lansing Shoal and the north shore off Summer Island and St. Martin Island, he would anchor in the lee of Washington Island until the gale moderated or the winds shifted.

It was then that something strange and unexplained happened. It was as though a compulsive but subconscious force was directing him. Against all the accepted rules of cautious seamanship, common sense, tradition, and the procedures normally dictated by the existing weather conditions, he heard himself ordering the course altered drastically . . . to take his ship down the east shore of Lake Michigan, the dreaded Manitou Passage. Once headed for Grays Reef and the "gut" between Middle Shoal and East Shoal, the seas, building up the whole width of Lake Michigan, began to punish the *William Nelson* unmercifully. They rose as high as the steering pole and swept her broadside with agonizing frequency. She rolled abominably, smothered with white water every few seconds. In the galley, dishes cascaded from their racks. The pans on the old coal range slid off on the deck. In the firehold the men were hard put to keep their footing, let alone feed their boilers. Loose coal slid from side to side in miniature avalanches that swept up the slice bars and spare shovels. The crew must have been confounded by Captain Mohr's decision. It just didn't make sense. Nevertheless, the *William Nelson* wallowed on down the fearful passage beyond Big Sable Point and Ludington, sustaining damage with every mile. Her afterhouse was jolted with every sea that came calling. Glass in the portholes was shattered.

Watertight doors, even though "dogged down," were sprung. The bulkheads were bent in. Forward, the steel companionways between the Texas deck and the pilothouse had been wrenched loose.

On the eastern shore of Lake Michigan shortly after noon on that day, a group of people were watching the effects of the awesome gale and the tremendous seas it brought thundering and breaking on the beach. One member of the party was an old friend of Captain Mohr, a Mr. Joseph A. Sadony,[1] a gentleman who had often puzzled people with his ability to discern or know what was happening in distant places and to predict future happenings with astounding accuracy. Nowadays it is called extrasensory perception. Mr. Sadony, who had spent his lifetime studying this personal phenomenon, had often demonstrated this "sixth sense," to the amazement of others.

As the gale raged and whipped clouds of white sand around them, one member of the party wondered aloud if any ships were caught out on the lake.

"There is one sailing ship to the northwest I would not want to be on," said Sadony.

Another commented that he didn't believe there were any sailing ships still plying the Great Lakes.

Sadony, however, insisted that his vision was correct, further describing the vessel's sorry plight . . . her hold filling steadily, her sails shredded, and the rigging hopelessly fouled. He also remarked that the ship was far off the normal course of any other vessel, but he also sensed the presence of a cigar-shaped ship, which, if her captain followed his hunch, would come across the sinking schooner.

On the *William Nelson*, the unexplained forces that had compelled Captain Mohr to take the dangerous east-shore

1 Joseph A. Sadony's experiences and documented accounts of his strange "sixth-sense" or extrasensory perception are recounted in his book, *Gates of the Mind*, published by Exposition Press, New York.

course, manifested themselves again. South of Ludington he once more altered course drastically, hauling hard to starboard and steering directly west toward the far-distant Wisconsin shore. Butting into the huge seas that now assaulted her head to, the steamer suffered still more damage. Her fo'c'sle deck was pushed inward about six inches, bending the stanchions and beams. Then the pilothouse windows were plucked out, one by one, by the wind and seas boarding her over the bow. Captain Mohr, still guided by that strange and subconscious force, kept her headed due west.

Daylight had failed to produce a rescue vessel. The *Our Son* was still wallowing deep in the troughs of the seas, her torn sails trailing over the starboard bulwarks. There was plenty of time for a reflective Captain Nelson to brood over the fate of his ship and dwell upon her past. To him she was much more than a creaking old wind-grabber . . . she was practically the last of the Great Lakes sailing ships, a dying symbol of the "glory" days of sail when nearly two thousand such craft spread their canvas to the winds and brought home the cargoes that nurtured industry at a hundred ports. Only because she was such a "handy" ship to sail had she outlasted all but one of her kind.[2] Her name itself, and its bestowing, was history. She was built at Lorain, Ohio, in 1875, by Captain Henry Kelley. One of Captain Kelley's small sons, playing near the slip where the schooner was being completed, fell into the Black River and was drowned. In his honor the captain had christened her "*Our Son*." Strangely, too, although she had several owners in her over half century of service, her name was never changed. Whether sentiment and the memory of the tragic event that inspired her name influenced her subsequent owners is not known. One hun-

2 The *Our Son* is often referred to as the last of the Great Lakes sailing ships. She was not. The *J. T. Wing*, another three-master, served as a commercial carrier in the sawlog and pulpwood trade until 1937 or 1938. She was later donated to the Detroit Sea Scouts and renamed the *Oliver H. Perry*, after the Great Lakes naval hero of the War of 1812.

dred and eighty-five feet long, with a beam of thirty-five feet, she could carry one thousand tons of iron ore or 40,000 bushels of grain. With a favorable breeze she could make from twelve to fifteen knots, faster than many steamers of her day. When she could no longer compete with the growing fleets of big steel bulk carriers, she took to other cargoes—salt, lumber, shingles, fence posts, saw logs, and pulpwood. She had sailed on her first voyage with one-armed Captain Hugh Morrison, of Milan, Ohio, in command. Now, a victim of the worst gale of the season, she was about to end her days in the vast loneliness of Lake Michigan, with Captain Fred Nelson and his crew of six perishing with her.

Aboard the schooner, where, above, the distress flag still snapped taut in the howling wind, the men were doing the idle, seemingly senseless things men do when waiting for the end, but not knowing when it will come. One toyed fretfully with frayed bits of rope and rigging, as if subconsciously wanting everything in order for a supreme final inspection. Another, with detached dedication, picked steadily at the putty around a cabin window that had long since surrendered its glass to the sea. Others just hung on and stared out over the heaving gray seas, lost in a myriad of private thoughts and treasured memories. Down below, the cook, Tom Larsen, up to his knees in water, kept fishing out pots and pans, moving them to the top of the ancient galley stove. Every roll of the ship dislodged them again, and Tom, muttering to himself, patiently retrieved them. He had refused to leave the galley when Captain Nelson had pointed out the futility of staying there. But, the captain had decided, there was no point in pursuing the matter. They were going to be lost anyway, and the galley was as good a place as any to meet the Supreme Navigator.

And so, at three o'clock, and in such a state, the *William Nelson* found them.

It really shouldn't have surprised Captain Mohr to see the

sinking schooner ahead. The hero of many rescues, he seemed a man destined to be in the right place at the right time, although, in that connotation, the present situation left room for doubt.

In June of 1922, when he was skipper of the *E. W. Oglebay*, he saved two men, two women, and three children from a sinking yacht in Georgian Bay. A devoted family man himself, the event had made a deep impression on the Captain.[3]

In November, four years later, as master of the *E. G. Mathiott*, he saved three men on a disabled yacht in Lake Erie.

The following year he had rescued the crew of the yacht, *Mildred*, in a Lake Erie snowstorm. There were three almost naked men aboard the *Mildred*. They had soaked their clothing in gasoline to make flares and signal torches, meanwhile drifting helplessly for three days.

In July of 1929 he happened upon and rescued four men and two women, adrift after their yacht had capsized. Again it was in Lake Erie, near Kelleys Island.

Now, the *Our Son* was out there before him, toiling sluggishly as though the burden of water and pulpwood in her hold would finish her at any moment. She was tired, very tired, and her slow, agonizing recoveries bespoke a vessel ready to lay her head down on the bosom of the seas to seek her eternal rest. Captain Mohr knew that saving the people of the *Our Son* would be far different from any of the other rescues. His own ship was already damaged, and he envisioned more before the day was done. He wasn't quite sure he could pull it off. The people on the schooner were in no position to help themselves. Launching the *William Nelson*'s lifeboats in such a lather of towering seas would be suicidal. No, if he were going to get them off, he would have to go

[3] Captain Mohr was the father of two children, Addison Mohr, now of St. Louis, Missouri, and Mrs. E. J. (Lee) King, Jr., of Montague, Michigan.

right in beside her, risking fatal damage to his own ship should they crash together as both rolled heavily. There was the distinct possibility that both vessels might go down.

As soon as his decision was made, Captain Mohr sent out an SOS. He was quite certain that he would need help for his own ship ere long, and wanted another vessel standing by, just in case. The *Pere Marquette Car Ferry No. 22* flashed word that she was coming to his assistance with as much speed as the heavy seas would permit. When the smoke from the oncoming car ferry could be seen, Captain Mohr prepared to spread storm oil. Slowly circling the battered schooner, the steamer spread a film of oil on the water, taking the crests off the breaking seas. Captain Nelson anticipated what Captain Mohr had in mind. He was going to bring his steamer up against the schooner for brief seconds . . . seconds in which he and his men must leap for their lives. He gathered them on the port side, abaft the foremast, even reluctant Tom Larsen who had finally left his beloved galley. Slowly, as the crew of the circling car ferry watched entranced, the *William Nelson* came on. In those frightening seconds of contact, when the steamer's starboard bow nuzzled up against the rolling schooner, with a sound of splintering wood and tortured plating, they leaped. Then, with a blast of triumph from her whistle, the steamer backed off.

Minutes later in the pilothouse of the *William Nelson*, Captain Fred Nelson, wringing the hand of his rescuer, was most graphic in describing the *Our Son*'s plight.

"The waves were thirty, forty . . . yes, and some fifty feet high. But still Tom Larsen wouldn't come out of the galley until I told him a ship was coming to save us."

Resuming his course to the west, Captain Mohr reached the lee of the Wisconsin shore after dark and hauled to port, on the South Chicago track. He and his battered ship were safe now. Elsewhere the gale was taking its toll. North of Muskegon the stone barge *Salvor*, under tow, went ashore when the heavy towing hawser between her and the tug, *Fitzgerald*, snapped. Five persons on the *Salvor* died that night. South of Muskegon the fruit boat, *North Shore*, St. Joseph to Milwaukee, with 10,000 baskets of grapes, foundered with a loss of six lives. All along the Michigan shore, from Ludington to Sleeping Bear Point, as the lake was churned into frightful wrath, the breakers brought ashore timbers from a hundred old wrecks. Joining them were some from the *Our Son*, and a quantity of cordwood from her last cargo.

Word of the rescue, wirelessed by the *Pere Marquette No. 22*, brought the press and radio people out in force when the *William Nelson* docked at South Chicago at 5:30 on the afternoon of the twenty-seventh. Captain Mohr, Captain Nelson, and the *Our Son*'s crew were interviewed extensively. Captain Nelson, a shy, modest man, was finally pressed into telling of the long, black night of horror as the cold seas swept over his vessel and her torn sails snapped in the gale like pistol shots.

"There would be times of silence," he recounted, "when we were down in the deep valleys or troughs between the seas. The crests would be high above us on either side and the wind would be whistling over them. But down where we were, it was awful quiet at times."

Captain Nelson had been a sailor all his life, and knew another real sailor when he met him. Of Captain Mohr's daring rescue he could say only: "A magnificent feat . . . the kind only a superb shipmaster like Captain Mohr could carry out."

As a result of his fearless action in rescuing the crew of the *Our Son*, Captain Mohr was later given a Congressional Medal for what was termed "One of the most daring pieces of expert seamanship in the history of navigation." The medal, awarded by the U.S. Department of the Treasury, by authorization of Congress, was presented to Captain Mohr, with suitable ceremonies, in the clubrooms of the International Shipmasters' Association in Cleveland. It was the only such medal ever bestowed on a Great Lakes shipmaster.

It was some time later that the captain learned from his good friend, Joseph Sadony, of his "mental visions" of the sinking schooner and a rescue vessel that afternoon of September twenty-sixth, as the group stood near the shore, watching the storm.

Sometime earlier, during a long conversation, the Captain and Sadony had agreed that each would follow his hunches, and someday compare notes. Their recounting of visions, actions, hunches, and events of that particular day would have left the casual listener dumbfounded. One thing was certain, be it extrasensory perception or something equally unexplainable, it was weird. But for Mr. Sadony's vision and the strange, unaccountable forces that compelled Captain Mohr to deviate from the accepted route down Lake Michigan, the *Our Son* would have become another "ghost ship" of the Great Lakes.

"In this case it was three-way mental contact," maintained Captain Mohr.

Mr. Sadony's convictions, inspired by his unusual mental powers, were purely impersonal. One day many years earlier, he had stated to John A. (Lex) Chisholm, a Muskegon newspaperman, that he (Sadony) would die in his eighty-fourth year—1960.

He did.

Bibliography

Bentor Harbor Michigan *News-Palladium*—"Mystery Still Shrouds Sinking of Local Steamer," January 2, 1958.

Brennan, Bert C.—"The Tale of Twin Cities," *Inland Seas*, Fall-Winter, 1955.

Carmichael, W. J.—"Service Recalls *Waubuno* Disaster," Midland, Ontario, *County Herald*, November 28, 1962.

Chisholm, John A.—"The Chisholm Trail," the *Muskegon Chronicle*, April 1, 8; September 9, 1967.

Cleveland, Ohio, *Plain Dealer*—October 23, 25, 28, 1905.

Conneaut, Ohio, *News-Herald*—December 9, 10, 11, 12, 1909.

Detroit *Marine Historian*—"Ships That Never Die," February, 1955.

Dunkirk, New York, *Evening Observer*—Issues of December, 1950, and January, September, and October, 1951.

Fleming, Roy F.—"The Sinking of the S.S. *Asia*," Manitoulin *Expositor*.

Gould, Filomena—"A Sixth Great Lake," *Inland Seas*; Summer, 1967.

Gore Bay, Ontario, *Recorder*—"Vivid Tale of the Wreck of the *Asia*," May, 1953.

Grand Haven, Michigan, *Daily Tribune*—September 12, November 1, 1929.

Grand Rapids, Michigan, *Press*—"Recalls 1895 Shipwreck," January 10, 1964.

Gravenhurst, Ontario, *Banner*—"Anchor from *Waubuno* Recalls Tragic History," 1962.

Great Lakes Protective Association—Annual Report, 1959.

Hilton, George W.—"The Great Lakes Car Ferries," Howell-North, 1962.

Kenosha, Wisconsin, *Evening News*—October 29, 1959.

Kingston, Ontario, *Daily Whig*—December 2, 1902.

Labadie, C. Patrick—"The Iron Wisconsin," Telescope; Vol. 13, No. 10, October, 1964.

Landon, Fred—"Loss of the Steamer *Waubuno* in 1879," London, Ontario *Free Press*; January 30, 1965.

Landon, Fred—"The Loss of the *Bannockburn*," *Inland Seas*; Winter, 1957.

London, Ontario, *Free Press*—September 17, 1949.

Mansfield, J. B.—"History of the Great Lakes," J. H. Beers and Co., Chicago, 1899.

Marine Review—August 13, 1896.

McKean, F. K.—"Trinity Church of Parry Sound," Parry Sound *North Star*, 1965.

McLeod, M. A.—"The Wreck of the *Jane Miller*."

Meakin, Rev. Alexander C.—"A History of the Great Lakes Towing Company," 1966.

Midland, Ontario, *County Herald*—February 8, 1963.

Murphy, Rowley W.—"Ghost Ships," *Inland Seas*; Summer, 1961.

Myers, Frank A.—"The Mysterious Fate of the *Waubuno*."

Painesville, Ohio, *Telegraph*—October 26; November 2, 1905.

Patten, T. J.—"Early Days in Little Current and Vicinity," Manitoulin *Expositor*; May 5, 1932.

Plumb, R. G.—"The Goodrich Line," *Inland Seas*; April, 1945.

Port Huron, Michigan, *Times*—October and November issues, 1905.

Remick, Teddy—"The Finding of the Vanished *Waubuno*," *Inland Seas*; Winter, 1960.

Robinson, Comdr. S. S.—"Manual of Wireless Telegraphy," U.S. Naval Institute, 1913.

Saugatuck, Michigan, *Commercial Record*—"Anniversary of *Chicora* Sinking," January 25, 1963.

Snider, C. H. J.—"Rough Night on Lakes Ended a Long Road," from *Schooner Days*.

Sturgeon Bay, Wisconsin, *Door County Advocate*—"*Clifton* Disaster," October 2, 1924.

Thorp, H. W., and H. W., Jr.—"History of the S.S. *Wisconsin*."

Toronto, Ontario, *Globe*—November 28, 29, 1902.

U.S. Lifesaving Service—Annual Report, 1881.

Vargo, George A.—"The Great Storm of October, 1929," *Inland Seas*; April, 1946.

Walmsley, Leo—"British Ports and Harbours," Collins; London, 1942.

White, James, F.R.G.S.—"Papers and Records of Ontario Historical Society," Vol. XI, 1913.

Wiarton, Ontario, *Echo*—November 25, 1881.

Williams, W. R.—"Shipwrecks at Isle Royale," *Inland Seas*; Winter, 1956.

Young, Anna G.—"A Canaller's Soliloquy," *Inland Seas*; Spring, 1967.

Index